PHILLIPS'
Awesome
COLLECTION OF
QUIPS & QUOTES

BOB PHILLIPS

HARVEST HOUSE PUBLISHERS
Eugene, Oregon 97402

Cover by Terry Dugan and Associates, Minneapolis, Minnesota

PHILLIPS' AWESOME COLLECTION OF QUIPS AND QUOTES
Copyright © 2001 by Bob Phillips
Published by Harvest House Publishers
Eugene, Oregon 97402

Library of Congress Cataloging-in-Publication Data
Phillips, Bob, 1940-
    Phillips' awesome collection of quips and quotes / Bob Phillips
        p. cm.
    ISBN 0-7369-0618-5
    1. Quotations, English. I. Title: Collection of awesome quotations. II. Title.

PN6081 .P47 2001
082—dc21   00-047119

Printed in the United States of America

01 02 03 04 05 06 07 / BC-MS / 10 9 8 7 6 5 4 3 2 1

CONTENTS

Contents

5

Morning
Mothers
Moths
Motives
Mouth
Movies
Music
Must

Name-dropping
Narcissists
National Debt
National Defense
National Honor
Nations
Necessity
Neighbors
Neurosis
Neutrality
Newspapers
Nicknames
No
Nonessentials
Normal Times
Nothing

Obedience
Obscenity
Obstacles
Old Age
Old Couples

Once
Openness
Opera
Opinion
Opportunities
Optimists
Original Sin
Originality
Others
Oxen

Pain
Paradox
Pardoning
Parents
Parties
Passing Away
Passion
Passiveness
Past
Patches
Patience
Patriotism
Peace
Peace of Mind
Peacemakers
People
Perfection
Performance
Perseverance
Persistence
Personal Preferences

Standing Still
Stars
States
Statesmen
Statistics
Staying
Stories
Storms
Strangers
Strength
Strenuous Life
Stress
Strong Defense
Struggle
Success
Suffering
Supporting
Surprise
Suspense
Suspicion
Swearing

T 370

Tact
Talent
Talk Shows
Talking
Tasks
Taxes
Teachers
Teaching
Teamwork
Tears

Teenagers
Television
Temper
Temptation
Ten Commandments
Tenacity
Theories
Thieves
Things
Thinking
Thoughts
Tigers
Time
Today
Tolerance
Tombs
Tongue
Toupee
Trade
Tradition
Tranquility
Travel
Treachery
Treason
Trees
Trials
Triumph
Trivial Matters
Trouble
Trust
Truth
Truthfulness
Tyranny

Absent

The absent are always in the wrong.

The absent are like children, helpless to defend themselves.
CHARLES READE

Greater things are believed of those who are absent.
TACITUS

The absent are never without fault. Nor the present without excuse.
BENJAMIN FRANKLIN

Abuse

There is none more abusive to others than they that lie most open to it themselves.
SENECA

Acceptance

You gotta play the hand that's dealt you. There may be pain in that hand, but you play it. And I've played it.
JAMES BRADY

Gladly accept the gifts of the present hour.
HORACE

Peace of mind is that mental condition in which you have accepted the worst.
LIN YUTANG

Acceptance says, True, this is my situation at the moment. I'll look unblinkingly at the reality of it. But I'll also open my hands to accept willingly whatever a loving Father sends me.

CATHERINE MARSHALL

Acceptance of what has happened is the first step to overcoming the consequence of any misfortune.

WILLIAM JAMES

Because you're not what I would have you be, I blind myself to who, in truth, you are.

Accomplishment

Accomplishment will prove to be a journey, not a destination.

DWIGHT D. EISENHOWER

Let us develop the resources of our land, call forth its powers, build up its institutions, promote all its great interests, and see whether we also, in our day and generation, may not perform something worthy to be remembered.

DANIEL WEBSTER

Man can climb to the highest summits but cannot dwell there long.

GEORGE BERNARD SHAW

Accuracy

Accuracy is the twin brother of honesty; inaccuracy, of dishonesty.

CHARLES SIMMONS

Achievement

My most brilliant achievement was my ability to persuade my wife to marry me.

SIR WINSTON CHURCHILL

Four steps to achievement: plan purposefully, prepare prayerfully, proceed positively, pursue persistently.

WILLIAM A. WARD

It isn't the incompetent who destroy an organization. The incompetent never get in a position to destroy it. It is those who have achieved something and want to rest upon their achievements who are forever clogging things up.

F.M. YOUNG

Action

When we have fully discovered the scientific laws that govern life, we shall realize that the one person who has more illusions than the dreamer is the man of action.   OSCAR WILDE

Better that we should err in action than wholly refuse to perform. The storm is so much better than the calm, as it declares the presence of a living principle. Stagnation is something worse than death. It is corruption also.

WILLIAM GILMORE SIMMS

Thought is the blossom; language the bud; action the fruit behind it.   RALPH WALDO EMERSON

The most drastic, and usually the most effective, remedy for fear is direct action.   WILLIAM BURNHAM

People avoid action often because they are afraid of the consequences, for action means risk and danger. Danger seems terrible from a distance: it is not so bad if you have a close look at it. And often it is a pleasant companion, adding to the zest and delight of life.   JAWAHARLAL NEHRU

Action is eloquence.

SHAKESPEARE

All the good maxims have been written. It only remains to put them into practice.

BLAISE PASCAL

I have never heard anything about the resolutions of the apostles, but a great deal about their acts.

HORACE MANN

Well done is better than well said.

BENJAMIN FRANKLIN

I think there is something more important than believing: action! The world is full of dreamers; there aren't enough who will move ahead and begin to take concrete steps to actualize their vision.

W. CLEMENT STONE

The finest eloquence is that which gets things done.

DAVID LLOYD GEORGE

We are face to face with our destiny, and we must meet it with a high and resolute courage. For us is the life of action, of strenuous performance of duty; let us live in the harness, striving mightily; let us rather run the risk of wearing out than rusting out.

THEODORE ROOSEVELT

There is something healthy and invigorating about direct action.

HENRY MILLER

The world is sown with good; but unless I turn my glad thoughts into practical living and till my own field, I cannot reap a kernel of the good.

HELEN KELLER

Actions

Whenever you are to do a thing, though it can never be known but to yourself, ask yourself how you would act were all the world looking at you and act accordingly.

THOMAS JEFFERSON

I have ever judged of the religion of others by their lives. It is in our lives, and not from our words, that our religion must be read. By the same test the world must judge me.

THOMAS JEFFERSON

I'd rather see a sermon than hear one any day;
I'd rather one should walk with me than merely show the way.
The eye's a better pupil and more willing than the ear;
Fine counsel is confusing, but example's always clear.
And the best of all preachers are the men who live their creeds,
For to see the good in action is what everybody needs.
I can soon learn how to do it if you'll let me see it done;
I can watch your hands in action, but your tongue too fast may run.
And the lectures you deliver may be very wise and true,
But I'd rather get my lesson by observing what you do.
For I may misunderstand you and the high advice you give,
But there's no misunderstanding how you act and how you live.

THE LOOKOUT

Do not expect a "well done" if you have not done well.

D. JAMES KENNEDY

Activity

Activity is contagious.

RALPH WALDO EMERSON

Our nature consists in motion; complete rest is death.

BLAISE PASCAL

Actors

Some of the greatest love affairs I've ever known involved one actor, unassisted.

Admonishment

Admonish your friends privately, but praise them openly.
PUBLILIUS SYRUS

Adolescence

Adolescence is a kind of emotional seasickness. Both are funny, but only in retrospect.
ARTHUR KOESTLER

Adultery

Can a man scoop fire into his lap without his clothes being burned? Can a man walk on hot coals without his feet being scorched? So is he who sleeps with another man's wife.
THE BIBLE: PROVERBS 6:27-29

Whoso committeth adultery with a woman lacketh understanding: he that doeth it destroyeth his own soul.
THE BIBLE: PROVERBS 6:32 KJV

Advantage

Next to knowing when to seize an opportunity, the most important thing in life is to know when to forego an advantage.
BENJAMIN DISRAELI

Adventure

Every forward step achieved by man has been due to the adventurous attitude. This attitude inspires dissatisfaction with the world as it is; it arouses the desire to change and improve things. The attitude of adventure is the flame that lights the fuse to explode new ideas.

WILFRED A. PETERSON

Adversity

Into each life some rain must fall.

HENRY W. LONGFELLOW

Adversity is easier borne than prosperity forgot.

Prosperity doth best discover vice, but adversity doth best discover virtue.

FRANCIS BACON

Anyone who proposes to do good must not expect people to roll stones out of his way, but must accept his lot calmly if they roll a few more upon it.

ALBERT SCHWEITZER

Adversity makes a man wise, not rich.

The brook would lose its song if we removed the rocks.

Prosperity is a great teacher; adversity is a greater. Possession pampers the mind; privation trains and strengthens it.

WILLIAM HAZLITT

The good things of prosperity are to be wished; but the good things that belong to adversity are to be admired.

SENECA

Prosperity is not a just scale; adversity is the only balance in which to weigh friends.

PLUTARCH

I would never have amounted to anything were it not for adversity. I was forced to come up the hard way.

J.C. PENNEY

Adversity not only draws people together, but brings forth that beautiful inward friendship.

SØREN KIERKEGAARD

Adversity is the first path to Truth.

LORD BYRON

Sweet are the uses of adversity.

WILLIAM SHAKESPEARE

He that is down needs fear no fall.

JOHN BUNYAN

A clay pot sitting in the sun will always be a clay pot. It has to go through the white heat of the furnace to become porcelain.

MILDRED W. STRUVEN

Times of general calamity and confusion have ever been productive of the greatest minds. The purest ore is produced from the hottest furnace, and the brightest thunderbolt is elicited from the darkest storms.

CHARLES CALEB COLTON

The beauty of the soul shines out when a man bears with composure one heavy mischance after another, not because he does not feel them, but because he is a man of high and heroic temper.

ARISTOTLE

Advertising

Advertising is a racket...its constructive contribution to humanity is exactly minus zero.   F. SCOTT FITZGERALD

Advice

I always pass on good advice. It is the only thing to do with it. It is never any use to oneself.   OSCAR WILDE

We give advice by the bucket, but take it by the grain.   W.R. ALGER

How is it possible to expect mankind to take advice when they will not so much as take warning?   JONATHAN SWIFT

No one wants advice—only corroboration.   JOHN STEINBECK

The easiest way to escape being hated is to mind your own business and refrain from giving good advice.   W. BURTON BALDRY

The advice of the aged will not mislead you.

One piece of good advice is better than a bagful.

Give neither advice nor salt until you are asked for it.

Whatever your advice, make it brief.   HORACE

Never trust the advice of a man in difficulties.

AESOP

Some folks won't ask for advice for fear of giving the impression they need it.

Advice is like snow; the softer it falls, the longer it dwells upon, and the deeper it sinks into the mind.

SAMUEL TAYLOR COLERIDGE

Advice is a stranger; if welcome he stays for the night; if not welcome he returns home the same day.

The true secret of giving advice, is after you have honestly given it, to be perfectly indifferent whether it is taken or not and never persist in trying to set people right.

HANNAH WHITALL SMITH

Most of us ask for advice when we know the answer but want a different one.

IVERN BELL

No one is wise enough to advise himself.

Advisers

For lack of guidance a nation falls, but many advisers make victory sure.

THE BIBLE: PROVERBS 11:14

Advocate

The first duty of a wise advocate is to convince his opponents that he understands their arguments, and sympathizes with their just feelings.

SAMUEL TAYLOR COLERIDGE

Affairs

Before undergoing a surgical operation, arrange your temporal affairs. You may live.

AMBROSE BIERCE

Affliction

Affliction comes to us all not to make us sad, but sober; not to make us sorry, but wise; not to make us despondent, but by its darkness to refresh us, as the night refreshes the day; not to impoverish, but to enrich us, as the plough enriches the field; to multiply our joy, as the seed, by planting, is multiplied a thousand-fold.

HENRY WARD BEECHER

Age

If wrinkles must be written upon our brows, let them not be written upon the heart. The spirit should never grow old.

JAMES A. GARFIELD

Age is like love; it cannot be hid.

THOMAS DEKKER

The older I grow, the more I distrust the familiar doctrine that age brings wisdom.

H.L. MENCKEN

I refuse to admit I'm more than fifty-two, even if that does make my sons illegitimate.

LADY ASTOR

Age does not depend upon years, but upon temperament and health. Some men are born old, and some never grow so.

TRYON EDWARDS

Agitation

Those who profess to favor freedom, and yet depreciate agitation, are men who want rain without thunder and lightning. They want the ocean without the roar of its many waters.

FREDERICK DOUGLASS

Agnostic

An agnostic found himself in trouble, and a friend suggested he pray. "How can I pray when I do not know whether or not there is a God?" he asked. "If you are lost in the forest," his friend replied, "you do not wait until you find someone before shouting for help."

DAN PLIES

Agreement

Ah, don't say that you agree with me. When people agree with me, I always feel that I must be wrong.

OSCAR WILDE

Agriculture

I think our governments will remain virtuous for many centuries; as long as they are chiefly agricultural; and this will be as long as there shall be vacant lands in any part of America. When they get piled upon one another in large cities, as in Europe, they will become corrupt as in Europe.

THOMAS JEFFERSON

Earth here is so kind, that just tickle her with a hoe and she laughs with a harvest.

DOUGLAS JERROLD

Farming looks mighty easy when your plow is a pencil, and you're a thousand miles from the cornfield.

DWIGHT D. EISENHOWER

Ailments

For every ailment under the sun,
There is a remedy, or there is none;
If there be one, try to find it;
If there be none, never mind it.

DALE CARNEGIE

We are so fond of each other because our ailments are the same.

JONATHAN SWIFT

Aloneness

In Genesis it says that it is not good for a man to be alone, but sometimes it is a great relief.

JOHN BARRYMORE

Language has created the word "loneliness" to express the pain of being alone, and the word "solitude" to express the glory of being alone.

PAUL TILLICH

Ambition

Ambition often puts men upon doing the meanest offices: So climbing is performed in the same posture as creeping.

JONATHAN SWIFT

I have found some of the best reasons I ever had for remaining at the bottom simply by looking at the men at the top.

FRANK MOORE COLBY

In a great river, great fish are found;
but take heed lest you be drowned.

Most people would succeed in small things, if they were not troubled with great ambitions.

HENRY W. LONGFELLOW

Keep away from people who try to belittle your ambitions. Small people always do that, but the really great make you feel that you, too, can become great.

MARK TWAIN

He that is fond of building will soon ruin himself without the help of enemies.

PLUTARCH

What seems to be generosity is often no more than disguised ambition, which overlooks a small interest in order to secure a great one.

FRANÇOIS DE LA ROCHEFOUCAULD

America

Let our object be our country, our whole country, and nothing but our country. And, by the blessing of God, may that country itself become a vast and splendid monument, not of oppression and terror, but of wisdom, of peace, and of liberty, upon which the world may gaze with admiration forever.

DANIEL WEBSTER

America is not a mere body of traders; it is a body of free men. Our greatness is built upon our freedom—it is moral, not material. We have a great ardor for gain; but we have a deep passion for the rights of man.

WOODROW WILSON

I am certain that however great the hardships and the trials which loom ahead, our America will endure and the cause of human freedom will triumph.

CORDELL HULL

America is like a gigantic boiler. Once the fuse is lighted under it, there is no limit to the power it can generate.

SIR WINSTON CHURCHILL

What's right about America is that although we have a mess of problems, we have great capacity—intellect and resources—to do something about them.

HENRY FORD II

America's beauty is not only in its features; its beauty is in the character underneath those features.

LUCI SWINDOLL

We have been the recipients of the choicest bounties of Heaven. We have been preserved, these many years, in peace and prosperity. We have grown in numbers, wealth and power, as no other nation has ever grown. But we have forgotten God. We have forgotten the gracious hand which preserved us in peace, and multiplied and enriched and strengthened us; and we have vainly imagined, in the deceitfulness of our hearts, that all these blessings were produced by some superior wisdom and virtue of our own. Intoxicated with unbroken success, we have become too self-sufficient to feel the necessity of redeeming and preserving grace, too proud to pray to the God that made us!

ABRAHAM LINCOLN

I sought for the greatness and genius of America in her commodious harbors and her ample rivers—and it was not there...in her fertile fields and boundless forests—and it was not there...in her rich mines and her vast world commerce—and it was not there...in her democratic Congress and her matchless Constitution—and it was not there. Not until I went into the churches of America and heard her pulpits flame with righteousness did I understand the secret of her genius and power. America is great because she is good, and if America ever ceases to be good, America will cease to be great.

ALEXIS DE TOCQUEVILLE

America is the only country ever founded on the printed word.

MARSHALL MCLUHAN

And so, my fellow Americans: Ask not what your country can do for you—ask what you can do for your country. My fellow citizens of the world: Ask not what America will do for you, but what together we can do for the freedom of man.

JOHN F. KENNEDY

With malice toward none, with charity for all, with firmness in the right—as God gives us to see the right—let us strive on to finish the work we are in, to bind up the nation's wounds, to care for him who shall have borne the battle and for his widow and his orphan—to do all which may achieve and cherish a just and lasting peace among ourselves and with all nations.

ABRAHAM LINCOLN

The second day of July 1776, will be the most memorable epoch in the history of America. I am apt to believe that it will be celebrated by succeeding generations as the great anniversary festival. It ought to be commemorated as the day of deliverance, by solemn acts of devotion to God Almighty. It ought to be solemnized with pomp and parade, with shows, games, sports, guns, bells, bonfires, and illustrations, from one end of this continent to the other, from this time forward forevermore.

JOHN ADAMS

It having pleased the Almighty ruler of the Universe propitiously to defend the cause of the United American States and finally by raising us up a powerful friend among the princes of the earth to establish our liberty and independence upon lasting foundations, it becomes us to set apart a day for gratefully acknowledging the divine goodness and celebrating the important event which we owe to His benign Interposition.

There is nothing wrong with America that the faith, love of freedom, intelligence, and energy of her citizens cannot cure.

DWIGHT D. EISENHOWER

Give me your tired, your poor,
Your huddled masses yearning to breathe free,
The wretched refuse of your teeming shore;
Send these, the homeless, tempest-tossed to me.
I lift my lamp beside the golden door!   EMMA LAZARUS

Whatever America hopes to bring to pass in the world must first come to pass in the heart of America.
DWIGHT D. EISENHOWER

The only foes that threaten America are the enemies at home, and these are ignorance, superstition, and incompetence.
ELBERT HUBBARD

If we do not make a common cause to save the good old ship of the Union on this voyage, nobody will have a chance to pilot her on another voyage.   ABRAHAM LINCOLN

Nothing will ruin the country if the people themselves will undertake its safety; and nothing can save it if they leave that safety in any hands but their own.   DANIEL WEBSTER

Then conquer we must, for our cause it is just, and this be our motto: "In God is our trust!"   FRANCIS SCOTT KEY

The winds that blow through the wide sky in these mountains—the winds that sweep from Canada to Mexico, from the Pacific to the Atlantic—have always blown on free men.
FRANKLIN D. ROOSEVELT

America is the only country in the world where a man can afford to build a four-bedroom house by the time all of his children are old enough to go to college.

The United States never lost a war or won a conference.

WILL ROGERS

There is nothing wrong with America that together we can't fix.

RONALD REAGAN

God had a divine purpose in placing this land between two great oceans to be found by those who had a special love of freedom and courage.

RONALD REAGAN

How little do my countrymen know what precious blessings they are in possession of, and which no other people on earth enjoy. I confess I had no idea of it myself. While we shall see multiplied instances of Europeans going to live in America, I will venture to say no man now living will ever see an instance of an American removing to settle in Europe and continuing there.

THOMAS JEFFERSON

If there be one principle more deeply rooted than any other in the mind of every American, it is that we should have nothing to do with conquest.

THOMAS JEFFERSON

The United States is the only country with a known birthday.

JAMES G. BLAINE

I believe in America because we have great dreams—and because we have the opportunity to make those dreams come true.

WENDELL L. WILLKIE

America is the great melting pot.

ISRAEL ZANGWILL

Double—no triple—our troubles and we'd still be better off than any other people on earth.

The fabulous country—the place where miracles not only happen, but where they happen all the time.

THOMAS WOLFE

Americanism

Americanism means the virtues of courage, honor, justice, truth, sincerity, and hardihood—the virtues that made America. The things that will destroy America are prosperity-at-any-price, peace-at-any-price, safety-first instead of duty-first, the love of soft living and the get-rich-quick theory of life.

THEODORE ROOSEVELT

There can be no fifty-fifty Americanism in this country. There is room here for only 100-percent Americanism, only for those who are Americans and nothing else.

THEODORE ROOSEVELT

Americans

An American is one who will sacrifice property, ease, and security in order that he and his children may retain the rights of free men.

HAROLD ICKES

Cut an American into a hundred pieces and boil him down, you will find him all fourth of July.

WENDELL PHILLIPS

I was born an American: I will live an American; I shall die an American; and I intend to perform the duties incumbent upon me in that character to the end of my career. I mean to do this, with absolute disregard of personal consequences. What are personal consequences? What is the individual man, with all the good or evil that may betide him, in comparison with the good or evil which may befall a great country in a crisis like this, and in the midst of great transactions which concern that country's fate? Let the consequences be what will, I am careless.

No man can suffer too much, and no man can fall too soon, if he suffers or if he falls in defense of the liberties and Constitution of his country.

DANIEL WEBSTER

When at first you don't succeed, remember the last four letters of American.

[An Englishman is] a person who does things because they have been done before. [An American is] a person who does things because they haven't been done before.

MARK TWAIN

Not many Americans have been around the world but their money sure has.

WALTER SLEZAK

Let us have done with British-Americans and Irish-Americans and German-Americans, and so on, and all be Americans...If a man is going to be an American at all let him be so without any qualifying adjectives; and if he is going to be something else, let him drop the word American from his personal description.

HENRY CABOT LODGE

If I were to attempt to put my political philosophy tonight into a single phrase, it would be this: Trust the people. Trust their good sense, their decency, their fortitude, their faith. Trust them with the facts. Trust them with the great decisions. And fix as our guiding star the passion to create a society where people can fulfill their own best selves—where no American is held down by race or color, by worldly condition or social status, from gaining what his character earns him as an American citizen, as a human being and as a child of God.

ADLAI STEVENSON

Ancient Times

Let others praise ancient times; I am glad I was born in these.

OVID

Anger

He best keeps from anger who remembers that God is always looking upon him.

PLATO

He that is slow to anger is better than the mighty; and he that ruleth his spirit than he that taketh a city.

THE BIBLE: PROVERBS 16:32 KJV

Two things a man should never be angry at: what he can help, and what he cannot help.

He that would be angry and sin not, must not be angry with anything but sin.

THOMAS SECKER

Frequent fits of anger produce in the soul a propensity to be angry; which oftentimes ends in choler, bitterness, and morosity, when the mind becomes ulcerated, peevish, and querulous, and is wounded by the least occurrence.

PLUTARCH

To be angry is to revenge the faults of others on ourselves.
ALEXANDER POPE

The intoxication of anger, like that of the grape, shows us to others, but hides us from ourselves. We injure our own cause in the opinion of the world when we too passionately defend it.
CHARLES CALEB COLTON

Anger begins with folly, and ends with repentance.
H.G. BOHN

Anger makes dull men witty, but it keeps them poor.
FRANCIS BACON

He who conquers his anger has conquered an enemy.

Anger is never without a reason, but seldom a good one.
BENJAMIN FRANKLIN

Anger has no counsel.

Anger has no eyes.

The size of a man can be measured by the size of the thing that makes him angry.
JOHN MORLEY

Animals

Animals are such agreeable friends—they ask no questions, they pass no criticisms.
GEORGE ELIOT

Answers

To every answer you can find a new question.

For many years now, you and I have been shushed like children and told there are no simple answers to the complex problems that are beyond our comprehension. Well, the truth is, there are simple answers. There are just not easy ones.

RONALD REAGAN

A man has joy in an apt answer, and how delightful is a timely word!

THE BIBLE: PROVERBS 15:23 NASB

Antagonists

He that wrestles with us, strengthens our nerves, and sharpens our skill. Our antagonist is our helper.

EDMUND BURKE

I am bound to furnish my antagonists with arguments but not with comprehension.

BENJAMIN DISRAELI

Anticipation

Nothing is so wretched or foolish as to anticipate misfortunes. What madness is it to be expecting evil before it comes.

SENECA

If pleasures are greatest in anticipation, just remember that this is also true of trouble.

ELBERT HUBBARD

Anticipation is often greater than realization.

R.E. PHILLIPS

Ants

None preaches better than the ant, and she says nothing.

BENJAMIN FRANKLIN

Anvil and Hammer

If you are an anvil, bear the strokes, and if you become a hammer, strike.

Anxiety

The thinner the ice, the more anxious is everyone to see whether it will bear.

JOSH BILLINGS

Appearance

Appear always what you are and a little less.

Appeasement

An appeaser is one who feeds a crocodile hoping it will eat him last.

SIR WINSTON CHURCHILL

Appetite

Appetite comes with eating.

Always rise from the table with an appetite, and you will never sit down without one.

WILLIAM PENN

Scientists have not yet found a better way of putting flavor into food than a five-mile hike before dinner.

It is difficult to satisfy one's appetite by painting pictures of cakes.

Applause

When someone does something good, applaud! You will make two people happy.

SAMUEL GOLDWYN

Appreciation

A word or a nod from the good has more weight than the eloquent speeches of others.

PLUTARCH

The deepest principle in human nature is the craving to be appreciated.

WILLIAM JAMES

Arbitration

Four out of five potential litigants will settle their disputes the first day they come together, if you will put the idea of arbitration into their heads.

MOSES HENRY GROSSMAN

Arguments

They are yet but ear-kissing arguments.

WILLIAM SHAKESPEARE

Art

Abstract art? A product of the untalented, sold by the unprincipled to the utterly bewildered.

Artists

Nobody can count themselves an artist unless they can carry a picture in their head before they paint it.

CLAUDE MONET

Assassination

Assassination is the extreme form of censorship.

GEORGE BERNARD SHAW

Assumptions

All miscommunication is the result of differing assumptions.

Atheism

To be an atheist requires an infinitely greater measure of faith than to receive all the great truths which atheism would deny.

JOSEPH ADDISON

The three great apostles of practical atheism that make converts without persecuting, and retain them without preaching, are health, wealth, and power.

CHARLES CALEB COLTON

An atheist is a man who has no invisible means of support.

JOHN BUCHAN

Attacks

As a general rule, I abstain from reading the reports of attacks upon myself, wishing not to be provoked by that to which I cannot properly offer an answer.

Attention

People who come with problems don't want solutions—they want attention.

Attitude

Nothing can work me damage except myself. The harm that I sustain I carry about with me, and am never a real sufferer but by my own fault.

BERNARD OF CLAIRVAUX

A perverse and fretful disposition makes any state of life unhappy.

CICERO

It is not he who gives abuse that affronts, but the view that we take of it as insulting; so that when one provokes you it is your own opinion which is provoking.

EPICTETUS

We sing "Make a Joyful Noise Unto the Lord" while our faces reflect the sadness of one who has just buried a rich aunt who left everything to her pregnant hamster.

ERMA BOMBECK

Sunshine is delicious, rain is refreshing, wind braces us up, snow is exhilarating; there is really no such thing as bad weather, only different kinds of good weather.

JOHN RUSKIN

Arrange whatever pieces come your way.

VIRGINIA WOOLF

It is no use to grumble and complain;
It's just as cheap and easy to rejoice;
When God sorts out the weather and sends rain—
Why, rain's my choice.

JAMES WHITCOMB RILEY

A man's as miserable as he thinks he is.

SENECA

Life is 10 percent what you make it, and 90 percent how you take it.
                                        IRVING BERLIN

It is our relation to circumstances that determines their influence over us. The same wind that carries one vessel into port may blow another off shore.
                                        CHRISTIAN NESTELL BOVEE

What you can't get out of, get into wholeheartedly.
                                        MIGNON MCLAUGHLIN

The really happy man is one who can enjoy the scenery on a detour.

If the sky falls, we shall catch larks.

I don't think of all the misery, but of all the beauty that still remains.
                                        ANNE FRANK

He shall fare well who confronts circumstances aright.
                                        PLUTARCH

The art of life is to know how to enjoy a little and to endure much.
                                        WILLIAM HAZLITT

I have resolved that from this day on, I will do all the business I can honestly, have all the fun I can reasonably, do all the good I can willingly, and save my digestion by thinking pleasantly.
                                        ROBERT LOUIS STEVENSON

We are not troubled by things, but by the opinion which we have of things.
                                        EPICTETUS

He who is in the shade doesn't know that another is in the sun.

Everything can be taken from a man but one thing: the last of human freedoms—to choose one's attitude in any given set of circumstances—to choose one's own way.

VIKTOR FRANKL

What a man thinks of himself, that it is which determines, or rather indicates, his fate.

HENRY DAVID THOREAU

Audience
Always make the audience suffer as much as possible.

ALFRED HITCHCOCK

Authors
The two most engaging powers of an author are, to make new things familiar, and familiar things new.

SAMUEL JOHNSON

What I like in a good author is not what he says, but what he whispers.

LOGAN PEARSALL SMITH

I don't want to be a doctor and live by men's diseases, nor a minister to live by their sins, nor a lawyer to live by their quarrels. So I don't see there's anything left for me but to be an author.

NATHANIEL HAWTHORNE

Avenging
The best manner of avenging ourselves is by not resembling him who has injured us.

JANE PORTER

Avoidance

We run away all the time to avoid coming face to face with ourselves.

Babies

Babies are such a nice way to start people.

DON HEROLD

Backbone

The individual activity of one man with backbone will do more than a thousand men with a mere wishbone.

WILLIAM J.H. BOETCKER

Bad Luck

I never knew an early-rising, hard-working, prudent man, careful of his earnings, and strictly honest, who complained of bad luck. A good character, good habits, and iron industry are impregnable to the assaults of all the ill-luck that fools ever dreamed of.

JOSEPH ADDISON

Bad Men

Even though you become the enemy of a good man, don't become the friend of a bad man.

A bad man is worse when he pretends to be a saint.

FRANCIS BACON

Bait

Every man has his price. This is not true. But for every man there exists a bait which he cannot resist swallowing.

FRIEDRICH NIETZSCHE

Ballot

The ballot is stronger than the bullet.

ABRAHAM LINCOLN

Baloney

No matter how thin you slice it, it's still baloney.

ALFRED E. SMITH

Beach

A place where people slap you on the back and ask how you're peeling.

Beauty

No one can live on beauty, but they can die for it.

Think of all the beauty still left around you and be happy.

ANNE FRANK

Beauty, in a modest woman, is like fire, or a sharp sword at a distance: neither doth the one burn, nor the other wound those that come not too near them.

MIGUEL DE CERVANTES

Beauty may be said to be God's trademark in creation.

HENRY WARD BEECHER

Beginning

More powerful than the will to win is the courage to begin.

The beginning is half of every action.

All beginnings are difficult.

THE TALMUD

Behavior

Behavior is a mirror in which every one displays his image.

JOHANN WOLFGANG VON GOETHE

Belief

He does not believe that does not live according to his belief.

THOMAS FULLER

Man's most valuable trait is a judicious sense of what not to believe.

EURIPIDES

Belly

He who does not mind his belly will hardly mind anything else.

SAMUEL JOHNSON

The belly overrules the head.

Benevolence

I never knew a child of God being bankrupted by his benevolence. What we keep we may lose, but what we give to Christ we are sure to keep.

THEODORE LEDYARD CUYLER

The true source of cheerfulness is benevolence. The soul that perpetually overflows with kindness and sympathy will always be cheerful.

PARKE GODWIN

Best

I have never had a policy. I have simply tried to do what seemed best each day, as each day came.

ABRAHAM LINCOLN

Any man's life will be filled with constant and unexpected encouragement if he makes up his mind to do his level best each day.

BOOKER T. WASHINGTON

I do the very best I know how—the very best I can; and I mean to keep on doing so until the end.

ABRAHAM LINCOLN

On God for all events depend;
You cannot want when God's your friend.
Weigh well your part and do your best;
Leave to your Maker all the rest.

NATHANIEL COTTON

Good, better, best; never rest till "good" be "better" and "better" "best".

MOTHER GOOSE

Better

Better inside a cottage than outside a castle.

War with your vices, at peace with your neighbors, and let New Year find you a better man.

BENJAMIN FRANKLIN

Bible

The best evidence that the Bible is the inspired word of God is to be found within its covers. It proves itself.

CHARLES HODGE

I have made it a practice for several years to read the Bible in the course of every year.

JOHN QUINCY ADAMS

All that I am I owe to Jesus Christ, revealed to me in His divine Book.

DAVID LIVINGSTONE

The book to read is not the one which thinks for you, but the one which makes you think. No book in the world equals the Bible for that.

JAMES MCCOSH

No man ever did, or ever will become most truly eloquent without being a constant reader of the Bible, and admirer of the purity and sublimity of its language.

FISHER AMES

It was the Lord who put into my mind (I could feel His hand upon me) the fact that it would be possible to sail from here to the Indies. All who heard of my project rejected it with laughter, ridiculing me. There is no question that the inspiration was from the Holy Spirit, because He comforted me with rays of marvelous inspiration from the Holy Scriptures.

CHRISTOPHER COLUMBUS

When you have read the Bible, you will know it is the Word of God, because you will have found it the key to your own heart, your own happiness, and your own duty.

WOODROW WILSON

The Bible is one of the greatest blessings bestowed by God on the children of men. It has God for its author; salvation for its end; and truth without any mixture for its matter. It is all pure, all sincere; nothing too much; nothing wanting.

JOHN LOCKE

Read Demosthenes or Cicero; read Plato, Aristotle, or any others of that class; I grant you that you will be attracted, delighted, moved, enraptured by them in a surprising manner; but if, after reading them, you turn to the perusal of the sacred volume, whether you are willing or unwilling, it will affect you so powerfully, it will so penetrate your heart, and impress itself so strangely on your mind that, compared with its energetic influence, the beauties of rhetoricians and philosophers will almost entirely disappear; so that it is easy to perceive something divine in the sacred Scriptures, which far surpasses the highest attainments and ornaments of human industry.

JOHN CALVIN

So great is my veneration for the Bible, that the earlier my children begin to read it the more confident will be my hopes that they will prove useful citizens to their country and respectable members of society.

JOHN QUINCY ADAMS

I speak as a man of the world to men of the world; and I say to you, Search the Scriptures! The Bible is the book of all others, to be read at all ages, and in all conditions of human life; not to be read once or twice or thrice through, and then laid aside, but to be read in small portions of one or two chapters every day, and never to be intermitted, unless by some overruling necessity.

JOHN QUINCY ADAMS

The Bible is God's chart for you to steer by, to keep you from the bottom of the sea, and to show you where the harbor is, and how to reach it without running on rocks or bars.

HENRY WARD BEECHER

In regard to this great Book, I have but to say, it is the best gift God has given to man. All the good the Savior gave to the world was communicated through this book. But for it we could not know right from wrong.   ABRAHAM LINCOLN

The Bible is a window in this prison-world, through which we may look into eternity.   TIMOTHY DWIGHT

I would advise no one to send his child where the Holy Scriptures are not supreme. Every institution that does not unceasingly pursue the study of God's word becomes corrupt.   MARTIN LUTHER

It is impossible to mentally or socially enslave a Bible-reading people. The principles of the Bible are the groundwork of human freedom.   HORACE GREELEY

Bigots

How it infuriates a bigot, when he is forced to drag into the light his dark convictions.   LOGAN PEARSALL SMITH

Bill of Rights

It does not require a lawyer to interpret the provisions of the Bill of Rights. They are as clear as the Ten Commandments.   HERBERT HOOVER

Billboards

I think that I shall never see
A billboard lovely as a tree.
Indeed, unless the billboards fall
I'll never see a tree at all.

   OGDEN NASH

Bipartisanship

Whenever a fellow tells me he's bipartisan, I know he's going to vote against me.

HARRY S. TRUMAN

Blarney

Baloney is the unvarnished lie laid on so thick you hate it. Blarney is flattery laid on so thin you love it.

FULTON J. SHEEN

Blessings

Reflect upon your present blessings, of which every man has many: not on your past misfortunes, of which all men have some.

CHARLES DICKENS

Blockheads

A learned blockhead is a greater blockhead than an ignorant one.

BENJAMIN FRANKLIN

Boasting

He who boasts of his accomplishments will reap ridicule.

Don't place too much confidence in a man who boasts of being as honest as the day is long. Wait until you meet him at night.

BOB EDWARDS

With all his tumid boasts, he's like the swordfish, who only wears his weapon in his mouth.

SAMUEL MADDEN

The empty cask makes the most sound.

JACOB CATS

Boldness

Avoiding danger is no safer in the long run than outright exposure. The fearful are caught as often as the bold.

HELEN KELLER

When you cannot make up your mind which of two evenly balanced courses of action you should take—choose the bolder.

W.J. SLIM

Don't be afraid to take a big step if one is indicated. You can't cross a chasm in two small jumps.

DAVID LLOYD GEORGE

In difficult situations, when hope seems feeble, the boldest plans are safest.

LIVY

Put a grain of boldness into everything you do.

BALTASAR GRACIAN

I hate to see things done by halves. If it be right, do it boldly— if it be wrong leave it undone.

BERNARD GILPIN

Bondage

Great nations rise and fall. The people go from bondage to spiritual truth to great courage, from courage to liberty, from liberty to abundance, from abundance to selfishness, from selfishness to complacency, from complacency to apathy, from apathy to dependence, from dependence back again to bondage.

BENJAMIN DISRAELI

Books

Everything comes to him who waits. Except a loaned book.

KIN HUBBARD

How many a man had dated a new era in his life from the reading of a book.

HENRY DAVID THOREAU

When I get a little money, I buy books; and if any is left, I buy food and clothes.

ERASMUS

Books are embalmed minds.

CHRISTIAN NESTELL BOVEE

He that loves not books before he comes to thirty years of age, will hardly love them enough afterward to understand them.

EDWARD HYDE

There is more treasure in books than in all the pirates' loot on Treasure Island…and best of all, you can enjoy these riches every day of your life.

WALT DISNEY

Read the best books first, or you may not have a chance to read them all.

HENRY DAVID THOREAU

Outside of a dog, a book is man's best friend. Inside of a dog, it's too dark to read.

GROUCHO MARX

Of making many books there is no end, and much study wearies the body.

THE BIBLE: ECCLESIASTES 12:12

If we encountered a man of rare intellect, we should ask him what books he read.

RALPH WALDO EMERSON

I cannot live without books.

THOMAS JEFFERSON

Books are the bees which carry the quickening pollen from one to another mind.

JAMES RUSSELL LOWELL

Bookstore

Where is human nature so weak as in the bookstore!

HENRY WARD BEECHER

Boredom

Broadly speaking, human beings may be divided into three classes: those who are billed to death, those who are worried to death, and those who are bored to death.

SIR WINSTON CHURCHILL

Bores

A healthy male adult bore consumes each year one-and-a-half times his own weight in other people's patience.

JOHN UPDIKE

There are few wild beasts more to be dreaded than a talking man having nothing to say.

JONATHAN SWIFT

Perhaps the world's second worst crime is boredom. The first is being a bore.

CECIL BEATON

Borrowing

When I lent, I was a friend; and when I asked, I was unkind.

The borrower is servant to the lender.

THE BIBLE: PROVERBS 22:7

Boss

The question "Who ought to be boss?" is like asking, "Who ought to be the tenor in the quartet?" Obviously, the man who can sing tenor.

HENRY FORD

I've always found that the speed of the boss is the speed of the team.

LEE IACOCCA

Boys

When I grow up, I want to be a little boy.

A good way to get a boy to cut the grass is to forbid him to touch the lawn mower.

Bragging

Generally when a man brags about his pedigree he has nothing else to brag about.

REFLECTIONS OF A BACHELOR

Brains

The biggest human brain on record was that of an idiot; one of the smallest was that of the gifted French writer Anatole France.

ASHLEY MONTAGU

Bravery

This will remain the land of the free only so long as it is the home of the brave.

We could never learn to be brave and patient if there were only joy in the world.

It is easy to be brave from a safe distance.

Bravery is the capacity to perform properly even when scared half to death.
OMAR BRADLEY

Physical bravery is an animal instinct; moral bravery is a much higher and truer courage.

Brevity

Brevity is the best recommendation of speech, whether in a senator or an orator.
CICERO

Bumblebees

According to the theory of aerodynamics, as may be readily demonstrated through wind tunnel experiments, the bumblebee is unable to fly. This is because the size, weight, and shape of its body in relation to the total wingspread make flying impossible. But the bumblebee, being ignorant of these scientific truths, goes ahead and flies anyway—and makes a little honey every day.
RALPH L. WOODS

Bungee Jumping

Whoever invented bungee jumping must have watched a lot of Roadrunner cartoons.
NICK ARNETTE

Burdens

It has been well said that no man ever sank under the burden of the day. It is when tomorrow's burden is added to the burden of today that the weight is more than a man can bear.
GEORGE MACDONALD

"What is life's heaviest burden?" asked a youth of a sad and lonely old man. "To have nothing to carry," he answered.
E. SCOTT O'CONNOR

Business

Business is like a wheelbarrow. Nothing ever happens until you start pushing.

Business is like riding a bicycle. Either you keep moving or you fall down.
JOHN DAVID WRIGHT

I remember that a wise friend of mine did usually say, "That which is everybody's business is nobody's business."
IZAAK WALTON

Never fear the want of business. A man who qualifies himself well for his calling, never fails of employment in it.
THOMAS JEFFERSON

Busy Man

The busy man has few idle visitors; to the boiling pot the flies come not.
BENJAMIN FRANKLIN

Busyness

Too many bricklayers make a lopsided house. Some are very busy and yet do nothing.

But

Oh, now comes that bitter word—but, which makes all nothing that was said before that smooths and wounds, that strikes and dashes more than a flat denial, or a plain disgrace.

SAMUEL DANIEL

Buying

Let the buyer beware.
Caveat emptor (Latin).

Tell me what you are eager to buy, and I will tell you what you are.

He who buys what he needs not, may have to sell what he needs.

Calamity

Calamity is the perfect glass wherein we truly see and know ourselves.

SIR WILLIAM DAVENANT

Calm

They sicken of the calm, who know the storm.

DOROTHY PARKER

Campaign Speech

The presidential campaign speech is, like jazz, one of the few truly American art forms. It is not, of course, unknown in other democratic countries, but nowhere else has it achieved the same degree of virtuosity; nowhere else is it so accurate a reflection of national character: by turns solemn or witty, pompous or deeply moving, full of sense or full of wind.

Candor

All faults may be forgiven of him who has perfect candor.

WALT WHITMAN

Canons

A DECALOGUE OF CANONS FOR OBSERVATION IN PRACTICAL LIFE:

1. Never put off till tomorrow what you can do today.
2. Never trouble another for what you can do yourself.
3. Never spend your money before you have it.
4. Never buy what you do not want because it is cheap; it will be dear to you.
5. Pride costs us more than hunger, thirst, and cold.
6. We never repent of having eaten too little.
7. Nothing is troublesome that we do willingly.
8. How much pain have cost us the evils which have never happened.
9. Take things always by their smooth handle.
10. When angry, count to ten before you speak; if very angry, a hundred.

THOMAS JEFFERSON

Capability

Treat people as if they were what they ought to be and you help them to become what they are capable of being.

JOHANN WOLFGANG VON GOETHE

Capableness

Men are men before they are lawyers or physicians or merchants or manufacturers; and if you make them capable and sensible men, they will make themselves capable and sensible lawyers or physicians.

JOHN STUART MILL

Capitalism

Capitalism and communism stand at opposite poles. Their essential difference is this: The communist, seeing the rich and his fine home says: "No man should have so much." The capitalist, seeing the same thing, says: "All men should have as much."

PHELPS ADAMS

Captains

Too many captains run the ship aground.

Car Alarms

They erupt like indignant metal jungle birds, and they whoop all night. They make American cities sound like lunatic rain forests, all the wildlife affrighted, violated, outraged, shrieking...In a neighborhood of apartment buildings, one such beast rouses sleepers by the hundreds, even thousands. They wake, roll over, moan, jam pillows on their ears and try to suppress the adrenaline. Car thieves, however, pay no attention to the noise.

LANCE MORROW

Care

[Cast] all your care upon him; for he careth for you.

THE BIBLE: 1 PETER 5:7 KJV

Cats

When the cat has gone, the rats come out to stretch themselves.

Cause

The greater the cause, the greater the possibility for collision.

No man is worth his salt who is not ready at all times to risk his well-being, to risk his body, to risk his life, in a great cause.

THEODORE ROOSEVELT

Caution

The chief danger in life is that you may take too many precautions.

ALFRED ADLER

Celebrities

The nice thing about being a celebrity is that when you bore people, they think it's their fault.

HENRY KISSINGER

Challenge

We gain nothing by being with such as ourselves: We encourage each other in mediocrity. I am always longing to be with men more excellent than myself.

CHARLES LAMB

Change

We need courage to throw away old garments which have had their day and no longer fit the requirements of the new generations.

FRIDTJOF NANSEN

Change is our ally, and we face squarely those who fight change because the status quo has been good to them. The divine right of the successful is as false a notion as the divine right of Kings.

WILLARD WIRTZ

Changing of works is lighting of hearts.

If we lose touch with the river of change and enter a backwater, become self-centered and self-satisfied, and ostrichlike ignore what happens elsewhere, we do so at our peril.

JAWAHARLAL NEHRU

The only time a woman really succeeds in changing a man is when he's a baby.

NATALIE WOOD

If you want to make enemies, try to change something.

WOODROW WILSON

Everything changes continually. What is history, indeed, but a record of change. And if there had been very few changes in the past, there would have been little of history to write.

JAWAHARLAL NEHRU

Nothing in the world that is alive remains unchanging. All Nature changes from day to day and minute to minute, only the dead stop growing and are quiescent. Fresh water runs on, and if you stop it, it becomes stagnant. So also is it with the life of man and the life of a nation.

JAWAHARLAL NEHRU

In prosperity prepare for a change; in adversity hope for one.

JAMES BURGH

Nothing is permanent but change.

HERACLITUS

The absurd man is he who never changes.

AUGUSTE BARTHELEMY

Nobody told me how hard and lonely change is.

JOAN GILBERTSON

The world hates change, yet it is the only thing that has brought progress.

CHARLES KETTERING

When you're through changing, you're through.

BRUCE BARTON

With me a change of trouble is as good as a vacation.

WILLIAM LLOYD GEORGE

Innovation is resisted by individuals who are unwilling to risk the status they have achieved and jealously guard their own job against any change.

WILLIAM T. BRADY

There is a certain relief in change, even though it be from bad to worse.

WASHINGTON IRVING

All is change; all yields its place and goes.

EURIPIDES

All changes, even the most longed for, have their melancholy; for what we leave behind us is a part of ourselves; we must die to one life before we can enter into another.

ANATOLE FRANCE

We are restless because of incessant change, but we would be frightened if change were stopped.

LYMAN LLOYD BRYSON

After you've done a thing the same way for two years, look it over carefully. After five years, look at it with suspicion. And after ten years, throw it away and start all over.

ALFRED EDWARD PERLMAN

Change is the law of life, and those who look only to the past or the present are certain to miss the future.

JOHN F. KENNEDY

Everything flows, nothing stays still.   HERACLITUS

One must change one's tactics every ten years if one wishes to maintain one's superiority.   NAPOLEON BONAPARTE

Just when I think I have learned the way to live, life changes.

HUGH PRATHER

Change is what people fear most.

FYODOR DOSTOYEVSKY

Everyone thinks of changing the world, but no one thinks of changing himself.   LEO TOLSTOY

Character

A man lays the foundation of true greatness when he becomes more concerned with building his character than with expanding his reputation.   WILLIAM ARTHUR WARD

Resolved: never to do anything which I should be afraid to do if it were the last hour of my life.   JONATHAN EDWARDS

A good character is more valuable than gold.

There is no character, howsoever good and fine, but it can be destroyed by ridicule, howsoever poor and witless. Observe the ass, for instance: His character is about perfect; he is the choicest spirit among all the humbler animals; yet see what ridicule has brought him to. Instead of feeling complimented when we are called an ass, we are left in doubt.

MARK TWAIN

Character contributes to beauty. It fortifies a woman as her youth fades. A mode of conduct, a standard of courage, discipline, fortitude, and integrity can do a great deal to make a woman beautiful.

JACQUELINE BISSET

Good character is more to be praised than outstanding talent. Most talents are to some extent a gift. Good character, by contrast, is not given to us. We have to build it piece by piece...by thought, choice, courage, and determination.

JOHN LUTHER LONG

Character is what you are in the dark.

DWIGHT L. MOODY

Education commences at the mother's knee, and every word spoken within the hearing of little children tends towards the formation of character.

HOSEA BALLOU

You can't tell what a man is like or what he is thinking when you are looking at him. You must get around behind him and see what he has been looking at.

WILL ROGERS

Character is like a tree, and reputation is like a shadow. The shadow is what we think of it; the tree is the real thing.

ABRAHAM LINCOLN

Every man is a volume, if you know how to read him.

WILLIAM ELLERY CHANNING

Be more concerned with your character than with your reputation. Your character is what you really are while your reputation is merely what others think you are.

JOHN WOODEN

Character builds slowly, but it can be torn down with incredible swiftness.

FAITH BALDWIN

Talents are best nurtured in solitude; character is best formed in the stormy billows of the world.

JOHANN WOLFGANG VON GOETHE

A man of character will make himself worthy of any position he is given.

MAHATMA GANDHI

A dwarf is small, even if he stands on a mountain; a colossus keeps his height, even if he stands in a well.

SENECA

A sound body is a first-class thing; a sound mind is an even better thing; but the thing that counts for most in the individual as in the nation, is character, the sum of those qualities which make a man a good man and a woman a good woman.

THEODORE ROOSEVELT

A good name lost is seldom regained. When character is gone, all is gone, and one of the richest jewels of life is lost forever.

JOEL HAWES

He who acts wickedly in private life can never be expected to show himself noble in public conduct. He that is base at home will not acquit himself with honor abroad; for it is not the man, but only the place that is changed.

AESCHINES

A man's character is the reality of himself. His reputation is the opinion others have formed of him. Character is in him, reputation is from other people; that is the substance, this is the shadow.

HENRY WARD BEECHER

The best advertisement of a workshop is first class work. The strongest attraction to Christianity is a well-made Christian character.

THEODORE LEDYARD CUYLER

Ugliness with a good character is better than beauty.

MARION DE VELDER

I have a dream that my four little children will one day live in a nation where they will not be judged by the color of their skin, but by the content of their character.

MARTIN LUTHER KING JR.

Gross and obscure natures, however decorated, seem impure shambles; but character gives splendor to youth and awe to wrinkled skin and gray hairs.

RALPH WALDO EMERSON

Charity

The best thing to give to your enemy is forgiveness; to an opponent, tolerance; to a friend, your heart; to your child, a good example; to a father, deference; to your mother, conduct that will make her proud of you; to yourself, respect; to all men, charity.

FRANCIS MAITLAND BALFOUR

Though I speak with the tongues of men and of angels, and have not charity, I am become as sounding brass, or a tinkling cymbal.

THE BIBLE: 1 CORINTHIANS 13:1 KJV

If you haven't any charity in your heart, you have the worst kind of heart trouble.

BOB HOPE

Charity is also a habit.

Charm

The basic thing which contributes to charm is the ability to forget oneself and be engrossed in other people.

ELEANOR ROOSEVELT

All charming people have something to conceal, usually their total dependence on the appreciation of others.

CYRIL CONNOLLY

Chase

With the catching ends the pleasures of the chase.

ABRAHAM LINCOLN

Cheating

I have found that if a young person cheats in school, he has a tendency to cheat in life. It starts a trend as he begins to harden his heart, and this becomes a terrible danger.

BILLY GRAHAM

Cheerfulness

Everyone must have felt that a cheerful friend is like a sunny day, which sheds its brightness on all around; and most of us can, as we choose, make of this world either a palace or a prison.

SIR JOHN LUBBOCK

A cheerful temper joined with innocence will make beauty attractive, knowledge delightful, and wit good-natured. It will lighten sickness, poverty, and affliction; convert ignorance into an amiable simplicity, and render deformity itself agreeable.

JOSEPH ADDISON

The cheerful live longest in years, and afterwards in our regards. Cheerfulness is the offshoot of goodness.

CHRISTIAN NESTELL BOVEE

A cheerful heart is a good medicine, but a downcast spirit dries up the bones.

THE BIBLE: PROVERBS 17:22 RSV

All of the days of the oppressed are wretched, but the cheerful heart has a continual feast.

THE BIBLE: PROVERBS 15:15

Wondrous is the strength of cheerfulness, and its power of endurance—the cheerful man will do more in the same time, will do it better, will persevere in it longer, than the sad or sullen.

THOMAS CARLYLE

Cheerfulness is like money well expended in charity; the more we dispense of it, the greater our possession.

VICTOR HUGO

Of cheerfulness, or a good temper—the more it is spent, the more it remains.

RALPH WALDO EMERSON

Children

There never was child so lovely but his mother was glad to get him asleep.

RALPH WALDO EMERSON

Don't threaten a child: Either punish him or forgive him.

The Talmud

Teach your child to hold his tongue; he'll learn fast enough to speak.

Benjamin Franklin

There's only one pretty child in the world, and every mother has it.

Many kiss the child for the nurse's sake.

John Heywood

Every child should have an occasional pat on the back as long as it is applied low enough and hard enough.

Fulton J. Sheen

In general my children refused to eat anything that hadn't danced on TV.

Erma Bombeck

Each day of our lives we make deposits in the memory banks of our children.

Charles Swindoll

Children require guidance and sympathy far more than instruction.

Annie Sullivan

It goes without saying that you should never have more children than you have car windows.

Erma Bombeck

Children have never been very good at listening to their elders, but they have never failed to imitate them.

James Baldwin

Let your children go if you want to keep them.
MALCOLM FORBES

Lo, children are an heritage of the Lord: and the fruit of the womb is his reward.
THE BIBLE: PSALM 127:3 KJV

Even when freshly washed and relieved of all obvious confections, children tend to be sticky.
FRAN LEBOWITZ

Genuine appreciation of other people's children is one of the rarer virtues.
HARLAN MILLER

One of the first things one notices in a backward country is that children are still obeying their parents.

Nature kindly warps our judgment about our children, especially when they are young, when it would be a fatal thing for them if we did not love them.
GEORGE SANTAYANA

Small children give you headache; big children, heartache.

Men are generally more careful of the breed of their horses and dogs than of their children.
WILLIAM PENN

One of the greatest pleasures a parent can experience is to gaze upon the children when they're fast asleep.

Better to be driven out from among men than to be disliked of children.
RICHARD HENRY DANA

One cannot see the evil deeds of one's own children.

The thing that impresses me most about America is the way parents obey their children.
                                    THE DUKE OF WINDSOR

The children now love luxury; they have bad manners, contempt for authority; they show disrespect for elders and love chatter in place of exercise. Children are now tyrants, not the servants of their households. They no longer rise when elders enter the room. They contradict their parents, chatter before company, gobble up dainties at the table, cross their legs, and tyrannize their teachers.
                                    SOCRATES

It seems as if I've been doing the same things since I was six years old. I'm a few inches taller, and I have a graying beard, but otherwise there's not much difference.
                                    MAURICE SENDAK

I know a lot about children. Not being an author, I'm a great critic.
                                    FINLEY PETER DUNNE

Vacation time is when kids get out of school and into your hair.

I kiss my kids "good night" no matter how late I have to wait up for them.

You can do anything with children if you only play with them.
                                    OTTO VON BISMARCK

Before I got married, I had six theories about bringing up children; now I have six children and no theories.
                                    LORD ROCHESTER

Any kid will run an errand for you, if you ask him at bedtime.
RED SKELTON

Choices

Look for your choices, pick the best one, then go with it.
PAT RILEY

Christianity

There never was found in any age of the world either philosopher, or sect, or law, or discipline which did so highly exalt the public good as the Christian faith.   FRANCIS BACON

There is one single fact which we may oppose to all the wit and argument of infidelity, namely, that no man ever repented of being a Christian on his death-bed.   HANNAH MORE

Christianity has not been tried and found wanting; it has been found difficult and not tried.   G.K. CHESTERTON

Christianity everywhere gives dignity to labor, sanctity to marriage, and brotherhood to man. Where it may not convince, it enlightens; where it does not convert, it restrains; where it does not renew, it refines; where it does not sanctify, it subdues and elevates. It is profitable alike for this world, and for the world that is to come.   SIR GEORGE LAWRENCE

When a man is opposed to Christianity, it is because Christianity is opposed to him. Your infidel is usually a person who resents the opposition of Christianity to that in his nature and life which Jesus came to rebuke and destroy.
ROBERT HALL

Whatever men may think of religion, the historic fact is, that in proportion as the institutions of Christianity lose their hold upon the multitudes, the fabric of society is in peril.

ARTHUR TAPPAN PIERSON

Christianity is the companion of liberty in all its conflicts, the cradle of its infancy, and the divine source of its claims.

ALEXIS DE TOCQUEVILLE

The distinction between Christianity and all other systems of religion consists largely in this, that in these others men are found seeking after God, while Christianity is God seeking after men.

THOMAS ARNOLD

Where science speaks of improvement, Christianity speaks of renovation; where science speaks of development, Christianity speaks of sanctification; where science speaks of progress, Christianity speaks of perfection.

JOSEPH PARRISH THOMPSON

The real security of Christianity is to be found in its benevolent morality; in its exquisite adaptation to the human heart; in the facility with which it accommodates itself to the capacity of every human intellect; in the consolation which it bears to every house of mourning; and in the light with which it brightens the great mystery of the grave.

THOMAS BABINGTON MACAULAY

Christians

Going to church doesn't make you a Christian any more than going to a garage makes you an automobile.

BILLY SUNDAY

Whatever makes men good Christians makes them good citizens.

DANIEL WEBSTER

The pagans do not know God, and love only the earth. The Jews know the true God, and love only the earth. The Christians know the true God, and do not love the earth.

BLAISE PASCAL

Circumstantial Evidence

Some circumstantial evidence is very strong, as when you find a trout in the milk.

HENRY DAVID THOREAU

Citizens

The true Christian is the true citizen, lofty of purpose, resolute in endeavor, ready for a hero's deeds, but never looking down on his task because it is cast in the day of small things; scornful of baseness, awake to his own duties as well as to his rights, following the higher law with reverence, and in this world doing all that in his power lies, so that when death comes he may feel that mankind is in some degree better because he lived.

THEODORE ROOSEVELT

A citizen first in war, first in peace, and first in the hearts of his countrymen.

HENRY LEE

The first requisite of a good citizen in this republic of ours is that he shall be able and willing to pull his weight.

THEODORE ROOSEVELT

Our average fellow-citizen is a sane and healthy man, who believes in decency and has a wholesome mind.

THEODORE ROOSEVELT

Civilizations

A great civilization is not conquered from without until it has destroyed itself within. The essential causes of Rome's decline lay in her people, her morals, her class struggle, her failing trade, her bureaucratic despotism, her stifling taxes, her consuming wars.

WILL DURANT

Now civilizations, I believe, come to birth and proceed to grow by successfully responding to successive challenges. They break down and go to pieces if and when a challenge confronts them which they fail to meet.

ARNOLD J. TOYNBEE

On this showing, the nature of the breakdown of civilizations can be summed up in three points: A failure of creative power in the minority, an answering withdrawal of mimesis on the part of the majority, and a consequent loss of social unity in the society as a whole.

ARNOLD J. TOYNBEE

Civilized Man

Anyone can be a barbarian; it requires a terrible effort to remain a civilized man.

LEONARD SIDNEY WOOLF

Clarity

"Then you should say what you mean," the March Hare went on.

"I do," Alice hastily replied; "at least—at least I mean what I say—that's the same thing, you know."

"Not the same thing a bit!" said the Hatter. "Why, you might as well say 'I see what I eat' is the same thing as 'I eat what I see'!"

Clear Vision

Give to us clear vision that we may know where to stand and what to stand for—because unless we stand for something we shall fall for anything.

PETER MARSHALL

Cleverness

It is very clever to know how to hide one's cleverness.

FRANÇOIS DE LA ROCHEFOUCAULD

The height of cleverness is to be able to conceal it.

FRANÇOIS DE LA ROCHEFOUCAULD

What cleverness hides, cleverness will reveal.

I always did think that cleverness was the art of hiding ignorance.

SHELLAND BRADLEY

Comedy

Comedy is in my blood. Frankly, I wish it were in my act!

RODNEY DANGERFIELD

Comedy has to be truth. You take the truth and put a little curlicue at the end.

SID CAESAR

Commands

There is a great force hidden in a sweet command.

What you cannot enforce, do not command.

SOPHOCLES

Common Appearance

The Lord prefers common-looking people. That is the reason
He makes so many of them.

ABRAHAM LINCOLN

Common Sense

Common sense is compelled to make its way without the
enthusiasm of anyone; all admit it grudgingly.

EDGAR WATSON HOWE

Communication

Think like a wise man but communicate in the language of the
people.

WILLIAM BUTLER YEATS

Communicate downward to subordinates with at least the same
care and attention as you communicate upward to superiors.

L.B. BELKER

What you can't communicate runs your life.

ROBERT ANTHONY

Good communication is as stimulating as black coffee, and just
as hard to sleep after.

ANNE MORROW LINDBERGH

Men who can speak a number of different tongues are noto-
rious for having little to say in any of them.

HOWARD HUGHES

Communists

What is a Communist? One who has yearning for equal divi-
sion of unequal earnings.

EBENEZER ELLIOT

It is necessary to be able to withstand all this, to agree to any and every sacrifice, and even—if need be—to resort to all sorts of stratagems, maneuvers, and illegal methods, to evasion and subterfuges in order to penetrate the trade unions, to remain in them, and to carry on Communist work in them at all costs.

V.I. LENIN

Communist: One who has nothing and is eager to share it with others.

If the Communists worked just as hard as they talked, they'd have the most prosperous style of government in the world.

WILL ROGERS

Company

A man is known by the company he keeps out of.

Cheerful company shortens the miles.

Compassion

Compassion will cure more sins than condemnation.

HENRY WARD BEECHER

Competition

Of all human powers operating on the affairs of mankind, none is greater than that of competition.

HENRY CLAY

Complaining

He that always complains is never pitied.

There are persons who constantly clamor. They complain of oppression, speculation, and pernicious influence of wealth. They cry out loudly against all banks and corporations, and a means by which small capitalists become united in order to produce important and beneficial results. They carry on mad hostility against all established institutions. They would choke the fountain of human civilization.

I must complain the cards are ill-shuffled till I have a good hand.
JONATHAN SWIFT

We have no more right to put our discordant states of mind into the lives of those around us and rob them of their sunshine and brightness than we have to enter their houses and steal their silverware.
JULIA MOSS SETON

Compliments

Everyone likes a compliment.
ABRAHAM LINCOLN

Compromise

Compromise makes a good umbrella, but a poor roof; it is a temporary expedient, often wise in party politics, almost sure to be unwise in statesmanship.
JAMES RUSSELL LOWELL

Conceit

Conceit is God's gift to little men.
BRUCE BARTON

The world tolerates conceit from those who are successful, but not from anybody else.
JOHN BLAKE

Conciliation

An infallible method of conciliating a tiger is to allow oneself to be devoured.

KONRAD ADENAUER

Conference

A conference is a gathering of important people who singly can do nothing, but together can decide that nothing can be done.

FRED ALLEN

No grand idea was ever born in a conference, but a lot of foolish ideas have died there.

F. SCOTT FITZGERALD

Confession

Confession is the first step to repentance.

He's half absolv'd who has confess'd.

MATTHEW PRIOR

Confession of our faults is the next thing to innocence.

PUBLILIUS SYRUS

A generous confession disarms slander.

THOMAS FULLER

The confession of evil works is the first beginning of good works.

AUGUSTINE

Conflict

It is well to remind ourselves that anxiety signifies a conflict, and so long as a conflict is going on, a constructive solution is possible.

ROLLO MAY

Tyranny, like hell, is not easily conquered; yet we have this consolation with us, that the harder the conflict the more glorious the triumph.

THOMAS PAINE

I have always found that to strive with a superior, is injurious; with an equal, doubtful; with an inferior, sordid and base; with any, full of unquietness.

JOSEPH HALL

No man resolved to make the most of himself can spare time for personal contention. Still less can he afford to take all the consequences, including the vitiating of his temper, and the loss of self-control. Yield larger things to which you can show no more than equal right; and yield lesser ones, though clearly your own. Better give your path to a dog than be bitten by him in contesting for the right. Even killing the dog would not cure the bite.

ABRAHAM LINCOLN

Congress

I am now here in Congress. I am at liberty to vote as my conscience and judgment dictate to be right, without the yoke of any party on me, or the driver at my heels, with his whip in hand, commanding me to gee-whoa-haw, just at his pleasure.

DAVY CROCKETT

I could study all my life and not think up half the amount of funny things they can think of in one session of Congress.

WILL ROGERS

You see, ordinarily you have got to work your way up as a humorist, and first get into Congress. Then you work your way up into the Senate and then, if your stuff is funny enough, it goes into the Congressional Record.

WILL ROGERS

Conscience

Cowardice asks, Is it safe? Expediency asks, Is it politic? Vanity asks, Is it popular? But Conscience asks, Is it right?

WILLIAM MORLEY PUNSHON

Conscience, true as the needle to the pole, points steadily to the pole-star of God's eternal justice, reminding the soul of the fearful realities of the life to come.

EZRA HALL GILLETT

It is astonishing how soon the whole conscience begins to unravel if a single stitch drops. One single sin indulged in makes a hole you could put your head through.

CHARLES BUXTON

Our greatest happiness does not depend on the condition of life in which chance has placed us, but is always the result of a good conscience, good health, occupation and freedom in all just pursuits.

THOMAS JEFFERSON

The only tyrant I accept in this world is the still voice within.

MAHATMA GANDHI

Preserve your conscience always soft and sensitive. If but one sin force its way into that tender part of the soul and is suffered to dwell there, the road is paved for a thousand iniquities.

ISAAC WATTS

If you would relish food, labor for it before you take it; if enjoy clothing, pay for it before you wear it; if you would sleep soundly, take a clear conscience to bed with you.

BENJAMIN FRANKLIN

Conscience is the root of all true courage; if a man would be brave let him obey his conscience.

JAMES FREEMAN CLARKE

I have noticed my conscience for many years, and I know it is more trouble and bother to me than anything else I started with.

MARK TWAIN

Labor to keep alive in your breast that little spark of celestial fire—conscience.

GEORGE WASHINGTON

A good conscience is a continual Christmas.

BENJAMIN FRANKLIN

A clear conscience sleeps during thunder.

Constitution

The United States Constitution has proved itself the most marvelous compilation of rules of government ever written.

FRANKLIN D. ROOSEVELT

It is too probable that no plan we propose will be adopted. Perhaps another dreadful conflict is to be sustained. If to please the people, we offer what we ourselves disapprove, how can we afterwards defend our work? Let us raise a standard to which the wise and the honest can repair. The event is in the hand of God.

GEORGE WASHINGTON

Don't interfere with anything in the Constitution. That must be maintained, for it is the only safeguard of our liberties.

ABRAHAM LINCOLN

To live under the American Constitution is the greatest political privilege that was ever accorded to the human race.

CALVIN COOLIDGE

The Constitution of the United States was made not merely for the generation that then existed, but for posterity—unlimited, undefined, endless, perpetual posterity.

HENRY CLAY

As the British Constitution is the most subtle organism which has proceeded from progressive history, so the American Constitution is the most wonderful work ever struck off at a given time by the brain and purpose of man.

WILLIAM GLADSTONE

The Constitution…is unquestionably the wisest ever yet presented to men.

THOMAS JEFFERSON

Contempt

Many can bear adversity, but few contempt.

Contentment

Be content with such things as ye have.

THE BIBLE: HEBREWS 13:5 KJV

He is richest who is content with the least, for content is the wealth of nature.

SOCRATES

The richest man, whatever his lot, is he who's content with what he has got.

He that's content hath enough; he that complains, hath too much.

BENJAMIN FRANKLIN

I had rather be shut up in a very modest cottage, with my books, my family, and a few old friends, dining on simple bacon, and letting the world roll on as it liked, than to occupy the most splendid post which any human power can give.

THOMAS JEFFERSON

There are nine requisites for contented living: Health enough to make work a pleasure. Wealth enough to support your needs. Strength to battle with difficulties and overcome them. Grace enough to confess your sins and forsake them. Patience enough to toil until some good is accomplished. Charity enough to see some good in your neighbor. Love enough to move you to be useful and helpful to others. Faith enough to make real the things of God. Hope enough to remove all anxious fears concerning the future.

JOHANN WOLFGANG VON GOETHE

Who is wise? He that learns from everyone. Who is powerful? He that governs his passions. Who is rich? He that is content. Who is that? Nobody.

BENJAMIN FRANKLIN

To be glad of life, because it gives you the chance to love and to work and to play and to look up at the stars; to be satisfied with your possessions, but not contented with yourself until you have made the best of them; to despise nothing in the world except falsehood and meanness, and to fear nothing except cowardice; to be governed by your admirations rather than by your disgusts; to covet nothing that is your neighbor's except his kindness of heart and gentleness of manners; to think seldom of your enemies, often of your friends, and every day of Christ; and to spend as much time as you can, with body and with spirit, in God's out-of-doors—these are little guideposts on the footpath to peace.

HENRY VAN DYKE

There are no conditions to which a man cannot become accustomed, especially if he sees that all those around him live the same way.

LEO TOLSTOY

Dwell upon the brightest parts in every prospect...and strive to be pleased with the present circumstances.

ABRAHAM TUCKER

Contentment with the divine will is the best remedy we can apply to misfortunes.

To be without some of the things you want is an indispensable part of happiness.

BERTRAND RUSSELL

The secret of contentment is knowing how to enjoy what you have, and to be able to lose all desire for things beyond your reach.

LIN YUTANG

Contribution

When you cease to make a contribution, you begin to die.

ELEANOR ROOSEVELT

Controversy

No great advance has ever been made in science, politics, or religion, without controversy.

LYMAN BEECHER

Conversation

For good or ill, your conversation is your advertisement. Every time you open your mouth you let men look into your mind. Do they see it well clothed, neat, businesslike?

BRUCE BARTON

The first ingredient in conversation is truth; the next, good sense; the third, good humor; and the fourth, wit.

SIR WILLIAM TEMPLE

One reason why we find so few people rational and agreeable in conversation is, that there is scarcely any one not rather thinking on what he is intending to say, than on answering exactly the question put to him. The cleverest and the most complaisant are satisfied if they only seem attentive, though we can discover in their eyes and distraction that they are wandering from what is addressed to them, and are impatient to return to what they were saying; whereas they should recollect that if they wish to please or convince others, they must not be overanxious to please themselves, and that to listen attentively, and to answer precisely, is the greatest perfection of conversation.

FRANÇOIS DE LA ROCHEFOUCAULD

The art of conversation is not in knowing what you ought to say, but what one ought not to say.

Ultimately the bond of all companionship, whether in marriage or in friendship, is conversation.

OSCAR WILDE

The most influential of all educational factors is the conversation in a child's home.

SIR WILLIAM TEMPLE

The world of conversationalists, in my experience, is divided into two classes: those who listen to what the other person has to say, and those who use the interval to plan their next remark.

BRUCE BLIVEN

A gossip is one who talks to you about others; a bore is one who talks to you about himself; and a brilliant conversationalist is one who talks to you about yourself.

LISA KIRK

I don't like to talk much with people who always agree with me. It is amusing to coquette with an echo for a little while, but one soon tires of it.

THOMAS CARLYLE

Conviction

A "No" uttered from deepest conviction is better and greater than a "Yes" merely uttered to please, or what is worse, to avoid trouble.

MAHATMA GANDHI

The height of your accomplishments will equal the depth of your convictions.

WILLIAM F. SCOLAVINO

Cooks

It is no wonder that diseases are innumerable: count the cooks.

SENECA

Cordless Phones

Cordless phones are great. If you can find them.

GLENN FOSTER

Correction

Correction is good when administered in time.

Counsel

Give neither counsel nor salt till you are asked for it.

Good counsel never comes too late.

Counselors

A counselor is one who simply articulates the human condition.

R.E. PHILLIPS

Without wise leadership, a nation is in trouble; but with good counselors there is safety.

THE BIBLE: PROVERBS 11:14 TLB

Country

Every country has its beauty.

Courage

Courage is more than standing for a firm conviction. It includes the risk of questioning that conviction.

JULIAN WEBER GORDON

We can never be certain of our courage till we have faced danger.

FRANÇOIS DE LA ROCHEFOUCAULD

Man cannot discover new oceans until he has courage to lose sight of the shore.

Be courageous!...I have seen many depressions in business. Always America has come out stronger and more prosperous. Be as brave as your fathers before you. Have faith! Go forward.

THOMAS EDISON

God grant me the courage not to give up what I think is right, even though I think it is hopeless.

CHESTER W. NIMITZ

On many of the great issues of our time, men have lacked wisdom because they have lacked courage.

WILLIAM BENTON

Last, but by no means least, courage—moral courage, the courage of one's convictions, the courage to see things through. The world is in a constant conspiracy against the brave. It's the age-old struggle—the roar of the crowd on one side and the voice of your conscience on the other.

DOUGLAS MACARTHUR

There is nothing in the world so much admired as a man who knows how to bear unhappiness with courage.

SENECA

He who loses wealth loses much; he who loses a friend loses more; but he who loses his courage loses all.

MIGUEL DE CERVANTES

Courage is the first of the human qualities because it is the quality which guarantees all the others.

SIR WINSTON CHURCHILL

It is courage, courage, courage, that raises the blood of life to crimson splendor. Live bravely and present a brave front to adversity!

HORACE

Wealth lost—something lost; Honor lost—much lost; Courage lost—all lost.

The hallmark of courage in our age of conformity is the capacity to stand on one's convictions—not obstinately or defiantly (these are gestures of defensiveness, not courage) nor as a gesture of retaliation, but simply because these are what one believes.

ROLLO MAY

One doesn't discover new lands without consenting to lose sight of the shore for a very long time.
                                                ANDRE GIDE

Courage is fear holding on a minute longer.
                                        GEORGE S. PATTON

Courage is almost a contradiction in terms. It means a strong desire to live taking the form of readiness to die.
                                        G.K. CHESTERTON

True courage is not the brutal force of vulgar heroes, but the firm resolve of virtue and reason.
                                ALFRED NORTH WHITEHEAD

This is the art of courage: to see things as they are and still believe that the victory lies not with those who avoid the bad, but those who taste, in living awareness, every drop of the good.
                                        VICTORIA LINCOLN

Courage is required not only in a person's occasional crucial decision for his own freedom, but in the little hour-to-hour decisions which place the bricks in the structure of his building of himself into a person who acts with freedom and responsibility.
                                        ROLLO MAY

Of those to whom much is given, much is required. And when at some future date the high court of history sits in judgment on each one of us—recording whether in our brief span of service we fulfilled our responsibilities to the state—our success or failure, in whatever office we may hold, will be measured by the answers to four questions: Were we truly men of courage? Were we truly men of judgment? Were we truly men of integrity? Were we truly men of dedication?
                                        JOHN F. KENNEDY

When we read, we fancy we could be martyrs; when we come to act, we cannot bear a provoking word.

HANNAH MORE

Keep your fears to yourself, but share your courage with others.

ROBERT LOUIS STEVENSON

A man of courage never wants weapons.

Success is never final; failure is never fatal; it is courage that counts.

SIR WINSTON CHURCHILL

It is better to die in battle than to die of hunger.

It often requires more courage to dare to do right than to fear to do wrong.

ABRAHAM LINCOLN

Money lost, nothing lost; courage lost, everything lost.

Courage is bearing one's own personal tragedies without dramatizing them to others.

WILLIAM FEATHER

One man with courage is a majority.

ANDREW JACKSON

Courage is grace under pressure.

ERNEST HEMINGWAY

Courage is doing what you're afraid to do. There can be no courage unless you're scared.

EDDIE RICKENBACKER

Courtesy

Nothing is ever lost by courtesy. It is the cheapest of pleasures, costs nothing, and conveys much. It pleases him who gives and receives and thus, like mercy, is twice blessed.

ERASTUS WIMAN

Life is not so short but that there is always time enough for courtesy.

RALPH WALDO EMERSON

Covetousness

The true way to gain much, is never to desire to gain too much. He is not rich that possesses much, but he that covets no more; and he is not poor that enjoys little, but he that wants too much.

FRANCIS BEAUMONT

When all sins grow old, covetousness is young.

Cowardice

Any coward can fight a battle when he's sure of winning.

GEORGE ELIOT

Avoiding danger is no safer in the long run than outright exposure. Life is either a daring adventure, or nothing.

HELEN KELLER

Creativity

Nothing makes a person respond more creatively than a level of discontent that approaches the unbearable.

Creativity has been built into every one of us; it's part of our design. Each of us lives less of the life God intended for us when we choose not to live out the creative powers we possess.

TED ENGSTROM

Creativity is the natural extension of our enthusiasm.

EARL NIGHTINGALE

Creator

All I have seen teaches me to trust the Creator for all I have not seen.

RALPH WALDO EMERSON

Credit

No man's credit is as good as his money.

EDGAR WATSON HOWE

The maxim of buying nothing without the money in our pocket to pay for it, would make of our country one of the happiest upon earth. Experience during the war proved this; as I think every man will remember that under all the privations it obliged him to submit to during that period he slept sounder and awaked happier than he can do now. Desperate of finding relief from a free course of justice, I look forward to the abolition of all credit as the only other remedy which can take place.

THOMAS JEFFERSON

Creed

HERE IS MY CREED.
I believe in one God, creator of the universe.
That He governs it by His providence.
That He ought to be worshiped.
That the most acceptable service we render Him is doing
  good to His other children.
That the soul of man is immortal and will be treated with
  justice in another life respecting its conduct in this.

BENJAMIN FRANKLIN

Crime

The accomplice is as bad as the thief.

The crime problem in New York is getting really serious. The other day the Statue of Liberty had both hands up.

JAY LENO

Small crimes always precede great ones. Never have we seen timid innocence pass suddenly to extreme licentiousness.

JEAN BAPTISTE RACINE

I grew up in a neighborhood so rough, I learned to read by the light of a police helicopter.

BILL JONES

New York is an exciting town where something is happening all the time, most of it unsolved.

JOHNNY CARSON

Crisis

The wise man does not expose himself needlessly to danger, since there are few things for which he cares sufficiently; but he is willing, in great crises, to give even his life—knowing that under certain conditions it is not worthwhile to live.

ARISTOTLE

Every little thing counts in a crisis.

JAWAHARLAL NEHRU

The nearer any disease approaches to a crisis, the nearer it is to a cure. Danger and deliverance make their advances together, and it is only in the last push that one or the other takes the lead.

THOMAS PAINE

Criticism

The trouble with most of us is that we would rather be ruined by praise than saved by criticism.

NORMAN VINCENT PEALE

Criticism may not be agreeable, but it is necessary. It fulfills the same function as pain in the human body: It calls attention to an unhealthy state of things.

SIR WINSTON CHURCHILL

People ask you for criticism, but they only want praise.

SOMERSET MAUGHAM

To escape criticism—do nothing, say nothing, be nothing.

ELBERT HUBBARD

If I were to attempt to answer all the criticisms and complaints I receive, I would have no time for any other business. From day to day I do the best I can and will continue to do so till the end. If in the end I come out all right, then the complaints and criticisms and what is said against me will make no difference. But, if the end brings me out wrong, then 10 angels coming down from heaven to swear I was right would still make no difference.

ABRAHAM LINCOLN

Critics

A critic is a gong at a railroad crossing clanging loudly and vainly as the train goes by.

CHRISTOPHER MORLEY

Pay no attention to what the critics say; there has never been set up a statue in honor of a critic.

JEAN SIBELIUS

A critic is someone who never actually goes to the battle yet who afterwards comes out shooting the wounded.

TYNE DALY

A critic is a legless man who teaches running.

CHANNING POLLOCK

Taking to pieces is the trade of those who cannot construct.

RALPH WALDO EMERSON

Dear Mrs. Jones:
Thank you for your letter. I shall try to do better.

CARL SANDBURG

[SANDBURG'S FORM LETTER FOR REPLYING TO CRITICAL LETTERS]

Cruelty

All cruel people describe themselves as paragons of frankness.

TENNESSEE WILLIAMS

Cruelty, like every other vice, requires no motive outside of itself; it only requires opportunity.

GEORGE ELIOT

Culture

Culture is only culture when the owner is not aware of its existence. Capture culture, hog tie it, and clap your brand upon it, and you did the shock that has killed the thing you loved. You can brand a steer, but you cannot brand deer.

ELBERT HUBBARD

Cunning

The greatest cunning is to have none at all.

CARL SANDBURG

Curiosity

Curiosity is one of the permanent and certain characteristics of a vigorous intellect.

SAMUEL JOHNSON

The important thing is not to stop questioning. Curiosity has its own reason for existing. One cannot help but be in awe when he contemplates the mysteries of eternity, of life, of the marvelous structure of reality. It is enough if one tries merely to comprehend a little of this mystery every day. Never lose a holy curiosity.

ALBERT EINSTEIN

Cynicism

A cynic is a man who knows the price of everything, and the value of nothing.

OSCAR WILDE

The cynic is one who never sees a good quality in a man, and never fails to see a bad one. He is the human owl, vigilant in darkness, and blind to light, mousing for vermin, and never seeing noble game.

HENRY WARD BEECHER

Give me six lines written by the most honorable of men, and I will find an excuse in them to hang him.

CARDINAL RICHELIEU

Danger

One ought never to turn one's back on a threatened danger and try to run away from it. If you do that, you will double the danger. But if you meet it promptly and without flinching, you will reduce the danger by half. Never run away from anything. Never!

SIR WINSTON CHURCHILL

People are in great danger when they know what they should do and refuse to act upon what they know.

JAMES BALDWIN

When the danger is past, God is forgotten.

DANIEL WEBSTER

Daring

Those who dare to fail miserably can achieve greatly.

ROBERT F. KENNEDY

Attacking is the only secret. Dare and the world always yields; or if it beats you sometimes, dare it again, and it will succumb.

WILLIAM MAKEPEACE THACKERAY

No one reaches a high position without daring.

PUBLILIUS SYRUS

Daughter

My son is my son till he have got him a wife,
But my daughter's my daughter all the days of her life.

THOMAS FULLER

Death

He who would teach men to die, would teach them to live.
                                MICHEL DE MONTAIGNE

We need to be reminded that there is nothing morbid about honestly confronting the thought of life's end and preparing for it so that we may go gracefully and peacefully. The fact is, we cannot truly face life until we have learned to face the fact that it will be taken away from us.   BILLY GRAHAM

Do not seek death. Death will find you. But seek the road which makes death a fulfillment.   DAG HAMMARSKJOLD

Death comes when memories become more powerful to us than dreams.

One may live as a conqueror, a king, or a magistrate; but he must die a man. The bed of death brings every human being to his pure individuality, to the intense contemplation of that deepest and most solemn of all relations—the relation between the creature and his Creator.   DANIEL WEBSTER

Death is the golden key that opens the palace of eternity.
                                JOHN MILTON

Let death be daily before your eyes, and you will never entertain any abject thought, nor too eagerly covet anything.
                                EPICTETUS

We picture death as coming to destroy; let us rather picture Christ as coming to save. We think of death as ending; let us rather think of life as beginning, and that more abundantly. We think of losing; let us think of gaining. We think of parting, let us think of meeting. We think of going away; let us think of arriving. And as the voice of death whispers "You must go from earth," let us hear the voice of Christ saying, "You are but coming to Me!"

NORMAN MACLEOD

Death softens all resentments, and the consciousness of a common inheritance of frailty and weakness modifies the severity of judgment.

JOHN GREENLEAF WHITTIER

He that dies pays all debts.

WILLIAM SHAKESPEARE

If my doctor told me I only had six minutes to live, I wouldn't brood. I'd type a little faster.

ISAAC ASIMOV

When death comes, the rich man has no money, the poor man no debt.

Let dissolution come when it will, it can do the Christian no harm, for it will be but a passage out of a prison into a palace; out of a sea of troubles into a haven of rest; out of a crowd of enemies, to an innumerable company of true, loving, and faithful friends; out of shame, reproach, and contempt, into exceeding great and eternal glory.

JOHN BUNYAN

Debt

Debt is the worst poverty.

THOMAS FULLER

Some people use one half their ingenuity to get into debt, and the other half to avoid paying it.

GEORGE D. PRENTICE

And to preserve our independence, we must not let our rulers load us with perpetual debt. We must make our election between economy and liberty, or profusion and servitude.

THOMAS JEFFERSON

Of all the freedoms a man may enjoy, none can quite match that which comes from being completely free of debt.

Debt is a bad companion.

Deception

We are inclined to believe those whom we do not know, because they have never deceived us.   SAMUEL JOHNSON

All deception in the course of life is indeed nothing else but a lie reduced to practice, and falsehood passing from words into things.

ROBERT SOUTHEY

It is double pleasure to deceive the deceiver.

JEAN DE LA FONTAINE

You can fool some of the people all of the time, and all of the people some of the time, but you cannot fool all the people all the time.

ABRAHAM LINCOLN

Decisions

Whenever you see a successful business, someone once made a courageous decision.

PETER DRUCKER

The moment one definitely commits oneself, then Providence moves too. All sorts of things occur to help that would never otherwise have occurred. A stream of events issues from the decision, raising unforeseen incidents and meetings and material assistance, which no man could have dreamt would have come his way.

W.H. MURRAY

Whenever I make a bum decision, I go out and make another one.

HARRY S. TRUMAN

Be willing to make decisions. That's the most important quality of a good leader. Don't fall victim to what I call the ready-aim-aim-aim syndrome. You must be willing to fire.

T. BOONE PICKENS

In forty hours I shall be in battle, with little information, and on the spur of the moment will have to make the most momentous decisions. But I believe that one's spirit enlarges with responsibility and that, with God's help, I shall make them, and make them right.

GEORGE S. PATTON

My father was my idol, I tried to emulate him not only as an ideal soldier but as a great man.

He used to say: "Gather all the facts possible and then make your decision on what you think is right, as opposed to what you think is wrong. Don't try to guess what others will think, whether they will praise or deride you. And always remember that at least some of your decisions will probably be wrong. Do this and you always will sleep well at night."

DOUGLAS MACARTHUR

A decision is what a man makes when he can't get anyone to serve on a committee.

FLETCHER KNEBEL

Give your decisions, never your reasons; your decisions may be right, but your reasons are sure to be wrong.

WILLIAM MURRAY

Decisiveness

Deliberate with caution, but act with decision and promptness.

CHARLES CALEB COLTON

It does not take much strength to do things, but it requires great strength to decide on what to do.

ELBERT HUBBARD

Don't fight the problem; decide it.

GEORGE C. MARSHALL

Men must be decided on what they will not do, and then they are able to act with vigor in what they ought to do.

MENCIUS

Dedication

Give me 100 men who fear nothing but sin and desire nothing but God, and I care not whether they be clergy or laymen; such men alone will shake the gates of hell and set up the Kingdom of Heaven on earth.

JOHN WESLEY

Deeds

Some people dream of worthy accomplishments, while others stay awake and do them.

As I grow older I pay less attention to what men say. I just watch what they do.

ANDREW CARNEGIE

The only measure of what you believe is what you do. If you want to know what people believe, don't read what they write, don't ask them what they believe, just observe what they do.

ASHLEY MONTAGU

Those who aim at great deeds must also suffer greatly.

PLUTARCH

To know what has to be done, then do it, comprises the whole philosophy of practical life.   SIR WILLIAM OSLER

By his deeds we know a man.

Men are alike in their promises. It is only in their deeds that they differ.

MOLIÉRE

What one does, one becomes.

Small deeds done are better than great deeds planned.

GEORGE C. MARSHALL

You can't try to do things; you simply must do them.

RAY BRADBURY

Defeat

It is defeat that turns bone to flint, and gristle to muscle, and makes men invincible, and formed those heroic natures that are now in ascendancy in the world. Do not then be afraid of defeat. You are never so near to victory as when defeated in a good cause.

HENRY WARD BEECHER

What is defeat? Nothing but education; nothing but the first step to something better.

WENDELL PHILLIPS

Never confuse a single defeat with a final defeat.

F. SCOTT FITZGERALD

Those who are prepared to die for any cause are seldom defeated.

JAWAHARLAL NEHRU

A man is not defeated by his opponents but by himself.

When Abraham Lincoln was a candidate for President of the United States, someone asked him about his aspiration to that high office. He answered that he did not fear his opponents. "But," he said, "there is a man named Lincoln of whom I am very much afraid. If I am defeated, it will be by that man."

DILLARD S. MILLER

Defects

Scoff not at the natural defects of any which are not in their power to amend. It is cruel to beat a cripple with his own crutches!

THOMAS FULLER

A man's personal defects will commonly have, with the rest of the world, precisely that importance which they have to himself. If he makes light of them, so will other men.

RALPH WALDO EMERSON

Deference

There is no quality of human nature so nearly royal as the ability to yield gracefully.

CHARLES CONRAD

Definitions

A large part of the discussions of disputants come from the want of accurate definition. Let one define his terms and then stick to the definition, and half the differences in philosophy

and theology would come to an end, and be seen to have no
real foundation.
                                            TRYON EDWARDS

Democracy

Democracy is based upon the conviction that there are extra-
ordinary possibilities in ordinary people.
                                      HARRY EMERSON FOSDICK

Too many people expect wonders from democracy, when the
most wonderful thing of all is just having it.
                                            WALTER WINCHELL

In a democracy, the individual enjoys not only the ultimate
power but carries the ultimate responsibility.
                                            NORMAN COUSINS

Man's capacity for justice makes democracy possible; but man's
inclination to injustice makes democracy necessary.
                                           REINHOLD NIEBUHR

Human dignity, economic freedom, individual responsibility,
these are the characteristics that distinguish democracy from
all other forms devised by man.
                                       DWIGHT D. EISENHOWER

Democracy, the practice of self-government, is a covenant
among free men to respect the rights and liberties of their fel-
lows.
                                       FRANKLIN D. ROOSEVELT

The measure of a democracy is the measure of the freedom of
its humblest citizens.
                                           JOHN GALSWORTHY

I am all kinds of a democrat, so far as I can discover—but the root of the whole business is this, that I believe in the patriotism and energy and initiative of the average man.

WOODROW WILSON

Departure

There is a time for departure even when there's no certain place to go.

TENNESSEE WILLIAMS

Depression

Depressed it is because I am living in the past.

Depression comes, not from having faults, but from the refusal to face them. There are tens of thousands of persons today suffering from fears which in reality are nothing but the effects of hidden sins.

FULTON J. SHEEN

Desires

If you don't get everything you want, think of the things you don't get that you don't want.

OSCAR WILDE

We soon believe what we desire.

Nobody speaks the truth when there's something they must have.

ELIZABETH BOWEN

If you desire many things, many things will seem but a few.

BENJAMIN FRANKLIN

Desire has no rest.

Desire will entice beyond the bounds of reason.

If your desires be endless, your cares and fears will be so too.

THOMAS FULLER

I count him braver who overcomes his desires than him who conquers his enemies; the hardest victory is the victory over self.

ARISTOTLE

Desk

The desk is a dangerous place from which to watch the world.

JOHN LE CARRÉ

Despair

Hope deferred maketh the heart sick.

THE BIBLE: PROVERBS 13:12 KJV

Despondency

How many feasible projects have miscarried through despondency, and been strangled in their birth by a cowardly imagination?

JEREMY COLLIER

Destiny

People are afraid of the future, of the unknown. If a man faces up to it, and takes the dare of the future, he can have some control over his destiny. That's an exciting idea to me, better than waiting with everybody else to see what's going to happen.

JOHN GLENN

Details

For want of a nail, the shoe was lost; for want of a shoe the horse was lost; and for want of a horse the rider was lost, being

overtaken and slain by the enemy, all for want of care about a horseshoe nail.
BENJAMIN FRANKLIN

Determination

This one thing I do...I press toward the mark.
THE BIBLE: PHILIPPIANS 3:14 KJV

It takes as much courage to have tried and failed as it does to have tried and succeeded.
ANNE MORROW LINDBERGH

No matter what business you're in, you can't run in place or someone will pass you by. It doesn't matter how many games you've won.
JIM VALVANO

Be like a postage stamp—stick to one thing until you get there.
JOSH BILLINGS

The real difference between men is energy. A strong will, a settled purpose, an invincible determination, can accomplish almost anything; and in this lies the distinction between great men and little men.
THOMAS FULLER

Firmness of purpose is one of the most necessary sinews of character, and one of the best instruments of success. Without it genius wastes its efforts in a maze of inconsistencies.
PHILIP DORMER STANHOPE

We fight to great disadvantage when we fight with those who have nothing to lose.
FRANCESCO GUICCIARDINI

If we are forced to fight, we must have the means and the determination to prevail or we will not have what it takes to secure the peace.
RONALD REAGAN

When one must, one can.

Don't forget to swing hard, in case you hit the ball.

WOODIE HELD

Devil

The devil is an optimist if he thinks he can make people meaner.

KARL KRAUS

Let the devil get into the church, and he will mount the altar.

It is easy to bid the devil be your guest, but difficult to get rid of him.

Better keep the devil at the door than turn him out of the house.

He that is embarked with the devil must sail with him.

The devil can quote Scripture.

Wherever God erects a house of prayer,
The devil always builds a chapel there;
And 'twill be found, upon examination,
The latter has the largest congregation.

DANIEL DEFOE

Difference

One lesson we learn early—that in spite of seeming difference, men are all of one pattern. In fact, the only sin which we never forgive in each other is difference of opinion.

RALPH WALDO EMERSON

Difficulties

There are two ways of meeting difficulties: You alter the difficulties or you alter yourself meeting them.

PHYLLIS BOTTOME

Difficulties strengthen the mind, as labor does the body.

SENECA

Difficulties are God's errands; and when we are sent upon them we should esteem it a proof of God's confidence—as a compliment from him.

HENRY WARD BEECHER

The habits of a vigorous mind are formed in contending with difficulties…great necessities call out great virtues.

ABIGAIL ADAMS

I am grateful for all my problems. After each one was overcome, I became stronger and more able to meet those that were still to come. I grew in all my difficulties.

J.C. PENNEY

A man's worst difficulties begin when he is able to do as he likes.

T.H. HUXLEY

Difficulty

Undertake something that is difficult; it will do you good. Unless you try to do something beyond what you have already mastered, you will never grow.

RONALD E. OSBORN

Nothing is particularly hard if you divide it into small jobs.

HENRY FORD

A fool often fails because he thinks what is difficult is easy, and a wise man because he thinks what is easy is difficult.

JOHN CHURTON COLLINS

Once we truly know that life is difficult—once we truly understand and accept it—then life is no longer difficult.

M. SCOTT PECK

Every difficulty slurred over will be a ghost to disturb your repose later on.

FREDERIC CHOPIN

Whatever you think it's gonna take, double it. That applies to money, time, stress. It's gonna be harder than you think and take longer than you think.

RICHARD A. CORTESE

The greater the difficulty, the more glory in surmounting it.

EPICURUS

Dignity

Originality and the feeling of one's own dignity are achieved only through work and struggle.

FYODOR DOSTOYEVSKY

There is a healthful hardiness about real dignity that never dreads contact and communion with others, however humble.

WASHINGTON IRVING

A plowman on his legs is higher than a gentleman on his knees.

BENJAMIN FRANKLIN

Diligence

What we hope ever to do with ease, we must learn first to do with diligence.

SAMUEL JOHNSON

Few things are impossible to diligence and skill...Great works are performed, not by strength, but perseverance.

SAMUEL JOHNSON

Teach us to number our days, that we may apply our hearts unto wisdom.

THE BIBLE: PSALM 90:12 KJV

For the diligent the week has seven todays, for the slothful seven tomorrows.

Diplomacy

A diplomat is one who can tell a man he's open-minded when he means he has a hole in his head.

Disagreement

The people to fear are not those who disagree with you, but those who disagree with you and are too cowardly to let you know.

NAPOLEON BONAPARTE

Discernment

After a spirit of discernment, the next rarest things in the world are diamonds and pearls.

JEAN DE LA BRUYÈRE

You've got to love what's lovable and hate what's hateable. It takes brains to see the difference.

ROBERT FROST

Discipline

Better the child should cry than the father.

The secret of discipline is motivation. When a man is sufficiently motivated, discipline will take care of itself.

SIR ALEXANDER PATERSON

You never will be the person you can be if pressure, tension, and discipline are taken out of your life.

JAMES G. BILKEY

Nothing can be more hurtful to the service than the neglect of discipline; for that discipline, more than numbers, gives one army the superiority over another.

GEORGE WASHINGTON

Sometimes mere words are not enough—discipline is needed. For words may not be heeded.

Discontent

Discontent is the first step in progress.

He that is discontented in one place will seldom be happy in another.

AESOP

There is no banquet but some dislike something in it.

THOMAS FULLER

Discord

Tranquility will roof a house, but discord can wear away the foundations of a city.

ERNEST BRAMAH

Discouragement

When down in the mouth, remember Jonah. He came out all right.

THOMAS EDISON

Discoveries

Great discoveries and improvements invariably involve the cooperation of many minds. I may be given credit for having blazed the trail but when I look at the subsequent developments I feel the credit is due to others rather than to myself.

ALEXANDER GRAHAM BELL

Discretion

Nothing is more dangerous than a friend without discretion; even a prudent enemy is preferable.

JEAN DE LA FONTAINE

Like a gold ring in a pig's snout is a beautiful woman who shows no discretion.

THE BIBLE: PROVERBS 11:22

If thou art a master, be sometimes blind; if a servant, sometimes deaf.

THOMAS FULLER

Better a lean agreement than a fat lawsuit.

Cowardice is not synonymous with prudence. It often happens that the better part of discretion is valor.

WILLIAM HAZLITT

Diseases

Physicians think they do a lot for a patient when they give his disease a name.

IMMANUEL KANT

A disease known is half cured.

Dishonesty

Dishonesty, cowardice and duplicity are never impulsive.

GEORGE A. KNIGHT

Disorder

At a press conference during the 1968 Democratic Party Convention in Chicago, mayor Richard Daley declared: "The police are here not to create disorder. They are here to preserve disorder."

Disorganization

He that is everywhere is nowhere.

THOMAS FULLER

Disparagement

All you need is to tell a man that he is no good ten times a day, and very soon he begins to believe it himself.

LIN YUTANG

Disposition

It isn't our position, but our disposition, that makes us happy.

The Constitution of America only guarantees pursuit of happiness—you have to catch up with it yourself. Fortunately, happiness is something that depends not on position but on disposition, and life is what you make it.

GILL ROBB WILSON

Disputes

If two friends ask you to judge a dispute, don't accept, because you will lose one friend; on the other hand, if two strangers come with the same request, accept because you will gain one friend.

AUGUSTINE

In private life I never knew any one to interfere with other people's disputes but that he heartily repented of it.

THOMAS CARLYLE

Casting the lot settles disputes and keeps strong opponents apart.

THE BIBLE: PROVERBS 18:18

An offended brother is more unyielding than a fortified city, and disputes are like the barred gates of a citadel.

THE BIBLE: PROVERBS 18:19

Dissent

Dissent does not include the freedom to destroy the system of law which guarantees freedom to speak, assemble, and march in protest. Dissent is not anarchy.

SEYMOUR F. SIMON

Distrust

What loneliness is more lonely than distrust?

GEORGE ELIOT

Diversity

If we cannot now end our differences, at least we can help make the world safe for diversity. For, in the final analysis, our most basic common link is that we all inhabit this small planet. We all breathe the same air. We all cherish our children's future. And we are all mortal.

JOHN F. KENNEDY

One man's meat is another man's poison.

Dividedness

This strange disease of modern life, with its sick hurry, its divided aims.

MATTHEW ARNOLD

A house divided against itself cannot stand.

ABRAHAM LINCOLN

Divine Life

Our imitation of God in this life…must be an imitation of God incarnate; our model is the Jesus, not only of Calvary, but of the workshop, the roads, the crowds, the clamorous demands and surly oppositions, the lack of all peace and privacy, the interruptions. For this, so strangely unlike anything we can attribute to the Divine life in itself, is apparently not only like, but is, the Divine life operating under human conditions.

C.S. LEWIS

Dogma

You can't teach an old dogma new tricks.

DOROTHY PARKER

The dogmas of the quiet past are inadequate to the stormy present. The occasion is piled high with difficulty, and we must rise with the occasion. As our case is new, so we must think anew and act anew.

ABRAHAM LINCOLN

Dogs

The dog was created specially for children. He is the god of frolic.

HENRY WARD BEECHER

I have always liked bird dogs better than kennel-fed dogs myself—you know, one that will get out and hunt for food rather than sit on his fanny and yell.

CHARLES E. WILSON

Doing

The Christian life is not merely knowing or hearing, but doing the will of Christ.

FREDERICK WILLIAM ROBERTSON

I feel that the greatest reward for doing is the opportunity to do more.

JONAS E. SALK

It is not the critic who counts; not the man who points out how the strong man stumbles, or where the doer of deeds could have done them better. The credit belongs to the man who is actually in the arena, whose face is marred by dust and sweat and blood; who strives valiantly; who errs, and comes short again and again, because there is no effort without error and shortcoming; but who does actually strive to do the deeds; who knows the great enthusiasms, the great devotions; who spends himself in a worthy cause; who at the best knows in the end the triumph of high achievement, and who at the worst, if he fails, at least fails while daring greatly, so that his place shall never be with those cold and timid souls who know neither victory nor defeat.

THEODORE ROOSEVELT

Doubt

I respect faith, but doubt is what gets you an education.

WILSON MIZNER

Man may doubt here and there, but mankind does not doubt. The universal conscience is larger than the individual conscience, and that constantly comes in to correct and check our infidelity.

HUGH REGINALD HAWEIS

Drama

Drama is life with the dull bits cut out.

ALFRED HITCHCOCK

A talent for drama is not a talent for writing, but is an ability to articulate human relationships.

GORE VIDAL

Dreams

The future belongs to those who believe in the beauty of their dreams.
                              ELEANOR ROOSEVELT

Dreams have only one owner at a time. That's why dreamers are lonely.
                              ERMA BOMBECK

It takes a lot of courage to show your dreams to someone else.
                              ERMA BOMBECK

All our dreams can come true—if we have the courage to pursue them.
                              WALT DISNEY

Drunkenness

The sight of a drunkard is a better sermon against that vice than the best that was ever preached on the subject.
                              JOHN FAUCIT SAVILLE

The best cure for drunkenness is while sober to see a drunken man.

Drunkenness is simply voluntary insanity.   SENECA

When the beer goes in, the wits go out.

Drunkenness is not a mere matter of intoxicating liquors; it goes deeper—far deeper. Drunkenness is the failure of a man to control his thoughts.
                              DAVID GRAYSON

I do the very best I know how—the very best I can; and I mean to keep doing so until the end. If the end brings me out all right, what is said against me won't amount to anything. If the end brings me out wrong, ten angels swearing I was right would make no difference. What you can't get out of, get into wholeheartedly.

ABRAHAM LINCOLN

Duties are not performed for duty's sake, but because their neglect would make the man uncomfortable. A man performs but one duty—the duty of contenting his spirit, the duty of making himself agreeable to himself.

MARK TWAIN

I am not bound to win, but I am bound to be true. I am not bound to succeed, but I am bound to live up to what light I have.

ABRAHAM LINCOLN

Early Rising

It is well to be up before daybreak, for such habits contribute to health, wealth, and wisdom.

ARISTOTLE

Next to temperance, a quiet conscience, a cheerful mind, and active habits, I place early rising as a means of health and happiness.

TIMOTHY FLINT

Ease

There has never yet been a man in our history who led a life of ease whose name is worth remembering.

THEODORE ROOSEVELT

Eating

Part of the secret of success in life is to eat what you like and let the food fight it out inside.

MARK TWAIN

I saw few die of hunger; of eating, a hundred thousand.

BENJAMIN FRANKLIN

To lengthen thy life, lessen thy meals.

BENJAMIN FRANKLIN

Eating Crow

"Eating crow" is never pleasant—no matter how much mustard and ketchup you put on it. But usually the sooner you eat it the less unpleasant it is to the taste!

NIDO QUBEIN

If you have to eat crow, eat it while it's hot.

ALBEN BARKLEY

Eavesdropping

The man who eavesdrops hears himself discussed.

Economists

In all recorded history there has not been one economist who has had to worry about where the next meal would come from.

PETER DRUCKER

Education

Very few people can stand the strain of being educated without getting superior over it.

STEPHEN LEACOCK

They say that we are better educated than our parents' generation. What they mean is that we go to school longer. They are not the same thing.

DOUGLAS YATES

An education isn't how much you have committed to memory, or even how much you know. It's being able to differentiate between what you do know and what you don't. It's knowing where to go to find out what you need to know; and it's knowing how to use the information you get.

WILLIAM FEATHER

You cannot teach a child to take care of himself unless you will let him try to take care of himself. He will make mistakes; and out of these mistakes will come his wisdom.

HENRY WARD BEECHER

The best education in the world is that gotten by struggling to get a living.

WENDELL PHILLIPS

Nothing in education is so astonishing as the amount of ignorance it accumulates in the form of inert facts.

HENRY ADAMS

Upon the subject of education, not presuming to dictate any plan or system respecting it, I can only say that I view it as the most important subject which we, as a people, can be engaged in.

ABRAHAM LINCOLN

The parents have a right to say that no teacher paid by their money shall rob their children of faith in God and send them

back to their homes skeptical or infidels or agnostics or athe-
ists.
         William Jennings Bryan

A man who has never gone to school may steal from a freight
car; but if he has a university education, he may steal the whole
railroad.
         Theodore Roosevelt

The chief wonder of education is that it does not ruin everybody concerned in it, teachers and taught.
         Henry Adams

Efficiency

It is more than probable that the average man could, with no
injury to his health, increase his efficiency fifty percent.
         Sir Walter Scott

Effort

Effort only fully releases its reward after a person refuses to
quit.
         Napoleon Bonaparte Hill

Ego

Many problems in business are caused by the ego interfering
with judgment.

I'd like to buy him at my price and sell him at his.

Peacock, look at your legs.

He fell in love with himself at first sight, and it is a passion to
which he has always remained faithful.
         Anthony Powell

Talk to a man about himself and he will listen for hours.
BENJAMIN DISRAELI

Never underestimate a man who overestimates himself.
FRANKLIN D. ROOSEVELT

Egotist, n. A person more interested in himself than in me.
AMBROSE BIERCE

Elderly

Why can't we build orphanages next to homes for the elderly? If someone's sitting in a rocker, it won't be long before a kid will be in his lap.
CLORIS LEACHMAN

Eloquence

True eloquence consists of saying all that should be said, and that only.
FRANÇOIS DE LA ROCHEFOUCAULD

Eloquence is the ability to say the right thing when you think of it.

Employment

The best time to fire a person is when you don't hire them. Likewise, the best time to ask a staff member to resign is when you don't select them on your staff.

When you hire people that are smarter than you are, you prove you are smarter than they are.
R.H. GRANT

Enablement

What God expects us to attempt, He also enables us to achieve.
STEPHEN OLFORD

Encouragement

Anxious hearts are very heavy, but a word of encouragement does wonders.

Endurance

One may go a long way after one is tired.

When you get into a tight place and everything goes against you till it seems as though you could not hold on a minute longer, never give up then, for that is just the place and time that the tide will turn.   HARRIET BEECHER STOWE

The secret of being able to take things as they come is to stagger the unpleasant ones far enough apart.

THE BOOK OF COMMON PRAYER

To endure is the first thing that a child ought to learn, and that which he will have the most need to know.

JEAN-JACQUES ROUSSEAU

To struggle when hope is banished.
To live when life's salt is gone!
To dwell in a dream that's vanished
To endure, and go calmly on!

BEN JONSON

Enemies

Am I not destroying my enemies when I make friends of them?
ABRAHAM LINCOLN

Forgive your enemies, but never forget their names.
JOHN F. KENNEDY

Do not fear when your enemies criticize you. Beware when they applaud.

VO DONG GIANG

If we could read the secret history of our enemies, we should find in each man's life sorrow and suffering enough to disarm all hostilities.

HENRY W. LONGFELLOW

Everyone needs a warm personal enemy or two to keep him free of rust in the movable parts of his mind.

GENE FOWLER

Better a thousand enemies outside the house than one inside.

Men of sense often learn from their enemies. Prudence is the best safeguard. This principle cannot be learned from a friend, but an enemy extorts it immediately. It is from their foes, not their friends, that cities learn the lesson of building high walls and ships of war. And this lesson saves their children, their homes, and their properties.

ARISTOPHANES

If you knew how cowardly your enemy is, you would slap him.

EDGAR WATSON HOWE

In order to have an enemy, one must be somebody. One must be a force before he can be resisted by another force. A malicious enemy is better than a clumsy friend.

ANNE SOPHIE SWETCHINE

No enemy is more dangerous than a friend who isn't quite sure he is for or against you.

I don't have a warm personal enemy left. They've all died off. I miss them terribly because they helped define me.

CLARE BOOTH LUCE

To have a good enemy, choose a friend; he knows where to strike.

DIANE DE POITIERS

Engagement

Better to break off an engagement than a marriage.

Enjoyment

Few people succeed in business unless they enjoy their work.

If your capacity to acquire has outstripped your capacity to enjoy, you are on the way to the scrap heap.

GLENN BUCK

Enthusiasm

We act as though comfort and luxury were the chief requirements of life, when all that we need to make us happy is something to be enthusiastic about.

CHARLES KINGSLEY

I prefer the errors of enthusiasm to the indifference of wisdom.

ANATOLE FRANCE

No one keeps up his enthusiasm automatically. Enthusiasm must be nourished with new actions, new aspirations, new efforts, new vision. Compete with yourself; set your teeth and dive into the job of breaking your own record.

When we accept tough jobs as a challenge and wade into them with joy and enthusiasm, miracles can happen.

GILBERT ARLAND

The most valuable thing I have or ever expect to have is enthusiasm, and I would rather pass this on to my children than anything else.

Almost anyone can develop enthusiasm—but the kind of enthusiasm that will get you somewhere is the kind that possesses you!

Nothing great was ever achieved without enthusiasm.

RALPH WALDO EMERSON

In things pertaining to enthusiasm, no man is sane who does not know how to be insane on proper occasions.

HENRY WARD BEECHER

No person who is enthusiastic about his work has anything to fear from life.

SAMUEL GOLDWYN

Next to getting enthusiastic about your job, the most important requirement to getting ahead is to become enthusiastic about your boss.

Most great men and women are not perfectly rounded in their personalities, but are instead people whose one driving enthusiasm is so great it makes their faults seem insignificant.

CHARLES A. CERAMI

Envy

The envious man does not die only once but as many times as the person he envies lives to hear the voice of praise.

BALTASAR GRACIAN

Envy always implies conscious inferiority wherever it resides.

PLINY THE ELDER

The envious praise only that which they can surpass; that which surpasses them they censure.

CHARLES CALEB COLTON

Men of noble birth are noted to be envious toward new men when they rise; for the distance is altered; it is like a deceit of the eye, that when others come on they think themselves go back.

FRANCIS BACON

Envy's memory is nothing but a row of hooks to hang up grudges on.

JOHN WATSON FOSTER

Envy is more irreconcilable than hatred.

FRANÇOIS DE LA ROCHEFOUCAULD

Nothing sharpens sight like envy.

THOMAS FULLER

As iron is eaten away by rust, so the envious are consumed by their own passion.

ANTISTHENES

Epigrams

An epigram is a half-truth so stated as to irritate the person who believes the other half.

SHAILER MATHEWS

Equality

We believe, as asserted in the Declaration of Independence, that all men are created equal; but that does not mean that all men are or can be equal in possessions, in ability, or in merit; it simply means that all shall stand equal before the law.

WILLIAM JENNINGS BRYAN

We hold these truths to be self-evident, that all men are created equal, that they are endowed by their Creator with certain unalienable Rights, that among these are Life, Liberty, and the pursuit of Happiness.

THOMAS JEFFERSON

Men are especially intolerant of serving, and being ruled by, their equals.

BARUCH SPINOZA

Americans are so enamored of equality that they would rather be equal in slavery than unequal in freedom.

ALEXIS DE TOCQUEVILLE

Error

Error is always more busy than truth.

HOSEA BALLOU

Errors

To admit errors sets one free as the truth always does.

HANS KUNG

It takes less time to do a thing right than it does to explain why you did it wrong.

HENRY W. LONGFELLOW

Essentials

Three great essentials to achieve anything worthwhile are, first, hard work; second, stick-to-itiveness; third, common sense.

THOMAS EDISON

Ethics

Divorced from ethics, leadership is reduced to management and politics to mere technique.

JAMES MACGREGOR BURNS

What a man has been is history; what he does is law; what he is is philosophy; what he ought to be is ethics.

EUGENE P. BERTIN

Everlasting Life

God so loved the world, that he gave his only begotten Son, that whosoever believeth in him should not perish, but have everlasting life.

THE BIBLE: JOHN 3:16 KJV

Evidence

There is not better evidence than something written on paper.

Evil

Evil events come from evil causes; and what we suffer, springs, generally, from what we have done.

ARISTOPHANES

He who passively accepts evil is as much involved in it as he who helps to perpetrate it.

MARTIN LUTHER KING JR.

It is the law of our humanity that man must know good through evil. No great principle ever triumphed but through much evil. No man ever progressed to greatness and goodness but through great mistakes.

FREDERICK W. ROBERTSON

Of two evils, choose neither.

CHARLES H. SPURGEON

He who is strong in evil deeds is also strong in good.

Evolution

There is no more reason to believe that man descended from some inferior animal than there is to believe that a stately mansion has descended from a small cottage.

WILLIAM JENNINGS BRYAN

The evolutionists seem to know everything about the missing.

Exaggeration

There are people so addicted to exaggeration they can't tell the truth without lying.

JOSH BILLINGS

Example

A good example is the best sermon.   BENJAMIN FRANKLIN

People look at you and me to see what they are supposed to be. And, if we don't disappoint them, maybe, just maybe, they won't disappoint us.

WALT DISNEY

I have learned silence from the talkative, toleration from the intolerant, and kindness from the unkind; yet strangely, I am ungrateful to these teachers.

KAHLIL GIBRAN

You are writing a gospel,
A chapter each day,
By deeds that you do,
By words that you say.

Men read what you write
Whether faithless or true.
Say! What is the gospel
According to you?

Excellence

The quality of a person's life is in direct proportion to their commitment to excellence, regardless of their chosen field of endeavor.

VINCE LOMBARDI

The less justified a man is in claiming excellence for his own self, the more ready is he to claim all excellence for his nation, his religion, his race, or his holy cause.

ERIC HOFFER

Excitement

Human nature, if it healthy, demands excitement; and if it does not obtain its thrilling excitement in the right way, it will seek it in the wrong. God never makes bloodless stoics; He makes no passionless saints.

OSWALD CHAMBERS

Excuses

An excuse is worse and more terrible than a lie; for an excuse is a lie guarded.

ALEXANDER POPE

Since excuses were invented, no one is ever in the wrong.

Several excuses are always less convincing than one.

ALDOUS HUXLEY

Exercise

I have never taken any exercise, except for sleeping and resting, and I never intend to take any. Exercise is loathsome.

MARK TWAIN

I'm not into working out. My philosophy: No pain, no pain.
CAROL LEIFER

Expectation

We part more easily with what we possess than with our expectations of what we hope for: expectation always goes beyond enjoyment.
LORD KAMES

The best part of our lives we pass in counting on what is to come.
WILLIAM HAZLITT

Men...always think that something they are going to get is better than what they have got.
JOHN OLIVER HOBBES

Experience

Experience is something you get too late to do anything about the mistakes you made while getting it.

Men are wise in proportion, not to their experience, but to their capacity for experience.
GEORGE BERNARD SHAW

Experience is not what happens to you; it is what you do with what happens to you.
ALDOUS HUXLEY

Experience is the best of schoolmasters, only the school fees are heavy.
THOMAS CARLYLE

Experience is the name everyone gives to his mistakes.
OSCAR WILDE

I have but one lamp by which my feet are guided, and that is the lamp of experience. I know of no way of judging the future but by the past.

PATRICK HENRY

Information's pretty thin stuff, unless mixed with experience.

CLARENCE DAY

Experts

Make three correct guesses consecutively, and you will establish a reputation as an expert.

LAURENCE J. PETER

Explanations

Never explain—your friends do not need it, and your enemies will not believe you anyway.

ELBERT HUBBARD

I wish no explanation made to our enemies. What they want is a squabble and a fuss, and that they can have if we explain, and they cannot have if we don't.

ABRAHAM LINCOLN

Expressions

The expression a woman wears on her face is far more important than the clothes she wears on her back.

DALE CARNEGIE

Eye Contact

Eye contact is crucial not only in making good communicational contact with a child, but in filling his emotional needs. Without realizing it, we use eye contact as a primary means of conveying love, especially to children. A child uses eye contact with his parents (and others) to feed emotionally. The more parents make eye contact with their child as a means of expressing their love, the more a child is nourished with love and the fuller is his emotional tank.   ROSS CAMPBELL

Eyes

An eye can threaten like a loaded and leveled gun, or it can insult like hissing or kicking; or, in its altered mood, by beams of kindness, it can make the heart dance for joy.

RALPH WALDO EMERSON

One eye of the master's sees more than ten of the servants'.

The eyes are the mirror of the soul.

Fables

Fables, like parables, are more ancient than formal arguments and are often the most effective means of presenting and impressing both truth and duty.   TRYON EDWARDS

Faces

He had the sort of face that, once seen, is never remembered.

OSCAR WILDE

You have such a February face, so full of frost, of storm, and cloudiness.   WILLIAM SHAKESPEARE

Facing It

Facing it—always facing it—that's the way to get through. Face it!

JOSEPH CONRAD

Facts

If a man will kick a fact out of the window, when he comes back he finds it again in the chimney corner.

RALPH WALDO EMERSON

There is no sadder sight in the world than to see a beautiful theory killed by a brutal fact.

T.H. HUXLEY

Once the facts are clear, the decisions jump out at you.

PETER DRUCKER

Facts do not cease to exist because they are ignored.

FRANKLIN FIELD

Facts are your friends.

NORM DANIELS

Facts are stubborn things; and whatever may be our wishes, our inclinations, or the dictates of our passions, they cannot alter the state of facts and evidence.

JOHN ADAMS

Failure

Failure is the opportunity to begin again more intelligently.

HENRY FORD

The person who succeeds is not the one who holds back, fearing failure, nor the one who never fails...but rather the one who moves on in spite of failure.

CHARLES SWINDOLL

Many of life's failures are people who did not realize how close they were to success when they gave up.

THOMAS EDISON

He who has never failed somewhere, that man cannot be great.

HERMAN MELVILLE

Failure is usually the line of least persistence.

WILFRED BEAVER

Never give a man up until he has failed at something he likes.

LEWIS E. LAWES

Don't waste energy trying to cover up failure. Learn from your failures and go on to the next challenge. It's O.K. to fail. If you're not failing, you're not growing.

H. STANLEY JUDD

I cannot give you the formula for success, but I can give you the formula for failure, which is: Try to please everybody.

HERBERT BAYARD SWOPE

I have told of my failings and mistakes, if only because I have found that failure is a far better teacher than success.

BERNARD BARUCH

We failed, but in the good providence of God, apparent failure often proves a blessing.

ROBERT E. LEE

Only those who dare to fail greatly can ever achieve greatly.

ROBERT F. KENNEDY

The greatest accomplishment is not in never falling, but in rising again after you fall.

VINCE LOMBARDI

While attempting to invent the incandescent lamp, Thomas Edison remarked after the 187th failure, "We are making progress. Now, at least, we know 187 things that won't work."

Faith

Faith is a gift of God.

BLAISE PASCAL

Faith is the divine evidence whereby the spiritual man discerneth God, and the things of God.

JOHN WESLEY

The primary cause of unhappiness in the world today is...lack of faith.

CARL JUNG

Faith is like radar that sees through the fog—the reality of things at a distance that the human eye cannot see.

CORRIE TEN BOOM

Pity the human being who is not able to connect faith within himself with the infinite...He who has faith has...an inward reservoir of courage, hope, confidence, calmness, and assuring trust that all will come out well—even though to the world it may appear to come out most badly.

B.C. FORBES

Faith makes the uplook good, the outlook bright, the inlook favorable, and the future glorious.

V. RAYMOND EDMAN

I have fought a good fight, I have finished my course, I have kept the faith.

THE BIBLE: 2 TIMOTHY 4:7 KJV

The just shall live by faith.

THE BIBLE: ROMANS 1:17 KJV

Skepticism has never founded empires, established principles, or changed the world's heart. The great doers in history have always been men of faith.
EDWIN HUBBEL CHAPIN

Any featherhead can have confidence in times of victory, but the test is to have faith when things are going wrong.
SIR WINSTON CHURCHILL

I admire the serene assurance of those who have religious faith. It is wonderful to observe the calm confidence of a Christian with four aces.
MARK TWAIN

Faith is a Fantastic Adventure In Trusting Him.
CORRIE TEN BOOM

God hasn't called me to be successful. He's called me to be faithful.
MOTHER TERESA

There is one inevitable criterion of judgment touching religious faith in doctrinal matters. Can you reduce it to practice? If not, have none of it.
HOSEA BALLOU

Faith is an outward and visible sign of an inward and spiritual grace.

The great act of faith is when man decides that he is not God.
OLIVER WENDELL HOLMES JR.

Faithfulness

Nothing is more noble, nothing more venerable than fidelity. Faithfulness and truth are the most sacred excellences and endowments of the human mind.
CICERO

Falsehood

The telling of a falsehood is like the cut of a sabre; for though the wound may heal, the scar of it will remain.

SA'DI, SHAIKH MUSLIH-UD-DIN

All that one gains by falsehood is, not to be believed when he speaks the truth.

ARISTOTLE

Falsehood often lurks upon the tongue of him, who, by self-praise, seeks to enhance his value in the eyes of others.

JAMES GORDON BENNETT

Falsehoods not only disagree with truths, but they usually quarrel among themselves.

DANIEL WEBSTER

Fame

The lust of fame is the last that a wise man shakes off.

TACITUS

Fame usually comes to those who are thinking about something else.

HORACE GREELEY

Let us satisfy our own consciences, and trouble not ourselves by looking for fame. If we deserve it, we shall attain it: If we deserve it not we cannot force it. The praise bad actions obtain dies soon away; if good deeds are at first unworthily received, they are afterward more properly appreciated.

SENECA

Fame is the perfume of heroic deeds.

SOCRATES

Familiarity

Familiarity is a magician that is cruel to beauty but kind to ugliness.

Ouida

Though familiarity may not breed contempt, it takes off the edge of admiration.

William Hazlitt

Family

Happy families are alike; every unhappy family is unhappy in its own way.

Leo Tolstoy

At the end only two things really matter to a man, regardless of who he is; and they are the affection and understanding of his family. Anything and everything else he creates is insubstantial; it is a ship given over to the mercy of the winds and tides of prejudice. But the family is an everlasting anchorage, a quiet harbor where a man's ship can be left to swing to the moorings of pride and loyalty.

Richard Byrd

Where can a man better be than with his family?

Jean-Francois Marmontel

There are no real difficulties in a home where the children hope to be like their parents one day.

William Lyon Phelps

Fashion

As to matters of dress, I would recommend one never to be first in the fashion nor the last out of it.

John Wesley

The custom and fashion of today will be the awkwardness and outrage of tomorrow—so arbitrary are these transient laws.

ALEXANDRE DUMAS

Every generation laughs at the old fashions, but follows religiously the new.

HENRY DAVID THOREAU

Fathers

By profession I am a soldier and take pride in that fact. But I am prouder—infinitely prouder—to be a father. A soldier destroys in order to build; the father only builds, never destroys. The one has the potentiality of death; the other embodies creation and life. And while the hordes of death are mighty, the battalions of life are mightier still. It is my hope that my son, when I am gone, will remember me not from the battle but in the home repeating with him our simple daily prayer.

DOUGLAS MACARTHUR

Tell me who your father is, and I'll tell you who you are.

The most important thing a father can do for his children is to love their mother.

THEODORE M. HESBURGH

Faults

There is so much good in the worst of us,
And so much bad in the best of us,
That it ill behooves any of us
To find fault with the rest of us.

Denying a fault doubles it.

We confess to little faults, only to persuade ourselves that we have no great ones.
FRANÇOIS DE LA ROCHEFOUCAULD

People in general will much better bear being told of their vices and crimes than of their failings and weaknesses.
LORD CHESTERFIELD

The fault, dear Brutus, is not in our stars, but in ourselves.
WILLIAM SHAKESPEARE

To reprove small faults with undue vehemence, is as absurd as if a man should take a great hammer to kill a fly on his friend's forehead.

Think of your faults the first part of the night when you are awake, and the faults of others the latter part of the night when you are asleep.

The camel never sees its own hump, but that of its brother is always before its eye.

We make more progress by owning our faults than by always dwelling on our virtues.
THOMAS BRACKETT REED

The greatest of faults is to be conscious of none.
THOMAS CARLYLE

Faults are thick where love is thin.
DANISH PROVERB

Favors

To accept a favor from a friend is to confer one.
JOHN CHURTON COLLINS

When you buy a vase cheap, look for the flaw; when someone offers favors, search for their purpose.

Fear

The most drastic and usually the most effective remedy for fear is direct action.
WILLIAM BURNHAM

It is only the fear of God that can deliver us from the fear of man.
JOHN WITHERSPOON

We must face what we fear; that is the case of the core of the restoration of health.
MAX LERNER

The fear of the LORD is the beginning of wisdom.
THE BIBLE: PSALM 111:10 KJV

If you wish to fear nothing, consider that everything is to be feared.
SENECA

There are many things that we would throw away, if we were not afraid that others might pick them up.
OSCAR WILDE

The man who fears suffering is already suffering from what he fears.
MICHEL DE MONTAIGNE

I sought the LORD, and He heard me, and delivered me from all my fears.
THE BIBLE: PSALM 34:4 KJV

Many of our fears are tissue paper-thin, and a single courageous step would carry us clear through them.

BRENDAN FRANCIS.

He who is feared by many, fears many.

Too much fear creates slavery.

Fearfulness

Don't make yourself a mouse, or the cat will eat you.

Feelings

One of the quickest ways to feel tired is to suppress your feelings.

SUE PATTON THOEK

Fighting

I have not yet begun to fight.

JOHN PAUL JONES

Rarely is a fight continued when the chief has fallen.

Finance

Alexander Hamilton originated the put and take system in our national treasury: the taxpayers put it in and the politicians take it out.

WILL ROGERS

If the American people ever allow private banks to control the issuance of their currency, first by inflation and then by deflation, the banks and corporations that will grow up around them will deprive the people of all their property until their children will wake up homeless on the continent their fathers conquered.

THOMAS JEFFERSON

If the nation is living within its income, its credit is good. If in some crisis it lives beyond its income for a year or two, it can usually borrow temporarily on reasonable terms. But if, like the spendthrift, it throws discretion to the winds, is willing to make no sacrifice at all in spending, extends its taxing to the limit of the people's power to pay, and continues to pile up deficits, it is on the road to bankruptcy.

FRANKLIN D. ROOSEVELT

Fishing

There is no use in your walking five miles to fish when you can depend on being just as unsuccessful near home.

MARK TWAIN

Flab

Muscles come and go; flab lasts.

BILL VAUGHAN

Flag

You're a grand old flag; you're a high-flying flag; and forever, in peace, may you wave. You're the emblem of the land I love, the home of the free and the brave . . .

GEORGE M. COHAN

Our flag has never waved over any community but in blessing.

WILLIAM MCKINLEY

Flattery

Flatterers are cats that lick before and scratch behind.

Whoever flatters his neighbor is spreading a net for his feet.
THE BIBLE: PROVERBS 29:5

Flattery is okay if you handle it right. It's like smoking ciga-rettes. Quite all right, as long as you don't inhale.
ADLAI STEVENSON

All are not friends that speak us fair.

We sometimes think we hate flattery, when we only hate the manner in which we have been flattered.
FRANÇOIS DE LA ROCHEFOUCAULD

Some there are who profess to despise all flattery, but even these are, nevertheless, to be flattered, by being told that they do despise it.
CHARLES CALEB COLTON

Flattery is never so agreeable as to our blind side; commend a fool for his wit, or a knave for his honesty, and they will receive you into their bosom.
HENRY FIELDING

He who praises everybody, praises nobody.
SAMUEL JOHNSON

Never trust a man who speaks well of everybody.
JOHN CHURTON COLLINS

Nothing is so great an instance of ill manners as flattery. If you flatter all the company, you please none; if you flatter only one or two, you affront the rest.
JONATHAN SWIFT

He that rewards flattery begs it.

Fleas

Elephants are always drawn smaller than life, but a flea always larger.

JONATHAN SWIFT

Focus

What we love to do we find time to do.

JOHN LANCASTER SPALDING

The shortest way to do many things is to do only one thing at a time.

RICHARD CECIL

When a man knows he is to be hanged in a fortnight, it concentrates his mind wonderfully.

SAMUEL JOHNSON

Foolishness

There is a foolish corner in the brain of the wisest man.

ARISTOTLE

Though the bear be gentle, don't bite him by the nose.

THOMAS D'URFEY

Fools

If I want to look at a fool, I have only to look in the mirror.

SENECA

I wasn't born a fool. It took work to get this way.

DANNY KAYE

Answer a fool according to his folly, lest he be wise in his own conceit.

THE BIBLE: PROVERBS 26:5 KJV

Fools rush in—and get all the best seats.

MARYBETH WESTON

Fools! Not to know how health and temperance bless the rustic swain, while luxury destroys her pampered train.

HESIOD

Even a fool has one accomplishment.

If a wise man goes to court with a fool, the fool rages and scoffs, and there is no peace.   THE BIBLE: PROVERBS 29:9

Like a lame man's legs that hang limp is a proverb in the mouth of a fool.   THE BIBLE: PROVERBS 26:7

Experience keeps a dear school, but fools will learn in no other.

Young men think old men are fools, but old men know young men are fools.

GEORGE CHAPMAN

Force
Force is all-conquering, but its victories are short-lived.

ABRAHAM LINCOLN

Forgetting
Clara Barton, founder of the American Red Cross, was once reminded of an especially cruel thing that had been done to her years before. But Miss Barton seemed not to recall it. "Don't you remember it?" her friend asked. "No," came the reply, "I distinctly remember forgetting the incident."

SUNSHINE MAGAZINE

And when he is out of sight, quickly also is he out of mind.

THOMAS À KEMPIS

The remedy for wrongs is to forget them.

PUBLILIUS SYRUS

We forget all too soon the things we thought we could never forget.

JOAN DIDION

Forgiveness

I firmly believe a great many prayers are not answered because we are not willing to forgive someone.

DWIGHT L. MOODY

If the other person injures you, you may forget the injury; but if you injure him you will always remember.

KAHLIL GIBRAN

One of the secrets of a long and fruitful life is to forgive everybody everything every night before you go to bed.

If thou wouldst find much favor and peace with God and man, be very low in thine own eyes. Forgive thyself little and others much.

ROBERT LEIGHTON

'Tis more noble to forgive, and more manly to despise, than to revenge an injury.

It is very easy to forgive others their mistakes; it takes more grit and gumption to forgive them for having witnessed your own.

JESSAMYN WEST

It is easier to forgive an enemy than to forgive a friend.

WILLIAM BLAKE

We can forgive almost anything except the person who has to forgive us.

To understand is to forgive.

FRENCH PROVERB

He that cannot forgive others breaks the bridge over which he must pass himself; for every man has need to be forgiven.

THOMAS FULLER

Let all bitterness, and wrath, and anger, and clamour, and evil speaking, be put away from you, with all malice: And be ye kind one to another, tenderhearted, forgiving one another, even as God for Christ's sake hath forgiven you.

THE BIBLE: EPHESIANS 4:31,32 KJV

Forgiveness is the oil of relationships.

JOSH MCDOWELL

Forgiveness means letting go of the past.

GERALD JAMPOLSKY

Forgiveness is not an elective in the curriculum of life. It is a required course, and the exams are always tough to pass.

CHARLES SWINDOLL

The more a man knows the more he forgives.

CATHERINE THE GREAT

Forgiveness needs to be accepted, as well as offered, before it is complete.

C.S. LEWIS

A Christian will find it cheaper to pardon than to resent. Forgiveness saves the expense of anger, the cost of hatred, the waste of spirits.

HANNAH MORE

If men wound you with injuries, meet them with patience: hasty words rankle the wound, soft language dresses it, forgiveness cures it, and oblivion takes away the scar. It is more noble by silence to avoid an injury than by argument to overcome it.

FRANCIS BEAUMONT

The weak can never forgive. Forgiveness is the attribute of the strong.

MAHATMA GANDHI

Forgiveness is the fragrance the violet sheds on the heel that has crushed it.

MARK TWAIN

Sometimes we find it hard to forgive. We forget that forgiveness is as much for us as for the other person. If you can't forgive it's like holding a hot coal in your hand—you're the one getting burned. The tension may be hurting you much more than the other person.

JENNIFER JAMES

Doing an injury puts you below your enemy; revenging one makes you but even with him; forgiving it sets you above him.

BENJAMIN FRANKLIN

Forgiveness is not a feeling but a promise or commitment to the following three things:
1. I will not use it against them in the future.
2. I will not talk to others about them.
3. I will not dwell on it myself.

JAY ADAMS

Fortune

He that waits upon fortune is never sure of a dinner.

BENJAMIN FRANKLIN

A man is never so on trial as in the moment of excessive good fortune.

LEW WALLACE

Foxes

Like Aesop's fox, when he had lost his tail, he would have all his fellow foxes cut off theirs.

ROBERT BURTON

Many foxes grow gray, but few grow good.

BENJAMIN FRANKLIN

Frankness

To say what you think will certainly damage you in society; but a free tongue is worth more than a thousand invitations.

LOGAN PEARSALL SMITH

Freedom

No man is free who is not a master of himself.

EPICTETUS

The greatest glory of a free-born people is to transmit that freedom to their children.

WILLIAM HAVARD

Still, if you will not fight for the right when you can easily win without bloodshed; if you will not fight when your victory will be sure and not too costly; you may come to the moment when you will have a fight with all the odds against you and only a precarious chance of survival. There may even be a worse case.

You may have to fight when there is no hope of victory, because it is better to perish than live as slaves.

SIR WINSTON CHURCHILL

We have confused the free with the free and easy.

ADLAI STEVENSON

If a man does only what is required of him, he is a slave. The moment he does more, he is a free man.

W. ROBERTSON

Freedom is not procured by a full enjoyment of what is desired, but by controlling that desire.

EPICTETUS

Our institutions of freedom will not survive unless they are constantly replenished by the faith that gave them birth.

JOHN FOSTER DULLES

We know that freedom cannot be served by the devices of the tyrant. As it is an ancient truth that freedom cannot be legislated into existence, so it is no less obvious that freedom cannot be censored into existence. And any who act as if freedom's defenses are to be found in suppression and suspicion and fear confess a doctrine that is alien to America.

DWIGHT D. EISENHOWER

Those who deny freedom to others deserve it not for themselves, and, under a just God, cannot long retain it.

ABRAHAM LINCOLN

For a people who are free, and who mean to remain so, a well-organized and armed militia is their best security.

THOMAS JEFFERSON

We in this country, in this generation, are—by destiny rather than choice—the watchman on the walls of world freedom. We ask, therefore, that we may be worthy of our power and responsibility, that we may exercise our strength with wisdom and restraint, and that we may achieve in our time and for all time the ancient vision of "peace on earth, good will toward men." That must always be our goal, and the righteousness of our cause must always underlie our strength. For as was written long ago: "Except the Lord keep the city, the watchman waketh but in vain."

JOHN F. KENNEDY

For what avail the plow or sail, or land or life, if freedom fail?

RALPH WALDO EMERSON

There is no longer any room for hope. If we wish to be free—if we mean to preserve inviolate those inestimable privileges for which we have been so long contending—if we mean not basely to abandon the noble struggle in which we have been so long engaged, and which we have pledged ourselves never to abandon, until the glorious object of our contest shall be obtained—we must fight! I repeat it, sir, we must fight! An appeal to arms and to the God of Hosts, is all that is left us!

PATRICK HENRY

Freedom is still expensive. It still costs money. It still costs blood. It still calls for courage and endurance, not only in soldiers, but in every man and woman who is free and who is determined to remain free.

HARRY S. TRUMAN

No man is entitled to the blessings of freedom unless he be vigilant in its preservation.

DOUGLAS MACARTHUR

Human freedom is not a gift of man. It is an achievement by man; and, as it was gained by vigilance and struggle, so it may be lost in indifference and supineness.

HARRY F. BYRD

There can be no greater good than the quest for peace, and no finer purpose than the preservation of freedom.

RONALD REAGAN

I intend no modification of my oft-expressed personal wish that all men everywhere could be free.

ABRAHAM LINCOLN

Better to die upright than to live on your knees.

Freedom means self-expression, and the secret of freedom is courage. No man ever remains free who acquiesces in what he knows to be wrong.

HAROLD J. LASKI

Those who expect to reap the blessings of freedom must, like men, undergo the fatigues of supporting it.

THOMAS PAINE

Let freedom never perish in your hands, but piously transmit it to your children.

JOSEPH ADDISON

Freedom of Speech

Without freedom of thought, there can be no such thing as wisdom; and no such thing as public liberty, without freedom of speech.

BENJAMIN FRANKLIN

Without an unfettered press, without liberty of speech, all the outward forms and structures of free institutions are a sham, a pretense—the sheerest mockery. If the press is not free; if speech is not independent and untrammeled; if the mind is shackled or made impotent through fear, it makes no difference under what form of government you live; you are a subject and not a citizen. Republics are not in and of themselves better than other forms of government except insofar as they carry with them and guarantee to the citizen that liberty of thought and action for which they were established.

WILLIAM E. BORAH

If the fires of freedom and civil liberties burn low in other lands, they must be made brighter in our own. If in other lands, the press and books and literature of all kinds are censored, we must redouble our efforts here to keep them free. If in other lands the eternal truths of the past are threatened by intolerance, we must provide a safe place for their perpetuation.

FRANKLIN D. ROOSEVELT

I have always been among those who believe that the greatest freedom of speech was the greatest safety, because if a man is a fool, the best thing to do is to encourage him to advertise the fact by speaking. It cannot be so easily discovered if you allow him to remain silent and look wise, but if you let him speak, the secret is out, and the world knows that he is a fool. So it is by the exposure of folly that it is defeated; not by the seclusion of folly, and in this free air of free speech men get into that sort of communication with one another which constitutes the basis of all common achievement.

The legislature of the United States shall pass no law on the subject of religion nor touching or abridging the liberty of the press.

CHARLES PINCKNEY

If men are to be precluded from offering their sentiments on a matter, which may involve the most serious and alarming consequences, that can invite the consideration of mankind, reason is of no use to us; the freedom of speech may be taken away, and, dumb and silent we may be led, like sheep, to the slaughter.

GEORGE WASHINGTON

But the character of every act depends upon the circumstances in which it is done. The most stringent protection of free speech would not protect a man in falsely shouting fire in a theater and causing a panic. It does not even protect a man from an injunction against uttering words that may have all the effect of force. The question in every case is whether the words used are used in such circumstances and are of such a nature as to create a clear and present danger that they will bring about the substantive evils that…Congress has a right to prevent. It is a question of proximity and degree.

OLIVER WENDELL HOLMES JR.

Fresh Air

I remember when people used to step outside a moment for a breath of fresh air. Now sometimes you have to step outside for days before you get it.   VICTOR BORGE

Friendliness

Lead the life that will make you kindly and friendly to everyone about you, and you will be surprised what a happy life you will live.   CHARLES M. SCHWAB

Take time to be friendly. It is the road to happiness.

Friends

Give me the avowed, the erect, the manly foe,
Bold I can meet, perhaps may turn his blow!
But of all plagues, good Heavens, thy wrath can send,
Save, save, oh save me from the candid friend!

GEORGE CANNING

Every man, however wise, needs the advice of some sagacious friend in the affairs of life.   PLAUTUS

He's a fine friend. He stabs you in the front.

LEONARD LOUIS LEVINSON

The happiest miser on earth is the man who saves up every friend he can make.

ROBERT E. SHERWOOD

Be slow in choosing a friend, slower in changing.

BENJAMIN FRANKLIN

A friend is someone you can do nothing with, and enjoy it.

One loyal friend is worth ten thousand relatives.

EURIPIDES

The friend of my adversity I shall always cherish most. I can better trust those who helped to relieve the gloom of my dark hours than those who are so ready to enjoy with me the sunshine of my prosperity.

ULYSSES S. GRANT

If we all told what we know of one another, there would not be four friends in the world.

BLAISE PASCAL

When the character of someone is not clear to you, look at that person's friends.

We shall never have friends if we expect to find them without fault.

THOMAS FULLER

Be careful the environment you choose for it will shape you; be careful the friends you choose for you will become like them.

W. CLEMENT STONE

The best way to keep your friends is not to give them away.
WILSON MIZNER

Friends agree best at a distance.

There are three kinds of friends: best friends, guest friends, and pest friends.
LAURENCE J. PETER

Two persons cannot long be friends if they cannot forgive each other's little failings.
JEAN DE LA BRUYÈRE

You can make more friends in two months by becoming interested in other people than you can in two years by trying to get other people interested in you.
DALE CARNEGIE

A friend is a present you give yourself.

A true friend unbosoms freely, advises justly, assists readily, adventures boldly, takes all patiently, defends courageously, and continues a friend unchangeably.
WILLIAM PENN

Don't tell your friends their social faults; they will cure the fault and never forgive you.
LOGAN PEARSALL SMITH

Choose your friends like your books: few but choice.

Tell me who your friends are, and I'll tell you who you are.

He who judges between two friends loses one of them.

Without friends no one would choose to live, though he had all other goods.

ARISTOTLE

Friendship

Friendship is the inexpressible comfort of feeling safe with a person, having neither to weigh thoughts nor measure words.

GEORGE ELIOT

Friendship doesn't make you wealthy, but true friendship will reveal the wealth within you.

True friendship comes when silence between two people is comfortable.

DAVE TYSON GENTRY

Don't flatter yourself that friendship authorizes you to say disagreeable things to your intimates. The nearer you come into relation with a person, the more necessary do tact and courtesy become.

OLIVER WENDELL HOLMES JR.

Distance preserves friendship.

Who friendship with a knave had made
Is judged a partner in the trade.

JOHN GAY

True friendship is a plant of slow growth and must undergo and withstand the shocks of adversity before it is entitled to the appellation.

GEORGE WASHINGTON

Friendship is only purchased with friendship.

Friendship is like money: easier made than kept.

SAMUEL BUTLER

The better part of one's life consists of his friendships.

ABRAHAM LINCOLN

Fulfillment

I firmly believe that any man's finest hour—his greatest fulfillment to all he holds dear—is that moment when he has worked his heart out in a good cause and lies exhausted on the field of battle victorious.

VINCE LOMBARDI

Fun

There is no fun in having nothing to do; the fun is having lots to do and not doing it.

FRANCIS HERBERT BRADLEY

The normal person living to age 70 has 613,200 hours of life. This is too long a period not to have fun.

Future

The strongest are those who renounce their own times and become a living part of those yet to come. The strongest, and the rarest.

MILOVAN DJILAS

I know of no way of judging the future but by the past.

PATRICK HENRY

Your future depends on many things, but mostly on you.

FRANK TAYLOR

The best thing about the future is that it comes only one day at a time.

ABRAHAM LINCOLN

The future has several names. For the weak, it is the impossible. For the fainthearted, it is the unknown. For the thoughtful and valiant, it is ideal.
VICTOR HUGO

The future is like heaven—everyone exalts it but no one wants to go there now.
JAMES BALDWIN

The future belongs to people who see possibilities before they become obvious.
TED LEVITT

When all else is lost, the future still remains.
CHRISTIAN NESTELL BOVEE

Gambling

I would hate to see legalized gambling in California, nor do I favor a lottery. We ought to finance the state by the strength of our people and not by their weakness.
RONALD REAGAN

It doesn't say much for society, if gambling is the main method of raising money for good causes.
BERTRAM TROY

Gardens

I have never had so many good ideas day after day as when I worked in the garden.
JOHN ERSKINE

Generalizations

All generalizations are false, including this one.

Generosity

One man gives freely, yet gains even more; another withholds unduly, but comes to poverty. A generous man will prosper; he who refreshes others will himself be refreshed.

THE BIBLE: PROVERBS 11:24,25

Genius

Men give me some credit for genius. All the genius I have lies just in this: When I have a subject in hand, I study it profoundly. Day and night it is before me. I explore it in all its bearings. My mind becomes pervaded with it. Then the effort which I make the people are pleased to call the fruit of genius. It is the fruit of labor and thought.

ALEXANDER HAMILTON

No great genius is without an admixture of madness.

ARISTOTLE

Never confuse activity, talk, or money with genius.

The main difference between a genius and the average man in the same profession is that the genius doesn't go to bed until he is a lot more tired.

Genius, in one respect, is like gold—numbers of persons are constantly writing about both, who have neither.

CHARLES CALEB COLTON

Genius is 1 percent inspiration and 99 percent perspiration.

THOMAS EDISON

Thousands of geniuses live and die undiscovered—either by themselves or by others.

MARK TWAIN

Gentleman

This is the final test of a gentleman: his respect for those who can be of no possible service to him.

WILLIAM LYON PHELPS

Getting Along

The secret of getting along with others consists in first mastering the art of getting along with yourself.

Gettysburg Address

Fourscore and seven years ago our fathers brought forth upon this continent a new nation, conceived in liberty and dedicated to the proposition that all men are created equal.

Now we are engaged in a great civil war, testing whether that nation, or any nation so conceived and so dedicated, can long endure. We are met on a great battlefield of that war. We are met to dedicate a portion of it as the final resting place of those who here gave their lives that that nation might live. It is altogether fitting and proper that we should do this.

But in a larger sense we cannot dedicate, we cannot consecrate, we cannot hallow this ground. The brave men, living and dead, who struggled here, have consecrated it far above our poor power to add or detract. The world will little note, nor long remember, what we say here, but it can never forget what they did here. It is for us, the living, rather, to be dedicated here to the unfinished work that they have thus far so nobly carried on.

It is rather for us to be here dedicated to the great task remaining before us, that from these honored dead we take increased devotion to that cause for which they here gave the last full measure of devotion; that we here highly resolve that these dead shall not have died in vain; that the nation shall, under God, have a new birth of freedom; and that government

of the people, by the people, for the people, shall not perish
from the earth.
ABRAHAM LINCOLN

Giving

It is more blessed to give than to receive.
THE BIBLE: ACTS 20:35 KJV

Blessed are those who can give without remembering, and take
without forgetting.
ELIZABETH BIBESCO

God loveth a cheerful giver.
THE BIBLE: 2 CORINTHIANS 9:7 KJV

We make a living by what we get, but we make a life by what
we give.
NORMAN MACEWAN

If there be any truer measure of a man than by what he does,
it must be by what he gives.
ROBERT SOUTHEY

As the purse is emptied, the heart is filled.
VICTOR HUGO

Feel for others—in your pocket.
CHARLES H. SPURGEON

Gladness

One can endure sorrow alone, but it takes two to be glad.
ELBERT HUBBARD

A glad heart makes a cheerful countenance.
THE BIBLE: PROVERBS 15:13 RSV

Glory

Real glory springs from the silent conquest of ourselves.

JOSEPH P. THOMPSON

Gluttons

The fool that eats till he is sick must fast till he is well.

GEORGE W. THORNBURY

Their kitchen is their shrine, the cook their priest, the table their altar, and their belly their god.

CHARLES BUCK

Goals

It must be borne in mind that the tragedy of life doesn't lie in not reaching your goal. The tragedy lies in having no goal to reach. It isn't a calamity to die with dreams unfulfilled, but it is a calamity to not dream. It is not a disgrace not to reach the stars, but it is a disgrace to have no stars to reach for. Not failure, but low aim is sin.

HELMUT SCHMIDT

In great attempts it is glorious even to fail.

VINCE LOMBARDI

Aim at the sun, and you may not reach it; but your arrow will fly far higher than if aimed at an object on a level with yourself.

JOEL HAWES

A man is not old as long as he is seeking something.

JEAN ROSTAND

He who aims at the moon may hit the top of a tree; he who aims at the top of a tree is unlikely to get off the ground.

In youth, everything seems possible, but we reach a point in the middle years when we realize that we are never going to reach all the shining goals we had set for ourselves. And in the end, most of us reconcile ourselves, with what grace we can, to living with our ulcers and arthritis, our sense of partial failure, our less-than-ideal families—and even our politicians!

ADLAI STEVENSON

Clearly define for yourself the long-range goals you aspire to, and you will find that all the obstacles in your way will become hills instead of mountains.

If a man does not know what port he is steering for, no wind is favorable to him.

SENECA

God

God is our refuge and strength, a very present help in trouble. Therefore will not we fear.

THE BIBLE: PSALM 46:1 KJV

God is not a cosmic bellboy for whom we can press a button to get things.

HARRY EMERSON FOSDICK

Two men please God—who serves Him with all his heart because he knows Him; who seeks Him with all his heart because he knows Him not.

NIKITA IVANOVICH PANIN

It is only from the belief of the goodness and wisdom of a Supreme Being, that our calamities can be borne in the manner which becomes a man.

HENRY MACKENZIE

In what way, or by what manner of working God changes a soul from evil to good—how he impregnates the barren rock with priceless gems and gold—is, to the human mind, an impenetrable mystery.   SAMUEL TAYLOR COLERIDGE

We have been the recipients of the choicest bounties of heaven; we have been preserved these many years in peace and prosperity; we have grown in number, wealth, and power as no other nation has ever grown. But we have forgotten God! Intoxicated with unbroken success, we have become too self-sufficient to feel the necessity of redeeming and preserving grace, too proud to pray to the God who made us.
                                                ABRAHAM LINCOLN

Belief in and dependence on God is absolutely essential. It will be an integral part of our public life as long as I am Governor.
                                                RONALD REAGAN

Sometimes a nation abolishes God, but fortunately God is more tolerant.   HERBERT V. PROCHNOW

Temptations which accompany the working day will be conquered on the basis of the morning breakthrough to God. Decisions, demanded by work, become easier and simpler where they are made not in the fear of men, but only in the sight of God. He wants to give us today the power which we need for our work.   DIETRICH BONHOEFFER

If we spend sixteen hours a day dealing with tangible things and only five minutes a day dealing with God, is it any wonder that tangible things are two hundred times more real to us than God?
                                                WILLIAM R. INGE

The God who gave us life, gave us liberty at the same time.
                                                THOMAS JEFFERSON

Often God has to shut a door in our face so that He can subsequently open the door through which He wants us to go.

CATHERINE MARSHALL

I know that the Lord is always on the side of the right. But it is my constant anxiety and prayer that I and this nation should be on the Lord's side.

ABRAHAM LINCOLN

No people can be bound to acknowledge and adore the Invisible Hand which conducts the affairs of men more than those of the United States.

GEORGE WASHINGTON

Government laws are needed to give us civil rights, and God is needed to make us civil.

RALPH W. SOCKMAN

Blessed is the nation whose God is the LORD.

THE BIBLE: PSALM 33:12 KJV

I believe in God in His wisdom and benevolence, and I cannot conceive that such a Being could make such a species as the human merely to live and die on this earth. If I did not believe [in] a future state, I should believe in no God.

JOHN ADAMS

Seek truth in all things. God reveals Himself through the created world.

THOMAS AQUINAS

I have lived, sir, a long time, and the longer I live, the more convincing proofs I see of this truth—God governs in the affairs of men. And if a sparrow cannot fall to the ground without His notice, is it probable that an empire can rise without His aid?

BENJAMIN FRANKLIN

Men are not flattered by being shown that there has been a difference of purpose between the Almighty and them.

ABRAHAM LINCOLN

The most successful men I know have always admitted that they would most surely have failed without God's help.

Gold

Gold is tested by fire; people are tested by gold.

If all the gold in the world were melted down into a solid cube it would be about the size of an eight-room house. If a man got possession of all that gold—billions of dollars' worth—he could not buy a friend, character, peace of mind, clear conscience, or a sense of eternity.

CHARLES F. BANNING

Gold begets in brethren hate;
Gold in families, debate;
Gold does friendship separate;
Gold does civil wars create.

ABRAHAM COWLEY

Gold goes in at any gate except heaven's.

Good

Do all the good you can, in all the ways you can, to all the souls you can, in every place you can, at all the times you can, with all the zeal you can, as long as ever you can.

JOHN WESLEY

He that does good to another does good also to himself, not only in the consequence, but in the very act. For the consciousness of well-doing is in itself ample reward.

SENECA

He who waits to do a great deal of good at once, will never do anything.
SAMUEL JOHNSON

The greatest pleasure I know is to do a good action by stealth, and to have it found out by accident.
CHARLES LAMB

There is never an instant's truce between virtue and vice.

Goodness is the only investment that never fails.
HENRY DAVID THOREAU

There is no odor so bad as that which arises from goodness tainted.
HENRY DAVID THOREAU

If you would be good, first believe you are bad.
EPICTETUS

Good Day
One good day often costs a hundred bad nights.

Good Enough
Good enough is the enemy of excellence.

Good Manners
Good manners and soft words have brought many a difficult thing to pass.
SIR JOHN VANBRUGH

If a man has good manners and is not afraid of other people, he will get by even if he is stupid.
SIR DAVID ECCLES

Good Nature

An inexhaustible good nature is one of the most precious gifts of heaven, spreading itself like oil over the troubled sea of thought, and keeping the mind smooth and equable in the roughest weather.

WASHINGTON IRVING

Good News

Like cold water to a weary soul is good news from a distant land.

PROVERBS 25:25

Goodwill

In war: resolution. In defeat: defiance. In victory: magnanimity. In peace: goodwill.

SIR WINSTON CHURCHILL

Gossip

Of every ten persons who talk about you, nine will say something bad, and the tenth will say something good in a bad way.

ANTOINE DE RIVAROL

Gossip is always a personal confession either of malice or imbecility.

JOSIAH GILBERT HOLLAND

Whoever gossips to you will gossip about you.

Who brings a tale takes two away.

Avoid a questioner, for he is also a tattler.

Gossiping and lying go together.

Shun the inquisitive, for you will be sure to find him leaky.
Open ears do not keep conscientiously what has been entrusted
to them; and a word once spoken flies, never to be recalled.

HORACE

Nobody will keep the thing he hears to himself, and nobody
will repeat just what he hears and no more.   SENECA

Gossip is a form of malicious talk indulged in by other people.

Without wood a fire goes out; without gossip a quarrel dies
down.   THE BIBLE: PROVERBS 26:20

A gossip betrays a confidence; so avoid a man who talks too
much.   THE BIBLE: PROVERBS 20:19

Governing

No man is good enough to govern another man without that
other's consent.   ABRAHAM LINCOLN

Nothing appears more surprising to those who consider
human affairs with a philosophical eye, than the ease with
which the many are governed by the few.   DAVID HUME

Government

The marvel of all history is the patience with which men and
women submit to burdens unnecessarily laid upon them by
their governments.   WILLIAM E. BORAH

The government is the only known vessel that leaks from the top.

JAMES RESTON

If you feel you are too busy to take an interest in government, feel that getting mixed up in politics is beneath your dignity or bad for business—then, at least take time for one thing: Teach your children to count foreign currency—they'll need to with the inheritance you're leaving them.

WILLARD M. WILSON

Many a person seems to think it isn't enough for the government to guarantee him the pursuit of happiness. He insists it also run interference for him.

The best of all governments is that which teaches us to govern ourselves.

JOHANN WOLFGANG VON GOETHE

Any people anywhere, being inclined and having the power, have the right to rise up and shake off the existing government and form a new one that suits them better. This is a most valuable, a most sacred right, a right which we hope and believe is to liberate the world. Nor is this right confined to cases in which the whole people of an existing government may choose to exercise it. Any portion of such people that can, may revolutionize and make their own of so much of the territory as they inhabit. More than this, a majority of any portion of such people may revolutionize, putting down a minority, intermingled with, or near about them, who may oppose their movement.

ABRAHAM LINCOLN

The essence of government is power; and power, lodged as it must be in human hands, will ever be liable to abuse.

JAMES MADISON

For thirty years, the Bible-believing Christians of America have been largely absent from the executive, legislative, and judicial branches of both federal and local government.

JERRY FALWELL

A wise and frugal government, which shall restrain men from injuring one another, shall leave them otherwise free to regulate their own pursuits of industry and improvement, and shall not take from the mouth of labor the bread it has earned. This is the sum of good government, and this is necessary to close the circle of our felicities.

THOMAS JEFFERSON

The best energies of my life have been spent in endeavoring to establish and perpetuate the blessings of free government.

ANDREW JOHNSON

Society in every state is a blessing, but government, even in its best stage, is a necessary evil; in its worst state an intolerable one.

THOMAS PAINE

Government exists to protect rights which are ours from birth: the right to life, to liberty, and the pursuit of happiness. A man may choose to sit and fish instead of working—that's his pursuit of happiness. He does not have the right to force his neighbors to support him in his pursuit because that interferes with their pursuit of happiness.

RONALD REAGAN

Why has government been instituted at all? Because the passions of men will not conform to the dictates of reason and justice, without constraint.

ALEXANDER HAMILTON

None of us here in Washington knows all or even half of the answers. You people out there in the fifty states had better understand that. If you love your country, don't depend on handouts from Washington for your information. If you cherish your freedom, don't leave it all up to big government.

BARRY GOLDWATER

I'm sure everyone feels sorry for the individual who has fallen by the wayside or who can't keep up in our competitive society, but my own compassion goes beyond that to those millions of unsung men and women who get up every morning, send the kids to school, go to work, try to keep up the payments on their house, pay exorbitant taxes to make possible compassion for the less fortunate, and as a result have to sacrifice many of their own desires and dreams and hopes. Government owes them something better than always finding a new way to make them share the fruit of their toils with others.

RONALD REAGAN

I go for all sharing the privileges of the government who assist in bearing its burdens.

ABRAHAM LINCOLN

When a people shall have become incapable of governing themselves, and fit for a master, it is of little consequence from what quarter he comes.

GEORGE WASHINGTON

The office of government is not to confer happiness, but to give men opportunity to work out happiness for themselves.

WILLIAM ELLERY CHANNING

Government is like a baby—an alimentary canal with a big appetite at one end and no sense of responsibility at the other.

RONALD REAGAN

The legitimate object of government is to do for a community of people whatever they need to have done, but cannot do at all, or can't so well do for themselves in their separate and individual capacities. In all that the people can individually do as well for themselves, government ought not to interfere.

ABRAHAM LINCOLN

If we can prevent the government from wasting the labors of the people, under the pretense of taking care of them, they must become happy.

THOMAS JEFFERSON

Whenever you have an efficient government you have a dictatorship.

HARRY S. TRUMAN

The government is the strongest of which every man feels himself a part.

THOMAS JEFFERSON

As the happiness of the people is the sole end of government, so the consent of the people is the only foundation of it, in reason, morality, and the natural fitness of things.

JOHN ADAMS

My reading of history convinces me that most bad government has grown out of too much government.

JOHN S. WILLIAMS

Never believe anything until it has been officially denied.

CLAUD COCKBURN

The will of the people is the only legitimate foundation of any government, and to protect its free expression should be our first object.

THOMAS JEFFERSON

In a free and republican government, you cannot restrain the voice of the multitude. Every man will speak as he thinks or, more properly, without thinking, and consequently will judge of effects without attending to their causes.

GEORGE WASHINGTON

The ideal social state is not that in which each gets an equal amount of wealth, but in which each gets in proportion to his contribution to the general stock.   Henry George

Any government, like any family, can for a year spend a little more than it earns. But you and I know that a continuation of that habit means the poorhouse.

Franklin D. Roosevelt

The government is mainly an expensive organization to regulate evildoers and tax those who behave; government does little for fairly respectable people except annoy them.

Edgar Watson Howe

Government is a trust, and the officers of the government are trustees; and both the trust and the trustees are created for the benefit of the people.   •   Henry Clay

You must not complicate your government beyond the capacity of its electorate to understand it. If you do, it will escape all control, turn corrupt and tyrannical, lose the popular confidence, offer real security to no man, and in the end it will let loose all the submerged antagonisms within the state.

Walter Lippmann

It is the duty of government to make it difficult for people to do wrong, easy to do right.   William Gladstone

Government Grants

You cannot get blood from a stone, but you can get a government grant to try.

Louis Phillips

Grace

The will of God will not take you where the grace of God cannot keep you.

You say grace before meals. All right. But I say grace before the concert and the opera, and grace before the play and pantomime, and grace before I open a book, and grace before sketching, painting, swimming, fencing, boxing, walking, playing, dancing and grace before I dip the pen in the ink.

G.K. CHESTERTON

God appoints our graces to be nurses to other men's weakness.

HENRY WARD BEECHER

Graceful Exits

Few men of action have been able to make a graceful exit at the appropriate time.

MALCOLM MUGGERIDGE

Grandmothers

If you would civilize a man, begin with his grandmother.

VICTOR HUGO

Gratitude

God gave you a gift of 86,400 seconds today. Have you used one to say "thank you"?

WILLIAM A. WARD

We can be thankful to a friend for a few acres, or a little money; and yet for the freedom and command of the whole earth, and for the great benefits of our being, our life, health, and reason, we look upon ourselves as under no obligation.

SENECA

Happiness cannot be traveled to, owned, earned, worn, or consumed. Happiness is the spiritual experience of living every minute with love, grace, and gratitude.

DENIS WAITLEY

The greatest saint in the world is not he who prays most or fasts most; it is not he who gives alms, or is most eminent for temperance, chastity, or justice. It is he who is most thankful to God.

WILLIAM LAW

Gratitude is one of the least articulate of the emotions, especially when it is deep.

FELIX FRANKFURTER

Next to ingratitude the most painful thing to bear is gratitude.

HENRY WARD BEECHER

If the only prayer you say in your whole life is "Thank you," that would suffice.

MEISTER ECKHART

This is the day which the LORD has made; let us rejoice and be glad in it.

THE BIBLE: PSALM 118:24 NASB

Gratitude is what shows whether a gift is appreciated.

Blessed is he who expects no gratitude, for he shall not be disappointed.

W.C. BENNETT

Gravity

It's a good thing there's gravity or else when birds died, they'd stay where they were.

STEVEN WRIGHT

Great Things

All the great things are simple, and many can be expressed in a single word: freedom; justice; honor; duty; mercy; hope.

SIR WINSTON CHURCHILL

Great Thoughts

1. You cannot bring about prosperity by discouraging thrift.
2. You cannot strengthen the weak by weakening the strong.
3. You cannot help small men up by tearing big men down.
4. You cannot help the poor by destroying the rich.
5. You cannot lift the wage-earner up by pulling the wage-payer down.
6. You cannot keep out of trouble by spending more than your income.
7. You cannot further the brotherhood of man by inciting class hatred.
8. You cannot establish sound social security on borrowed money.
9. You cannot build character and courage by taking away a man's initiative and independence.
10. You cannot help men permanently by doing for them what they could and should do for themselves.

ABRAHAM LINCOLN

Greatness

It is a grand mistake to think of being great without goodness, and I pronounce it as certain that there was never yet a truly great man that was not at the same time truly virtuous.

BENJAMIN FRANKLIN

Great men are little men expanded; great lives are ordinary lives intensified.

WILFRED A. PETERSON

Towers are measured by their shadows, great men by those who speak evil of them.

If any man seeks for greatness, let him forget greatness and ask for truth, and he will find both.

HORACE MANN

The price of greatness is responsibility.

SIR WINSTON CHURCHILL

If we are to be a really great people, we must strive in good faith to play a great part in the world. We cannot avoid meeting great issues. All that we can determine for ourselves is whether we shall meet them well or ill.

THEODORE ROOSEVELT

A man must first care for his own household before he can be of use to the state. But no matter how well he cares for his household, he is not a good citizen unless he also takes thought of the state. In the same way, a great nation must think of its own internal affairs; and yet it cannot substantiate its claim to be a great nation unless it also thinks of its position in the world at large.

THEODORE ROOSEVELT

Greed

Every crowd has a silver lining.

P.T. BARNUM

There is no fire like passion, there is no shark like hatred, there is no snare like folly, there is no torrent like greed.

Don't try to buy at the bottom and sell at the top. This can't be done—except by liars.

BERNARD BARUCH

He who is fed by another's hand seldom gets enough.

He that is greedy of gain troubleth his own house.

THE BIBLE: PROVERBS 15:27 KJV

Grief

There is no grief which time does not lessen and soften.

CICERO

The only cure for grief is action. GEORGE HENRY LEWES

The greatest griefs are those we cause ourselves.

SOPHOCLES

Patience, says another, is an excellent remedy for grief, but submission to the hand of him that sends it is far better.

CHARLES SIMMONS

We should publish our joys, and conceal our griefs.

Well it has been said that there is no grief like the grief which does not speak.

HENRY W. LONGFELLOW

Everyone can master a grief but he that has it.

WILLIAM SHAKESPEARE

Grief destroys even a hero.

Grievances

To have a grievance is to have a purpose in life.

ERIC HOFFER

Growth

Undertake something that is difficult; it will do you good. Unless you try to do something beyond what you have already mastered, you will never grow.   RONALD E. OSBORN

What is used, develops, and what is left unused, atrophies, or wastes away.

If we don't change, we don't grow. If we don't grow, we are not really living. Growth demands a temporary surrender of security.
      GAIL SHEEHY

Guests

The first day, a guest; the second, a burden; the third, a pest.
      EDOUARD R. LABOULAYE

Guilt

A guilty conscience needs no accuser.

Fear is the tax that conscience pays to guilt.
      GEORGE SEWELL

Suspicion always haunts the guilty mind.
      WILLIAM SHAKESPEARE

From the body of one guilty deed a thousand ghostly fears and haunting thoughts proceed.   WILLIAM WORDSWORTH

Gumperson's Law

The probability of anything happening is in inverse ratio to its desirability.
      JOHN W. HAZARD

Guts

One of man's finest qualities is described by the simple word "guts"—the ability to take it. If you have the discipline to stand fast when your body wants to run, if you can control your temper and remain cheerful in the face of monotony or disappointment, you have "guts" in the soldiering sense.

JOHN S. ROOSMAN

Habit

The mind unlearns with difficulty what has long been impressed on it.

SENECA

We are what we repeatedly do. Excellence, then, is not an act, but a habit.

ARISTOTLE

Habit is a cable; we weave a thread of it every day, and at last we cannot break it.

HORACE MANN

Habit is a shirt of iron.

Hairdos

It is an ill wind that blows when you leave the hairdresser.

PHYLLIS DILLER

Halftime

On Thanksgiving Day, all over America, families sit down to dinner at the same moment—halftime.

Half-truths

Half the truth is often a great lie.   BENJAMIN FRANKLIN

Hanging

We must all hang together, or assuredly we shall all hang separately.   BENJAMIN FRANKLIN

There is no man so good, who, were he to submit all his thoughts and actions to the law, would not deserve hanging ten times in his life.   MICHEL DE MONTAIGNE

Happiness

The U.S. Constitution doesn't guarantee happiness, only the pursuit of it. You have to catch up with it yourself.
      BENJAMIN FRANKLIN

One is happy as a result of one's own efforts—once one knows the necessary ingredients of happiness—simple tastes, a certain degree of courage, self-denial to a point, love of work, and, above all, a clear conscience.   GEORGE SAND

True happiness may be sought, thought, or caught—but never bought.

Happiness is good health and a bad memory.
      INGRID BERGMAN

Happiness is the only thing you can give without having.

All who would win joy, must share it; happiness was born a twin.   LORD BYRON

Do not worry; eat three square meals a day; say your prayers; be courteous to your creditors; keep your digestion good; exercise; go slow and easy. Maybe there are other things your special case requires to make you happy; but, my friend, these I reckon will give you a good lift.   ABRAHAM LINCOLN

All men have happiness as their object: there are no exceptions. However different the means they employ, they aim at the same end.   BLAISE PASCAL

Scatter seeds of kindness everywhere you go;
Scatter bits of courtesy—watch them grow and grow.
Gather buds of friendship, keep them till full-blown;
You will find more happiness than you have ever known.
     AMY R. RAABE

No one is happy all his life long.   EURIPIDES

The grand essentials of happiness are: something to do, something to love, and something to hope for.   ALLAN K. CHALMERS

A multitude of small delights constitute happiness.
     CHARLES BAUDELAIRE

Happiness isn't something you experience; it's something you remember.   OSCAR LEVANT

The best way to secure future happiness is to be as happy as is rightfully possible today.   CHARLES W. ELLIOT

The door to happiness opens outwards.
     SØREN KIERKEGAARD

In vain do they talk of happiness who never subdued an impulse in obedience to a principle. He who never sacrificed a present to a future good, or a personal to a general one, can speak of happiness only as the blind do of colors.

HORACE MANN

Happiness consists in being happy with what we have got and with what we haven't got.

CHARLES H. SPURGEON

All you need for happiness is a good gun, a good horse, and a good wife.

DANIEL BOONE

Happiness is the natural flower of duty.

PHILLIPS BROOKS

Happiness in this world, when it comes, comes incidentally. Make it the object of pursuit, and it leads us on a wild-goose chase, and is never attained. Follow some other object, and very possibly we may find that we have caught happiness without dreaming of it.

NATHANIEL HAWTHORNE

Happiness is a perfume you cannot pour on others without getting a few drops on yourself.

GEORGE BERNARD SHAW

May we never let the things we can't have, or don't have, or shouldn't have, spoil our enjoyment of the things we do have and can have. As we value our happiness, let us not forget it, for one of the greatest lessons in life is learning to be happy without the things we cannot or should not have.

RICHARD L. EVANS

Whoever is happy will make others happy too.

ANNE FRANK

A truly happy person is one who can smile from year to year.

A happy heart makes the face cheerful, but heartache crushes the spirit.
THE BIBLE: PROVERBS 15:13

There's an Oriental story about two friends who stood on a bridge watching the fish in a stream below. "How happy the fishes are," observed one. "You're not a fish," said his friend. "How can you know whether they're happy or not?" "You're not me," the first man replied. "How can you know whether I know whether fish are happy or not?" EDWIN WAY TEALE

No man is happy unless he believes he is.
PUBLILIUS SYRUS

Harvest

Those who have not sown anything during their responsible life will have nothing to reap in the future.
GEORGE GURDJIEFF

And let us not be weary in well doing: for in due season we shall reap, if we faint not.
THE BIBLE: GALATIANS 6:9 KJV

Haste

Some persons do first, think afterward, and then repent forever.
THOMAS SECKER

Haste is the sister of repentance.

Hate

Hate is a prolonged form of suicide.   DOUGLAS V. STEERE

Whom they have injured, they also hate.   SENECA

Hating people is like burning down your own house to get rid of a rat.   HARRY EMERSON FOSDICK

Now hatred is by far the longest pleasure; men love in haste, but they detest at leisure.   LORD BYRON

Health

If we could give every individual the right amount of nourishment and exercise, not too little and not too much, we would have found the safest way to health.

HIPPOCRATES

Half the spiritual difficulties that men and women suffer arise from a morbid state of health.   HENRY WARD BEECHER

Heart

The heart of a fool is in his mouth, but the mouth of the wise man is in his heart.   BENJAMIN FRANKLIN

He did it with all his heart, and prospered.
THE BIBLE: 2 CHRONICLES 31:21 KJV

Be careful what you set your heart upon—for it will surely be yours.   JAMES BALDWIN

When you paint a dragon, you paint his skin; it is difficult to paint the bones. When you know a man, you know his face but not his heart.

The heart is deceitful above all things and beyond cure. Who can understand it?   THE BIBLE: JEREMIAH 17:9

Heaven

If I ever reach heaven I expect to find three wonders there: first, to meet some I had not thought to see there; second, to miss some I had expected to see there; and third, the greatest wonder of all, to find myself there.   JOHN NEWTON

Heavy Heart

Like one who takes away a garment on a cold day…is one who sings songs to a heavy heart.   THE BIBLE: PROVERBS 25:20

Hell

There may be some doubt about hell beyond the grave but there is no doubt about there being one on this side of it.
          ED HOWE

Help

Time and money spent in helping men to do more for themselves is far better than mere giving.   HENRY FORD

It is easy to help him who is willing to be helped.

We're not primarily put on this earth to see through one another, but to see one another through.

PETER DE VRIES

Heroes

Show me a hero and I will write you a tragedy.

F. SCOTT FITZGERALD

How many illustrious and noble heroes have lived too long by one day!

JEAN-JACQUES ROUSSEAU

The world's battlefields have been in the heart chiefly; more heroism has been displayed in the household and the closet, than on the most memorable battlefields in history.

HENRY WARD BEECHER

The legacy of heroes is the memory of a great name and the inheritance of a great example.

BENJAMIN DISRAELI

The idol of today pushes the hero of yesterday out of our recollection; and will, in turn, be supplanted by his successor of tomorrow.

WASHINGTON IRVING

A boy doesn't have to go to war to be a hero; he can say he doesn't like pie when he sees there isn't enough to go around.

EDGAR WATSON HOWE

Calculation never made a hero.

JOHN HENRY NEWMAN

High Energy

Do not waste your high-energy hours. Invest them where they yield the highest payoff.

Hindsight

If a man had half as much foresight as he has twice as much hindsight, he'd be a lot better off.   ROBERT J. BURDETTE

History

The main thing is to make history, not to write it.
OTTO VON BISMARCK

History never looks like history when you are living through it. It always looks confusing and messy, and it always feels uncomfortable.   JOHN W. GARDNER

The illusion that the times that were are better than those that are, has probably pervaded all ages.   HORACE GREELEY

Holiness

A true love of God must begin with a delight in his holiness.
JONATHAN EDWARDS

Nothing can make a man truly great but being truly good, and partaking of God's holiness.   MATTHEW HENRY

The serene, silent beauty of a holy life is the most powerful influence in the world, next to the might of the Spirit of God.
BLAISE PASCAL

Home

I long for rural and domestic scenes, for the warbling of birds and the prattle of my children...As much as I converse with sages or heroes, they have very little of my love or admiration. I should prefer the delights of a garden to the dominion of a world.
JOHN ADAMS

No nation can be destroyed while it possesses a good home life.
JOSIAH GILBERT HOLLAND

Travel east or travel west, a man's own house is still the best.

Homosexual Behavior

It's only common sense. If God wanted people to be gay, He wouldn't have created Adam and Eve. He would have created Adam and Steve.
ARTHUR HARMON

Honesty

Make yourself an honest man, and then you may be sure there is one less rascal in the world.
THOMAS CARLYLE

I hope I shall always possess firmness and virtue enough to maintain what I consider the most enviable of all titles, the character of an "honest man."
GEORGE WASHINGTON

Honesty has come to mean the privilege of insulting you to your face without expecting redress.
JUDITH MARTIN

Never give 'em more than one barr'l to start with. But if they are foolish enough to ask for more, then give 'em the other barr'l right between the eyes.
JOHN WESLEY DAFOE

Never add the weight of your character to a charge against a person without knowing it to be true.
ABRAHAM LINCOLN

Honesty is one part of eloquence. We persuade others by being in earnest ourselves.

WILLIAM HAZLITT

A man can build a staunch reputation for honesty by admitting he was in error, especially when he gets caught at it.

ROBERT RUARK

Honor

Show me the man you honor, and I will know what kind of a man you are, for it shows me what your ideal of manhood is, and what kind of a man you long to be.

THOMAS CARLYLE

If honor be your clothing, the suit will last a lifetime; but if clothing be your honor, it will soon be worn threadbare.

WILLIAM ARNOT

You heard the story, haven't you, about the man who was tarred and feathered and carried out of town on a rail? A man in the crowd asked him how he liked it. His reply was that if it was not for the honor of the thing, he would much rather walk.

ABRAHAM LINCOLN
[WHEN ASKED HOW HE LIKED BEING PRESIDENT]

Great honors are great burdens.

Honorary Degrees

I find honorary degrees always tempting, and often bad for me: tempting because we all—even ex-politicians—hope to be mistaken for scholars, and bad because if you then make a speech the mistake is quickly exposed.

ADLAI STEVENSON

Hope

Hope is a waking dream.

ARISTOTLE

Now may the God of hope fill you with all joy and peace in believing, so that you will abound in hope.

THE BIBLE: ROMANS 15:13 NASB

Oh, what a valiant faculty is hope.

MICHEL DE MONTAIGNE

There is one thing which gives radiance to everything. It is the idea of something around the corner.

G.K. CHESTERTON

But those who hope in the LORD will renew their strength. They will soar on wings like eagles; they will run and not grow weary, they will walk and not be faint.

THE BIBLE: ISAIAH 40:31

Hope is itself a species of happiness, and, perhaps, the chief happiness which this world affords.

SAMUEL JOHNSON

There is no medicine like hope, no incentive so great, and no tonic so powerful as expectation of something tomorrow.

ORISON SWETT MARDEN

They sailed. They sailed. Then spake the mate:
"This mad sea shows its teeth tonight.
He curls his lip, he lies in wait,
With lifted teeth, as if to bite!
Brave Admiral, say but one good word:
What shall we do when hope is gone?"
The words leapt like a leaping sword:
"Sail on! sail on! sail on! and on!"

JOAQUIN MILLER

The grand essentials to happiness in this life are something to
do, something to love, and something to hope for.

JOSEPH ADDISON

Hope is grief's best music.

Hosts

People are either born hosts or born guests.

SIR MAX BEERBOHM

Hot Temper

Do not make friends with a hot-tempered man, do not associate with one easily angered, or you may learn his ways and
get yourself ensnared.   THE BIBLE: PROVERBS 22:24,25

Housework

I hate housework! You make the beds, you do the dishes—
and six months later you have to start all over again.

JOAN RIVERS

Human Behavior

There's nothing really consistent about human behavior except
its tendency to drift toward evil.

Human History

Mankind never loses any good things, physical, intellectual,
or moral, till it finds a better, and then the loss is a gain. No
steps backward, is the rule of human history. What is gained
by one man is invested in all men, and is a permanent investment for all time.

THEODORE PARKER

Human Nature

Knowledge of human nature is the beginning and end of political education.

HENRY ADAMS

Every man is an island, and often you row around and around before you find a place to land.

HARRY EMERSON FOSDICK

Human Spirit

The human spirit is stronger than anything that can happen to it.

GEORGE C. SCOTT

Humble Pie

If humble pie has to be eaten, that's the best way to eat it—bolt it whole.

MAURICE HEWLETT

Humility

A humble person is not himself conscious of his humility. Truth and the like perhaps admit of measurement, but not humility. Inborn humility can never remain hidden, and yet the possessor is unaware of its existence.

MAHATMA GANDHI

It is no great thing to be humble when you are brought low; but to be humble when you are praised is a great and rare attainment.

BERNARD OF CLAIRVAUX

To be humble to superiors, is duty; to equals, is courtesy; to inferiors, is nobleness; and to all, safety; it being a virtue that, for all its lowliness, commandeth those it stoops to.

SIR THOMAS MORE

Humor

The world is a perpetual caricature of itself; at every moment it is the mockery and the contradiction of what it is pretending to be. But as it nevertheless intends all the time to be something different and highly dignified, at the next moment it corrects and checks and tries to cover up the absurd thing it was; so that a conventional world, a world of masks, is superimposed on the reality, and passes in every sphere of human interest for the reality itself. Humor is the perception of this illusion, whilst the convention continues to be maintained, as if we had not observed its absurdity.

GEORGE SANTAYANA

If you could choose one characteristic that would get you through life, choose a sense of humor.

JENNIFER JAMES

The secret source of humor is not joy but sorrow.

MARK TWAIN

Whenever you find humor, you find pathos close by his side.

EDWIN PERCY WHIPPLE

Humor is the instinct for taking pain playfully.

MAX FORRESTER EASTMAN

If I had no sense of humor, I should long ago have committed suicide.

MAHATMA GANDHI

A cardinal rule of humor: Never say anything about anyone that the person can't change in five seconds. Use the AT&T test for stories and jokes—make sure it's Appropriate, Timely and Tasteful.

SUSAN ROANE

Against the assault of humor, nothing can stand.

MARK TWAIN

The man who has had the job I've had and didn't have a sense of humor wouldn't still be here.

HARRY S. TRUMAN

Husbands

A good husband makes a good wife.

The first thing a woman should do to make a successful husband out of a man is admire him.

All husbands are alike, but they have different faces so you can tell them apart.

Hustle

Things may come to those who wait, but only the things left by those who hustle.

ABRAHAM LINCOLN

Everything comes to him who hustles while he waits.

THOMAS EDISON

Hypocrisy

It is a shameful and unseemly thing to think one thing and speak another, but how odious to write one thing and think another.

SENECA

Idealism

Idealism increases in direct proportion to one's distance from the problem.

Ideals

Ideals are like the stars: we never reach them, but like the mariners of the sea, we chart our course by them.

CARL SCHURZ

With no ideas of diamonds, we settle for glass.

Ideas

A new idea is delicate. It can be killed by a sneer or a yawn; it can be stabbed to death by a quip and worried to death by a frown on the right man's brow.

CHARLES BROWER

Almost all new ideas have a certain aspect of foolishness when they are first produced.

ALFRED NORTH WHITEHEAD

Ideas are like rabbits. You get a couple and learn how to handle them, and pretty soon you have a dozen.

Ideas lose themselves as quickly as quail, and one must wing them the minute they raise out of the grass—or they are gone.

THOMAS KENNEDY

An idea isn't responsible for the people who believe in it.

DON MARQUIS

There is nothing in the world more powerful than an idea. No weapon can destroy it; no power can conquer it except the power of another idea.

JAMES ROY SMITH

Nothing helps to stretch one's mind like a good idea that you can get all excited about.

Above all, do not talk yourself out of good ideas by trying to expound them at haphazard meetings.

JACQUES BARZUN

Great minds discuss ideas, average minds discuss events, small minds discuss people.

Idleness

If the devil catch a man idle, he'll set him at work.

It is impossible to enjoy idling thoroughly unless one has plenty of work to do.

JEROME K. JEROME

There is no kind of idleness by which we are so easily seduced as that which dignifies itself by the appearance of business.

SAMUEL JOHNSON

Idols

A God who let us prove his existence would be an idol.

DIETRICH BONHOEFFER

The maker of idols does not worship them.

Ignorance

It is profound ignorance that inspires the dogmatic tone.

The voice of the intelligence…is drowned out by the roar of fear. It is ignored by the voice of desire. It is contradicted by the voice of shame. It is hissed away by hate and extinguished by anger. Most of all it is silenced by ignorance.

KARL MENNINGER

Ignorance is the mother of admiration.

GEORGE CHAPMAN

It takes a lot of things to prove you are smart, but only one thing to prove you are ignorant.

DON HEROLD

Imagination

Sometimes I've believed as many as six impossible things before breakfast.

LEWIS CARROLL

Imitation

When people are free to do as they please, they usually imitate each other.

ERIC HOFFER

Immortality

If your contribution has been vital there will always be somebody to pick up where you left off, and that will be your claim to immortality.

WALTER GROPIUS

The nearest approach to immortality on earth is a government bureau.

JAMES F. BYRNES

Impatience

I have not so great a struggle with my vices, great and numerous as they are, as I have with my impatience. My efforts

are not absolutely useless; yet I have never been able to conquer this ferocious wild beast.

JOHN CALVIN

Importance

Almost every man you meet feels himself superior to you in
some way; and a sure way to his heart is to let him realize that
you recognize his importance.

DALE CARNEGIE

Most of the trouble in the world is caused by people wanting
to be important.

T.S. ELIOT

One doesn't recognize in one's life the really important
moments—not until it's too late.

AGATHA CHRISTIE

Important Points

If you have an important point to make, don't try to be subtle
or clever. Use a pile driver. Hit the point once. Then come back
and hit it again. Then hit it a third time—a tremendous whack.

SIR WINSTON CHURCHILL

Imprisonment

Most men have a tendency to imprison themselves—without
the help of the authorities.

HENRY MILLER

Impulse

Since the generality of persons act from impulse much more
than from principle, men are neither so good nor so bad as
we are apt to think them.

AUGUSTUS AND JULIUS HARE

Inaction

Iron rusts from disuse; stagnant water loses its purity and in cold weather becomes frozen; even so does inaction sap the vigors of the mind.

LEONARDO DA VINCI

Income Tax

The hardest thing in the world to understand is income tax.

ALBERT EINSTEIN

Indecision

Nothing is so exhausting as indecision, and nothing is so futile.

BERTRAND RUSSELL

Independence

When I was young, my parents told me what to do; now that I am old, my children tell me what to do. I wonder when I will be able to do what I want to do.

Indignation

Moral indignation is in most cases 2 percent moral, 48 percent indignation and 50 percent envy.

VITTORIO DE SICA

Indiscretion

More trouble is caused in the world by indiscreet answers than by indiscreet questions.

SYDNEY J. HARRIS

Individuals

Society is continually pushing in on the individual. He has only a few areas in which he can be himself, free from external restraint or observation.

EDWARD VAUGHAN LONG

Industriousness

Go on deserving applause, and you will be sure to meet with it; and the way to deserve it is to be good and to be industrious.

THOMAS JEFFERSON

He that performs his own errand saves the messenger's hire.

Take care of the minutes, and the hours will take care of themselves.

If you have great talents, industry will improve them; if moderate abilities, industry will supply their deficiencies. Nothing is denied to well-directed labor; nothing is ever to be attained without it.

JOSHUA REYNOLDS

Plow deep while sluggards sleep,
And you shall have corn to sell and to keep.

BENJAMIN FRANKLIN

In the ordinary business of life, industry can do anything which genius can do, and very many things which it cannot.

HENRY WARD BEECHER

Industry keeps the body healthy, the mind clear, the heart whole, and the purse full.

CHARLES SIMMONS

Industry need not wish, and he that lives upon hopes will die fasting. There are no gains without pains. He that hath a trade hath an estate, and he that hath a calling hath an office of profit and honor; but then the trade must be worked at, and the calling followed, or neither the estate nor the office will enable us to pay our taxes. If we are industrious, we shall never starve; for, at the workingman's house hunger looks in, but dares not enter. Nor will the bailiff or the constable enter, for industry pays debts, while idleness and neglect increase them.

BENJAMIN FRANKLIN

Inequality

It is a wise man who said there is no greater inequality than the equal treatment of unequals.   FELIX FRANKFURTER

Inevitability

There is no good in arguing with the inevitable. The only argument available with an east wind is to put on your overcoat.

JAMES RUSSELL LOWELL

It is so. It cannot be otherwise.

Everything comes gradually and at its appointed hour.

OVID

Inferiority

No one can make you feel inferior without your consent.

ELEANOR ROOSEVELT

No man who says, "I'm as good as you," believes it. He would not say it if he did. The Saint Bernard never says it to the toy dog, nor the scholar to the dunce, nor the employable to the bum, nor the pretty woman to the plain. The claim to equality is made only by those who feel themselves to be in some way inferior. What it expresses is the itching, smarting awareness of an inferiority which the patient refuses to accept, and therefore resents.

C.S. LEWIS

Infidelity

The nurse of infidelity is sensuality.

RICHARD CECIL

Influence

The very essence of all power to influence lies in getting the other person to participate.

HARRY A. OVERSTREET

Ingenuity

Never tell people how to do things. Tell them what to do, and they will surprise you with their ingenuity.

GEORGE S. PATTON

Ingratitude

Ingratitude is always a form of weakness. I have never known a man of real ability to be ungrateful.

JOHANN WOLFGANG VON GOETHE

Inheritance

Never say you know a man till you have divided an inheritance with him.

JOHANN KASPAR LAVATER

The best blood will sometimes get into a fool or a mosquito.

AUSTIN O'MALLEY

If a man is fortunate he will, before he dies, gather up as much as he can of his civilized heritage and transmit it to his children.

WILL DURANT

We pay for the mistakes of our ancestors, and it seems only fair that they should leave us the money to pay with.

DON MARQUIS

Injuries

An individual, thinking himself injured, makes more noise than a state.

THOMAS JEFFERSON

Write injuries in dust, benefits in marble.

BENJAMIN FRANKLIN

No man ever did a designed injury to another, but at the same time he did a greater to himself.

LORD KAMES

Neglect will kill an injury sooner than revenge.

Injustice

Those who commit injustice bear the greatest burden.

HOSEA BALLOU

Innocence

Innocence is a desirable thing, a dainty thing, an appealing thing, in its place; but carried too far, it is merely ridiculous.

DOROTHY PARKER

Innovator

The entrepreneur finds a need and fills it. The innovator anticipates or creates a need and fills it.

DENIS E. WAITLEY AND ROBERT B. TUCKER

Inquiry

He that inquires much, learns much.

Let not the freedom of inquiry be shackled. If it multiplies contentions among the wise and virtuous, it exercises the charity of those who contend. If it shakes for a time the belief that is rested only on prejudice, it finally settles it on the broader and more solid basis of conviction.   HENRY KIRKE WHITE

Insanity

Insanity is often the logic of an accurate mind overtaxed.
OLIVER WENDELL HOLMES JR.

Insincerity

Nothing is more disgraceful than insincerity.   CICERO

Inspiration

Inspirations never go in for long engagements; they demand immediate marriage to action.   BRENDAN FRANCIS

Instinct

Trust your own instinct. Your mistakes might as well be your own, instead of someone else's.   BILLY WILDER

Insults

Whatever be the motive of an insult it is always best to overlook it; for folly scarcely can deserve resentment, and malice is punished by neglect.   SAMUEL JOHNSON

There are two insults no human being will endure: that he has no sense of humor, and that he has never known trouble.
SINCLAIR LEWIS

A graceful taunt is worth a thousand insults.
LOUIS NIZER

Insurance

Something that keeps you poor all your life so that you can die rich.

Insurrection

Insurrection of thought always precedes insurrection of arms.

WENDELL PHILLIPS

Integrity

Integrity is the glue that holds our way of life together.

BILLY GRAHAM

A little integrity is better than any career.

RALPH WALDO EMERSON

The supreme quality for leadership is unquestionably integrity. Without it, no real success is possible, no matter whether it is on a section gang, a football field, in an army, or in an office.

DWIGHT D. EISENHOWER

I have simply tried to do what seemed best each day, as each day came.

ABRAHAM LINCOLN

Intellectual

An intellectual is a man who takes more words than necessary to tell more than he knows.

DWIGHT D. EISENHOWER

Intelligence

There are plenty of the well-endowed, thank God....It strikes me as unfair, and even in bad taste, to select a few of them for boundless admiration, attributing superhuman powers of mind and character to them. This has been my fate, and the contrast between the popular estimate of my powers and achievements and the reality is simply grotesque.

ALBERT EINSTEIN

Intentions

Begin somewhere; you cannot build a reputation on what you intend to do.

LIZ SMITH

Interests

Our delight in any particular study, art, or science rises and improves in proportion to the application which we bestow upon it. Thus, what was at first an exercise becomes at length an entertainment.

JOSEPH ADDISON

What we love to do we find time to do.

JOHN LANCASTER SPALDING

Interrupting

There are two faults in conversations, which appear very different, yet arise from the same root, and are equally blamable; I mean an impatience to interrupt others and the uneasiness of being interrupted ourselves.

JONATHAN SWIFT

Introductions

Introductions. Nobody reads them. But our editor said, "Introduction?" And what he says goes. This is it.

WILLIAM COLE AND LOUIS PHILLIPS

Intuition

Intuition is given only to him who has undergone long preparation to receive it.

LOUIS PASTEUR

Intuition is a spiritual faculty and does not explain, but simply points the way.

FLORENCE SCOVEL SHINN

Inventing

Inventing is a combination of brains and materials. The more brains you use, the less materials you need.

CHARLES KETTERING

Jealousy

All jealousy must be strangled in its birth, or time will soon make it strong enough to overcome the truth.

SIR WILLIAM DAVENANT

Anger is cruel and fury overwhelming, but who can stand before jealousy?

THE BIBLE: PROVERBS 27:4

Anger and jealousy can no more bear to lose sight of their objects than love.

GEORGE ELIOT

Jealousy is...a tiger that tears not only its prey but also its own raging heart.

MICHAEL BEER

To jealousy, nothing is more frightful than laughter.

FRANÇOISE SAGAN

There is never jealousy where there is not strong regard.

WASHINGTON IRVING

Jealousy, that dragon which slays love under the pretence of keeping it alive.

HAVELOCK ELLIS

Jesus Christ

If Socrates would enter the room we should rise and do him honor. But if Jesus Christ came into the room we should fall down on our knees and worship Him.

NAPOLEON BONAPARTE

The great mistake of my life has been that I tried to be moral without faith in Jesus; but I have learned that true morality can only keep pace with trust in Christ as my Savior.

GERRIT SMITH

I search in vain in history to find the similar to Jesus Christ, or anything which can approach the gospel. Neither history, nor humanity, nor the ages, nor nature, offer me anything with which I am able to compare or explain it. There is nothing there which is not beyond the march of events and above the human mind. What happiness it gives to those who believe it! What marvels there which those admire who reflect upon it!

NAPOLEON BONAPARTE

As the print of the seal on the wax is the express image of the seal itself, so Christ is the express image—the perfect representation of God.

AMBROSE OF MILAN

In his life, Christ is an example, showing us how to live; in His death, He is a sacrifice, satisfying for our sins; in His resurrection, a conqueror; in His ascension, a king; in His intercession, a high priest.

MARTIN LUTHER

The sum of the whole matter is this, that our civilization cannot survive materially unless it be redeemed spiritually. It can be saved only by becoming permeated with the spirit of Christ and being made free and happy by the practices which spring out of that spirit.

WOODROW WILSON

To be like Christ is to be a Christian.

WILLIAM PENN

There is no greater drama in human record than the sight of a few Christians, scorned or oppressed by a succession of emperors, bearing all trials with a fierce tenacity, multiplying quietly, building order while their enemies generated chaos, fighting the sword with the word, brutality with hope, and at last defeating the strongest state that history has known. Caesar and Christ had met in the arena, and Christ had won.

WILL DURANT

The sages and heroes of history are receding from us. But time has no power over the name and deeds and words of Jesus Christ.

WILLIAM ELLERY CHANNING

Philosophical argument, especially that drawn from the vastness of the universe, in comparison with the apparent insignificance of this globe, has sometimes shaken my reason for the faith which is in me; but my heart has always assured me that the gospel of Jesus Christ must be divine reality. The Sermon on the Mount cannot be a mere human production. This belief enters into the very depth of my conscience. The whole history of man proves it.

DANIEL WEBSTER

[HIS EPITAPH, DICTATED THE DAY BEFORE HE DIED]

Jobs

To get a job well done, assign it to the man who has the most to lose, not to one who has everything to gain.

Every job is a self-portrait of the person who did it. Autograph your work with excellence.

Do your job and demand your compensation—but in that order.
CARY GRANT

Nothing helps you to enjoy your job like an independent income.

Jokes

There are things of deadly earnest that can only be safely mentioned under cover of a joke.
J.J. PROCTER

Were it not for my little jokes, I could not bear the burdens of this office.
ABRAHAM LINCOLN

Like a madman shooting firebrands or deadly arrows is a man who deceives his neighbor and says, "I was only joking!"
THE BIBLE: PROVERBS 26:18,19

Jones' Law

The man who smiles when things go wrong has thought of someone he can blame it on.

Journalism

The sole aim of journalism should be service. The press is a great power, but just as an unchained torrent of water submerges the whole countryside and devastates crops, even so an uncontrolled pen serves but to destroy. If the control is from without, it proves more poisonous than want of control. It can be profitable only when exercised from within. If this line of reasoning is correct, how many of the journals in the world would stand the test? But who would stop those that are useless? And who should be the judge? The useful and the useless must, like good and evil generally, go on together, and man must make his choice.

MAHATMA GANDHI

The only qualities for real success in journalism are ratlike cunning, a plausible manner, and a little literary ability. The capacity to steal other people's ideas and phrases...is also invaluable.

NICHOLAS TOMALIN

Journalism largely consists in saying, "Lord Jones Dead" to people who never knew Lord Jones was alive.

G.K. CHESTERTON

Journalists

Journalists do not live by words alone, although sometimes they have to eat them.

ADLAI STEVENSON

Journalists say a thing that they know isn't true, in the hope that if they keep on saying it long enough it will be true.

ARNOLD BENNETT

Joy

The joy of the heart makes the face fair.

One joy scatters a hundred griefs.

Joy has nothing to do with material things, or with a man's outward circumstance....a man living in the lap of luxury can be wretched, and a man in the depths of poverty can over-flow with joy.

WILLIAM BARCLAY

Weeping may endure for a night, but joy cometh in the morning.

THE BIBLE: PSALM 30:5 KJV

One filled with joy preaches without preaching.

MOTHER TERESA

Joy is the flag you fly when the Prince of Peace is in residence within your heart.

WILFRED PETERSON

Judge

Four things belong to a judge: to hear courteously, to answer wisely, to consider soberly, and to decide impartially.

SOCRATES

There is no greater indictment of a judge than the fact that honest men are afraid to go into court, while criminals swagger out its revolving doors.

THOMAS SOWELL

Judging

Judge not, that ye be not judged.

THE BIBLE: MATTHEW 7:1 KJV

It is well, when judging a friend, to remember that he is judging you with the same godlike and superior impartiality.

ARNOLD BENNETT

Judgment

Take each man's censure, but reserve thy judgment.

WILLIAM SHAKESPEARE

He has a good judgment that relies not wholly on his own.

Though reading and conversation may furnish us with many ideas of men and things, our own meditation must form our judgement.
ISAAC WATTS

Judiciousness

One man's word is no man's word; we should quietly hear both sides.
JOHANN WOLFGANG VON GOETHE

Justice

Justice and power must be brought together, so that whatever is just may be powerful, and whatever is powerful may be just.
BLAISE PASCAL

I tremble for my country when I reflect that God is just.
THOMAS JEFFERSON

We need to rectify this mockery of justice and seek to realign the imbalanced scales of justice that all too often subjugate the rights and safety of society to the privileged exploitations and atrocities by the criminal.
JOHN L. MCCLELLAN

Justice is the great interest of man on earth. It is the ligament which holds civilized beings and civilized nations together. Wherever her temple stands, and so long as it is duly honored, there is a foundation for social security, general happiness, and the improvement and progress of our race. And whoever labors on this edifice with usefulness and distinction, whoever clears its foundations, strengthens its pillars, adorns its entablatures, or contributes to raise its august dome still higher in the skies, connects himself, in name, and fame, and character, with that which is and must be as durable as the frame of human society.

DANIEL WEBSTER

If it is thought that justice is with us, it will give birth to courage.

ELMER DAVIS

Kindness

A kind heart is a fountain of gladness, making everything in its vicinity freshen into smiles.

WASHINGTON IRVING

A kind man benefits himself, but a cruel man brings trouble on himself.

THE BIBLE: PROVERBS 11:17

Kindness is in our power, even when fondness is not.

SAMUEL JOHNSON

Human kindness has never weakened the stamina or softened the fiber of a free people. A nation does not have to be cruel in order to be tough.

FRANKLIN D. ROOSEVELT

The cheapest of all things is kindness, its exercise requiring the least possible trouble and self-sacrifice.

SAMUEL SMILES

A more glorious victory cannot be gained over another man, than this, that when the injury began on his part, the kindness should begin on ours.

JOHN TILLOTSON

Don't be a noble fighter, 'cause kindness is righter.

POPEYE

Shall we make a new rule of life from tonight: always to try to be a little kinder than is necessary.

JAMES M. BARRIE

People who overlook little slights and keep reaching out to help one another with acts of kindness will have very little problem maintaining harmonious relationships.

RICHARD STRAUSS

Kindness in words creates confidence; kindness in thinking creates profoundness; kindness in giving creates love.

LAO-TZU

Constant kindness can accomplish much. As the sun makes ice melt, kindness causes misunderstanding, mistrust and hostility to evaporate.

ALBERT SCHWEITZER

Kind words can be short and easy to speak, but their echoes are truly endless.

MOTHER TERESA

Kings
Kings and such are just as funny as politicians.

Kisses
It is the passion that is in a kiss that gives to it its sweetness; it is the affection in a kiss that sanctifies it.

CHRISTIAN NESTELL BOVEE

The sound of a kiss is not so loud as that of a cannon, but its echo lasts a great deal longer.

OLIVER WENDELL HOLMES JR.

Knowledge

He knows so little and knows it so fluently.

ELLEN ANDERSON GHOLSON GLASGOW

The more extensive a man's knowledge of what has been done, the greater will be his power of knowing what to do.

BENJAMIN DISRAELI

The more we know of any one ground of knowledge, the further we see into the general domains of intellect.

LEIGH HUNT

One half of knowing what you want is knowing what you must give up before you get it.

SIDNEY HOWARD

Of all kinds of knowledge that we can ever obtain, the knowledge of God and the knowledge of ourselves are the most important.

JONATHAN EDWARDS

He who has no inclination to learn more will be very apt to think that he knows enough.

SIR JOHN POWELL

He that increaseth knowledge increaseth sorrow.

THE BIBLE: ECCLESIASTES 1:18 KJV

All wish to possess knowledge, but few, comparatively speaking, are willing to pay the price.

JUVENAL

If you have knowledge, let others light their candles at it.

THOMAS FULLER

Never try to tell everything you know. It may take too short a time.

NORMAN FORD

Labor

God sells us all things at the price of labor.

LEONARDO DA VINCI

Manual labor to my father was not only good and decent for its own sake, but as he was given to saying, it straightened out one's thoughts.

MARY ELLEN CHASE

Last Breath

Each person is born to one possession which outvalues all the others—his last breath.

MARK TWAIN

Last Minute

If it weren't for the last minute, nothing would get done.

Late Rising

He that riseth late must trot all day, and shall scarce overtake his business by night.

BENJAMIN FRANKLIN

Laughter

A laugh is a smile that bursts.

MARY H. WALDRIP

No one is laughable who laughs at himself.

SENECA

If you wish to glimpse inside a human soul and get to know a man, don't bother analyzing his ways of being silent, of talking, of weeping, or seeing how much he is moved by noble ideas; you'll get better results if you just watch him laugh. If he laughs well, he's a good man.

FYODOR DOSTOYEVSKY

With the fearful strain that is on me night and day, if I did not laugh I should die.

ABRAHAM LINCOLN

The fact is I have always believed that a good laugh was good for both the mental and the physical digestion.

ABRAHAM LINCOLN

I laugh because I must not weep—that's all, that's all.

ABRAHAM LINCOLN

The world is a looking glass and gives back to every man the reflection of his own face. Frown at it, and it will in turn look sourly upon you; laugh at it, and with it, and it is a jolly kind companion.

WILLIAM MAKEPEACE THACKERAY

Be sincere. Be simple in words, manners and gestures. Amuse as well as instruct. If you can make a man laugh, you can make him think and make him like and believe you.

ALFRED EMANUEL SMITH

Of all the things God created, I am often most grateful he created laughter.

CHARLES SWINDOLL

Laughter and tears are meant to turn the wheels of the same machinery of sensibility; one is a wind-power and the other water-power, that is all.

OLIVER WENDELL HOLMES JR.

Laughter is the sensation of feeling good all over, and showing it principally in one spot.
                                                        JOSH BILLINGS

Laughter is not a bad beginning for a friendship, and it is the best ending for one.
                                                        OSCAR WILDE

Law

And you experts in the law, woe to you, because you load people down with burdens they can hardly carry, and you yourselves will not lift one finger to help them.
                                        THE BIBLE: LUKE 11:46

The law turns on golden wheels.

Agree, for the law is costly.

Laws

When men are pure, laws are useless; when men are corrupt, laws are broken.
                                                        BENJAMIN DISRAELI

Lawyers

Here's an amazing story. A man in Orlando, Florida, was hit by eight cars in a row and only one stopped. The first seven drivers thought he was a lawyer. The eighth was a lawyer.
                                                        JAY LENO

A wise lawyer never goes to law himself.

I wanted to make it a law that only those lawyers and attorneys should receive fees who had won their cases. How much

litigation would have been prevented by such a measure!
NAPOLEON BONAPARTE

A lawyer's ink writes nothing until you have thrown silver into
it.

Laziness

Laziness travels so slowly that poverty soon overtakes him.
BENJAMIN FRANKLIN

Laziness is a secret ingredient that goes into failure. But it's
only kept a secret from the person who fails.
ROBERT HALF

The lazy man is not ashamed of begging.

A lazy boy and a warm bed are difficult to part.

Leaders

Where the chief walks, there questions are decided.

The final test of a leader is that he leaves behind him, in other
men, the conviction and the will to carry on.
WALTER LIPPMANN

Learning is the essential fuel for the leader, the source of high-
octane energy that keeps up the momentum by continually
sparking new understanding, new ideas, and new challenges.
It is absolutely indispensable under today's conditions of rapid
change and complexity. Very simply, those who do not learn
do not long survive as leaders.
WARREN BENNIS AND BURT NANUS

The ultimate responsibility of a leader is to facilitate other people's development as well as his own.   FRED PRYOR

The first responsibility of a leader is to define reality. The last is to say thank you. In between the leader is a servant.
         MAX DEPREE

A leader is a dealer in hope.   NAPOLEON BONAPARTE

Men make history and not the other way round. In periods where there is no leadership, society stands still. Progress occurs when courageous, skillful leaders seize the opportunity to change things for the better.   HARRY S. TRUMAN

We expect our leaders to be better than we are...and they should be—or why are we following them?
         PAUL HARVEY

A great leader never sets himself above his followers except in carrying responsibilities.   JULES ORMONT

A good leader inspires other men with confidence in him; a great leader inspires them with confidence in themselves.

Fail to honor people, they fail to honor you. But of a good leader, who talks little, when his work is done, his aim fulfilled, they will all say, "we did this ourselves."   LAO-TZU

When a leader makes a mistake, all the people suffer.

The best leader is the one who has the sense to surround himself with outstanding people and the self-restraint not to meddle with how they do their jobs.

There are no office hours for leaders.

JAMES GIBBONS

It is the capacity to develop and improve their skills that distinguishes leaders from their followers.

WARREN BENNIS AND BERT NANUS

Faith in the ability of a leader is of slight service unless it be united with faith in his justice.

GEORGE WASHINGTON GOETHALS

He that commands well shall be obeyed well.

An army of a thousand is easy to find, but, ah, how difficult to find a general.

Leadership

It is said that if Noah's ark had had to be built by a company, they would not have laid the keel yet; and it may be so. What is many men's business is nobody's business. The greatest things are accomplished by individual men.

CHARLES H. SPURGEON

Leadership is a word and a concept that has been more argued than almost any other I know. I am not one of the desk-pounding type that likes to stick out his jaw and look like he is bossing the show. I would far rather get behind and, recognizing the frailties and the requirements of human nature, I would rather try to persuade a man to go along, because once I have persuaded him he will stick. If I scare him, he will stay just as long as he is scared, and then he is gone.

DWIGHT D. EISENHOWER

Two captains sink a ship.

Get into the habit of asking yourself if what you're doing can be handled by someone else.

If anything goes bad, I did it. If anything goes semi-good, then we did it. If anything goes real good, then you did it. That's all it takes to get people to win football games for you.

BEAR BRYANT

I am compelled to take a more impartial and unprejudiced view of things. Without claiming to be your superior, which I do not, my position enables me to understand my duty in all these matters better than you possibly can, and I hope you do not yet doubt my integrity.

ABRAHAM LINCOLN

An institution is the lengthened shadow of one man...and all history resolves itself very easily into the biography of a few stout and earnest persons.

RALPH WALDO EMERSON

He that has not served knows not how to command.

Our chief want in life is somebody who shall make us do what we can.

To get people to follow the straight and narrow path, stop giving them advice and start leading the way.

Learning

We will be victorious if we have not forgotten how to learn.

ROSA LUXEMBURG

A teacher who is attempting to teach without inspiring the pupil with a desire to learn is hammering on a cold iron.

HORACE MANN

I've known countless people who were reservoirs of learning yet never had a thought.

WILSON MIZNER

He that stumbles twice over one stone, deserves to break his shins.

The best of all things is to learn. Money can be lost or stolen, health and strength may fail, but what you have committed to your mind is yours forever.

If you devote your time to study, you will avoid all the irksomeness of this life, nor will you long for the approach of night, being tired of the day; nor will you be a burden to yourself, nor your society insupportable to others.

SENECA

Seeing much, suffering much, and studying much, are the three pillars of learning.

BENJAMIN DISRAELI

Wear your learning, like your watch, in a private pocket. Do not pull it out merely to show that you have one. If asked what o'clock it is, tell it; but do not proclaim it hourly and unasked, like the watchman.

LORD CHESTERFIELD

Swallow all your learning in the morning, but digest it in company in the evening.

LORD CHESTERFIELD

Learning is acquired by reading books, but the much more necessary learning, the knowledge of the world, is only to be acquired by reading men and studying all the various facets of them.

LORD CHESTERFIELD

Legal Proceedings

The penalty for laughing in a courtroom is six months in jail; if it were not for this penalty, the jury would never hear the evidence.

H.L. MENCKEN

The first to present his case seems right, till another comes forward and questions him.

THE BIBLE: PROVERBS 18:17

Discourage litigation. Persuade your neighbors to compromise whenever you can.

ABRAHAM LINCOLN

What you have seen with your eyes do not bring hastily to court, for what will you do in the end if your neighbor puts you to shame? If you argue your case with a neighbor, do not betray another man's confidence, or he who hears it may shame you and you will never lose your bad reputation.

THE BIBLE: PROVERBS 25:7-10

Legislation

One of the greatest delusions in the world is the hope that the evils of this world can be cured by legislation. I am happy in the belief that the solution of the great difficulties of life and government is in better hands even than those of this body.

THOMAS BRACKETT REED

Lending

Lending is like throwing away; being paid is like finding something.

Lend never that thing you need most.

He that does lend does lose his money and friend.

Leopards

If you find a leopard in your house, make him your friend.

Letters

The present letter is a very long one, simply because I had no leisure to make it shorter.   BLAISE PASCAL

One of the pleasures of reading old letters is the knowledge that they need no answer.   LORD BYRON

Sir, more than kisses, letters mingle souls; For, thus friends absent speak.   JOHN DONNE

Liars

You can best reward a liar by believing nothing of what he says.   ARISTIPPUS

Half a fact is a whole falsehood. He who gives the truth a false coloring by his false manner of telling it, is the worst of liars.   ELIAS LYMAN MAGOON

He that once deceives, is ever suspected.

Even a liar tells a hundred truths to one lie; he has to, to make the lie good for anything.   HENRY WARD BEECHER

He that will lie, will steal.

Liberals

A liberal is a man who is willing to spend somebody else's money.   CARTER GLASS

A rich man told me recently that a liberal is a man who tells other people what to do with their money.

LEROI JONES

A liberal is a man who leaves the room when the fight begins.

HEYWOOD BROUN

A liberal is a person whose interests aren't at stake at the moment.

WILLIS PLAYER

A liberal mind is a mind that is able to imagine itself believing anything.

MAX EASTMAN

Hell hath no fury like a liberal scorned.

DICK GREGORY

Liberalism is the first refuge of political indifference and the last refuge of leftists.

HARRY ROSKOLENKO

Liberty

Every man has a property in his own person; this nobody has a right to but himself.

JOHN LOCKE

If we mean to support the liberty and independence which have cost us so much blood and treasure to establish, we must drive far away the demon of party spirit and local reproach.

GEORGE WASHINGTON

They that can give up essential liberty to obtain a little temporary safety, deserve neither liberty nor safety.

BENJAMIN FRANKLIN

God grants liberty only to those who love it and are always ready to guard and defend it.

DANIEL WEBSTER

True liberty consists only in the power of doing what we ought to will, and in not being constrained to do what we ought not to will.

JONATHAN EDWARDS

No people ever lost their liberties unless they themselves first became corrupt. The people are the safeguards of their own liberties, and I rely wholly on them to guard themselves.

ANDREW JACKSON

Our union is now complete; our constitution composed, established and approved. You are now the guardians of your own liberties.

SAMUEL ADAMS

I must study politics and war that my sons may have liberty to study mathematics and philosophy.

JOHN ADAMS

Liberty is the one thing you cannot love unless you are willing to give it to others.

WILLIAM ALLEN WHITE

The history of liberty is a history of resistance. The history of liberty is a history of the limitation of governmental power, not the increase of it.

WOODROW WILSON

I would remind you that extremism in the defense of liberty is no vice. And let me remind you also that moderation in the pursuit of justice is no virtue.

BARRY GOLDWATER

The inescapable price of liberty is an ability to preserve it from destruction.

DOUGLAS MACARTHUR

I would rather belong to a poor nation that was free than to a rich nation that had ceased to be in love with liberty. We shall not be poor if we love liberty.   WOODROW WILSON

The things required for prosperous labor, prosperous manufactures, and prosperous commerce are three. First, liberty; second, liberty; third, liberty.   HENRY WARD BEECHER

Is the relinquishment of the trial by jury and the liberty of the press necessary for your liberty? Will the abandonment of your most sacred rights tend to the security of your liberty? Liberty, the greatest of all earthly blessings—give us that precious jewel, and you may take everything else! Guard with jealous attention the public liberty. Suspect everyone who approaches that jewel.   PATRICK HENRY

When liberty is taken away by force, it can be restored by force. When it is relinquished voluntarily by default, it can never be recovered.   DOROTHY THOMPSON

Liberty, when it begins to take root, is a plant of rapid growth.   GEORGE WASHINGTON

Liberty exists in proportion to wholesome restraint; the more restraint on others to keep off from us, the more liberty we have.   DANIEL WEBSTER

Liberty is the proper end and object of authority, and cannot subsist without it; and it is a liberty to that only which is good, just, and honest.   JOHN WINTHROP

A free people ought not only to be armed, but disciplined.   GEORGE WASHINGTON

The whole history of the progress of human liberty shows that all concessions yet made to her august claims have been made of earnest struggle. If there is no struggle, there is no progress. Those who profess to favor freedom yet deprecate agitation, are men who want crops without plowing up the ground; they want rain without thunder and lightning. They want the ocean without the awful roar of its many waters. Power concedes nothing without a demand. It never did and it never will. The limits of tyrants are prescribed by the endurance of those whom they oppress.

FREDERICK DOUGLASS

He that would make his own liberty secure must guard even his enemy from oppression.

THOMAS PAINE

There is a just God who presides over the destinies of nations and who will raise up friends to fight our battles for us. The battle, sir, is not to the strong alone; it is to the vigilant, the active, the brave. It is vain, sir, to extenuate the matter. Gentlemen may cry, peace, peace—but there is no peace. The war is actually begun! The next gale that sweeps from the north will bring to our ears the clash of resounding arms! Our brethren are already in the field! Why stand we here idle? What is it that gentlemen wish? What would they have? Is life so dear, or peace so sweet, as to be purchased at the price of chains and slavery? Forbid it, almighty God! I know not what course others may take; but as for me, give me liberty, or give me death!

PATRICK HENRY

Our reliance is the love of liberty which God has planted in us. Our defense is in the spirit which prizes liberty as the heritage of all men, in all lands everywhere.

ABRAHAM LINCOLN

The tree of liberty must be refreshed from time to time with the blood of patriots and tyrants. It is its natural manure.

THOMAS JEFFERSON

Liberty is always dangerous, but it is the safest thing we have.
HENRY EMERSON FOSDICK

The true danger is when liberty is nibbled away, for expedients, and by parts.
EDMUND BURKE

Eternal vigilance is the price of liberty; power is ever stealing from the many to the few. The manna of popular liberty must be gathered each day, or it is rotten. The living sap of today outgrows the dead rind of yesterday. The hand entrusted with power becomes, either from human depravity or esprit de corps, the necessary enemy of the people. Only by continued oversight can the democrat in office be prevented from hardening into a despot; only by unintermitted agitation can a people be sufficiently awake to principle not to let liberty be smothered in material prosperity.
WENDELL PHILLIPS

It is a common observation here that our cause is the cause of all mankind, and that we are fighting for their liberty in defending our own.
BENJAMIN FRANKLIN

Liberty means responsibility. That is why most men dread it.
GEORGE BERNARD SHAW

Let every nation know, whether it wishes us well or ill, that we shall pay any price, bear any burden, meet any hardship, support any friend, oppose any foe to assure the survival and the success of liberty.
JOHN F. KENNEDY

If the true spark of religious and civil liberty be kindled, it will burn. Human agency cannot extinguish it. Like the earth's central fire, it may be smothered for a time; the ocean may overwhelm it; mountains may press it down; but its inherent and unconquerable force will heave both the ocean and the land, and at some time or other, in some place or other, the volcano will break out and flame up to heaven.

DANIEL WEBSTER

The spirit of liberty is the spirit which is not too sure that it is right; the spirit of liberty is the spirit which seeks to understand the minds of other men and women; the spirit of liberty is the spirit which weighs their interests alongside its own without bias; the spirit of liberty remembers that not even a sparrow falls to earth unheeded; the spirit of liberty is the spirit of Him who, near two thousand years ago, taught mankind that lesson it has never learned, but has never quite forgotten: that here is a kingdom where the least shall be heard and considered side by side with the greatest.

LEARNED HAND

Libraries

Libraries are the marketplaces of human thought.

TREVOR FAWCETT

Lies

Sin has many tools, but a lie is the handle that fits them all.

OLIVER WENDELL HOLMES JR.

He who tells a lie is not sensible how great a task he undertakes; for he must be forced to invent twenty more to maintain one.

ALEXANDER POPE

One deceit needs many others, and so the whole house is built in the air and must soon come to the ground.

BALTASAR GRACIAN

Every life is its own excuse for being, and to deny or refute the untrue things that are said of you is an error in judgment. All wrongs recoil upon the doer, and the man who makes wrong statements about others is himself to be pitied, not the man he vilifies. It is better to be lied about than to lie.

ELBERT HUBBARD

There is no worse lie than a truth misunderstood by those who hear it.

           WILLIAM JAMES

A lie always needs a truth for a handle to it. The worst lies are those whose blade is false, but whose handle is true.

           HENRY WARD BEECHER

Life

Live mindful of how brief your life is.

           HORACE

Life happens at the level of events, not words.

           ALFRED ADLER

Do not take life too seriously; you will never get out of it alive.

           ELBERT HUBBARD

The measure of life is not its duration, but its donation.

           PETER MARSHALL

The mere sense of living is joy enough.   EMILY DICKINSON

Life does not cease to be funny when people die any more than it ceases to be serious when people laugh.

           GEORGE BERNARD SHAW

Life is something to do when you can't get to sleep.

           FRAN LEBOWITZ

Life is a great canvas, and you should throw all the paint on it you can.

           DANNY KAYE

I like living. I have sometimes been wildly, despairingly, acutely miserable, racked with sorrow, but through it all I still know quite certainly that just to be alive is a grand thing.

           AGATHA CHRISTIE

Life is what happens to you while you're making other plans.
ROBERT BALZER

Every day is a little life, and our whole life is but a day repeated. Therefore live every day as if it would be the last. Those that dare lose a day, are dangerously prodigal; those that dare misspend it are desperate.
JOSEPH HALL

In the game of life, it's a good idea to have a few early losses, which relieve you of the pressure of trying to maintain an undefeated season.
BILL VAUGHAN

The trouble with life is it is so daily.

Only those are fit to live who do not fear to die; and none are fit to die who have shrunk from the joy of life and the duty of life. Both life and death are parts of the same Great Adventure.
THEODORE ROOSEVELT

Life is a foreign language; all men mispronounce it.
CHRISTOPHER MORLEY

In this world a man must either be anvil or hammer.
HENRY W. LONGFELLOW

Life is a two-stage rocket. The first is physical energy—it ignites, and we are off. As physical energy diminishes, the spiritual stage must ignite to boost us into orbit, or we will fall back or plateau.
W.F. SMITH

I worry that our lives are like soap operas. We can go for months and not tune in to them, then six months later we look in and the same stuff is still going on.
JANE WAGNER

Life is a disease, and the only difference between one man and another is the stage of the disease at which he lives.

GEORGE BERNARD SHAW

If life were predictable, it would cease to be life and would be without flavor.

ELEANOR ROOSEVELT

Someone should tell us right at the start that we are dying. Then we would be more inclined to live life to the limit every minute of every day.

MICHAEL LANDON

My life is like a stroll upon the beach,
As near the ocean's edge as I can go.

HENRY DAVID THOREAU

A life isn't significant except for its impact on other lives.

JACKIE ROBINSON

Liking People

Getting people to like you is merely the other side of liking them.

NORMAN VINCENT PEALE

Limitations

The man with insight enough to admit his limitations comes nearest to perfection.

JOHANN WOLFGANG VON GOETHE

Imposing limitations on yourself is cowardly because it protects you from having to try, and perhaps failing.

VLADIMIR ZWORYKIN

Lincoln

Lincoln is one of those peculiar men who perform with admirable skill everything which they undertake.

STEPHEN A. DOUGLAS

Not often in the story of mankind does a man arrive on earth who is both steel and velvet, who is as hard as rock and soft as drifting fog, who holds in his heart and mind the paradox of terrible storm and peace unspeakable and perfect.

CARL SANDBURG

Mr. Lincoln is like a waiter in a large eating house where all the bells are ringing at once; he cannot serve them all at once, and so some grumblers are to be expected.

JOHN BRIGHT

Listening

It takes a great man to make a good listener.

SIR ARTHUR HELPS

He who answers before listening—that is his folly and his shame.

THE BIBLE: PROVERBS 18:13

A good listener is not only popular everywhere but after a while he knows something.

WILSON MIZNER

One of the first things that every top executive learns is that a very high percentage of his salary goes just to pay him to listen.

The silent person is often worth listening to.

No man would listen to you talk if he didn't know it was his turn next.

EDGAR WATSON HOWE

Loan a man your ears and you will immediately open a pathway to his heart.

Literature

Literature is a very bad crutch but a very good walking stick.

CHARLES LAMB

Little-mindedness

Little-minded people's thoughts move in such a small circle that five minutes' conversation gives you an arc long enough to determine their whole curve.

OLIVER WENDELL HOLMES JR.

Living Well

He that lives well, is learned enough.

BENJAMIN FRANKLIN

Loneliness

People are lonely because they build walls instead of bridges.

JOSEPH F. NEWTON

Long Life

The secret of long life is double careers. One to about age sixty, then another for the next thirty years.   DAVID OGILVY

Looks

He gave her a look you could have poured on a waffle.

RING LARDNER

Love

Hatred stirreth up strifes: but love covereth all sins.

THE BIBLE: PROVERBS 10:12 KJV

Love makes one fit for any work.

Faith, like light, should always be simple and unbending; while love, like warmth, should beam forth on every side and bend to every necessity of our brethren.

MARTIN LUTHER

Perfect love casteth out fear.

THE BIBLE: 1 JOHN 4:18 KJV

Those who love deeply never grow old; they may die of old age, but they die young.

SIR ARTHUR WING PINERO

Greater love has no man than this, that a man lay down his life for his friends.

THE BIBLE: JOHN 15:13 RSV

Love is the free exercise of choice. Two people love each other only when they are quite capable of living without each other but choose to live with each other.

M. SCOTT PECK

They do not love that do not show their love.

WILLIAM SHAKESPEARE

Absence is to love what wind is to fire; it puts out the little, it kindles the great.

ROGER DE BUSSY-RABUTIN

You might as well withdraw love as threaten to withdraw it; to one who loves you, these are equal catastrophes.

The arithmetic of love is unique: Two halves do not make a whole; only two wholes make a whole.

JO COUDERT

If Jack's in love, he's no judge of Jill's beauty.

BENJAMIN FRANKLIN

Love does not dominate; it cultivates.

JOHANN WOLFGANG VON GOETHE

Nothing spoils the taste of peanut butter like unrequited love.

CHARLIE BROWN

Everybody forgets the basic thing: People are not going to love you unless you love them.

PAT CARROLL

Love is like the five loaves and fishes. It doesn't start to multiply until you give it away.

INSPIRATIONAL THOUGHTS

Love often makes a fool of the cleverest men, and as often gives cleverness to the most foolish.

'Tis impossible to love and be wise.

FRANCIS BACON

No woman ever hates a man for being in love with her, but many a woman hates a man for being a friend to her.

ALEXANDER POPE

He who covers over an offense promotes love, but whoever repeats the matter separates close friends.

THE BIBLE: PROVERBS 17:9

Love is not blind—it sees more, not less. But because it sees more, it is willing to see less.

JULIUS GORDON

You can always try to teach people to love you in your style, but never expect anyone, no matter how close, to read your mind and heart. Tell them what you want. The investment you make in surprise is often a hidden expectation that brings disappointment. Better yet, buy yourself your heart's desire. Don't turn special days into tests of love. Take care of yourself in the style you prefer—yours. Then, anything else you receive on that day will seem like extra love that you can enjoy without hurtful expectations.

JENNIFER JAMES

There is no greater invitation to love than loving first.

AUGUSTINE

Love is the delusion that one woman differs from another.

H.L. MENCKEN

Love is like the measles; we all have to go through it.

JEROME K. JEROME

Love does not die easily. It is a living thing. It thrives in the face of all life's hazards, save one—neglect.

JAMES D. BRYDEN

Love's a malady without a cure.

JOHN DRYDEN

He prayeth best who loveth best.

SAMUEL TAYLOR COLERIDGE

Loyalty

Loyalty means nothing unless it has at its heart the absolute principle of self-sacrifice.

WOODROW WILSON

Unless you can find some sort of loyalty, you cannot find unity and peace in your active living.

JOSIAH ROYCE

My kind of loyalty was loyalty to one's country, not to its institutions or its officeholders. The country is the real thing, the substantial thing, the eternal thing; it is the thing to watch over, and care for, and be loyal to.

MARK TWAIN

Lust

Lust is an enemy to the purse, a foe to the person, a canker to the mind, a corrosive to the conscience, a weakness of the wit, a besotter of the senses, and, finally, a mortal bane to all the body.

PLINY THE ELDER

Lust is bottomless.

Madness

When we remember we are all mad, the mysteries disappear and life stands explained.

MARK TWAIN

Majority

One, on God's side, is a majority.

WENDELL PHILLIPS

It is my principle that the will of the majority should always prevail.

THOMAS JEFFERSON

Malice

Malice swallows the greater part of its own venom.

PUBLILIUS SYRUS

Malice sucks up the greater part of her own venom, and poisons herself.

MICHEL DE MONTAIGNE

Malice drinks one-half of its own poison.

SENECA

I shall do nothing in malice. What I deal with is too vast for malicious dealing.

ABRAHAM LINCOLN

Managers

As a manager you're paid to be uncomfortable. If you're comfortable, it's a sure sign you're doing things wrong.

PETER DRUCKER

Mankind

Man is the only animal that can remain on friendly terms with the victims he intends to eat until he eats them.

SAMUEL BUTLER

Man was made at the end of the week's work when God was tired.

MARK TWAIN

Manliness

Manliness consists not in bluff, bravado or lordliness. It consists in daring to do the right and facing consequences, whether it is in matters social, political or other. It consists in deeds, not in words.

MAHATMA GANDHI

First find the man in yourself if you will inspire manliness in others.

AMOS BRONSON ALCOTT

Manners

Manners are a sensitive awareness of the feelings of others. If you have that awareness, you have good manners, no matter what fork you use.

EMILY POST

Good manners and good morals are sworn friends and fast allies.
CYRUS AUGUSTUS BARTOL

Marmalade

I got the blues thinking of the future, so I left off and made some marmalade. It's amazing how it cheers one up to shred oranges and scrub the floor.
D.H. LAWRENCE

Marriage

Men dream in courtship, but in wedlock wake.
ALEXANDER POPE

A successful marriage is an edifice that must be rebuilt every day.
ANDRE MAUROIS

Marriage is the greatest educational institution on earth.
CHANNING POLLOCK

The great secret of a successful marriage is to treat all disasters as incidents and none of the incidents as disasters.
HAROLD NICHOLSON

Marriage with a good woman is a harbor in the tempest of life; with a bad woman, it is a tempest in the harbor.
JOHN PETIT-SENN

In marriage it is all very well to say that "the two are made one." The question is: Which one?

A marriage is like a long trip in a tiny rowboat: If one passenger starts to rock the boat, the other has to steady it; otherwise they will go to the bottom together.
DAVID REUBEN

Often the difference between a successful marriage and a mediocre one consists of leaving about three or four things a day unsaid.

HARLAN MILLER

A happy marriage is a long conversation that seems all too short.

ANDRE MAUROIS

A good marriage would be between a blind wife and a deaf husband.

MICHEL DE MONTAIGNE

Success in marriage is much more than finding the right person; it is a matter of being the right person.

BARNETT ROBERT BRICKNER

Marriage is a lottery, but you can't tear up your ticket if you lose.

F.M. KNOWLES

Don't marry for money; you can borrow it cheaper.

SCOTTISH PROVERB

Only choose in marriage a woman whom you would choose as a friend if she were a man.

JOSEPH JOUBERT

Marriage is not just spiritual communion and passionate embraces; marriage is also three meals a day and remembering to carry out the trash.

JOYCE BROTHERS

When I was a young man, I vowed never to marry until I found the ideal woman. Well, I found her—but alas, she was waiting for the ideal man.

ROBERT SCHUMANN

Chains do not hold a marriage together. It is threads, hundreds of tiny threads, which sew people together through the years.

SIMONE SIGNORET

Successful marriage is always a triangle: a man, a woman, and God.

T. CECIL MYERS

Many a man in love with a dimple makes the mistake of marrying the whole girl.

STEPHEN LEACOCK

After a few years of marriage, a man can look right at a woman without seeing her—and a woman can see right through a man without looking at him.

HELEN ROWLAND

I would like to have engraved inside every wedding band: "Be kind to one another." This is the golden rule of marriage, and the secret of making love last through the years.

RANDOLPH RAY

It resembles a pair of shears, so joined that they cannot be separated, often moving in opposite directions, yet always punishing anyone who comes between them.

SYDNEY SMITH

The value of marriage is not that adults produce children, but that children produce adults.

PETER DE VRIES

All marriages are happy. It's the living together afterward that causes all the trouble.

Martyrs

It is more difficult, and calls for higher energies of soul, to live a martyr than to die one.

HORACE MANN

Mass Media

The mass media know their reports are worth nothing compared to the eye and voice of a serious writer. Like cowardly bulls, people in the mass media paw the ground when one comes near.

NORMAN MAILER

Maturity

To be mature means to face, and not evade, every fresh crisis that comes.

FRITZ KUNKEL

The way of a superior man is three-fold: virtuous, he is free from anxieties; wise, he is free from perplexities; bold, he is free from fear.

CONFUCIUS

It is the mark of a superior man that, left to himself, he is able endlessly to amuse, interest, and entertain himself out of his personal stock of meditations, ideas, criticisms, memories, philosophy, humor, and what not.

GEORGE JEAN NATHAN

The following qualities are criteria of emotional maturity: the ability to deal constructively with reality, the capacity to adapt to change, relative freedom from symptoms produced by tensions and anxieties, the capacity to find more satisfaction in giving than receiving, the capacity to relate to others in a consistent manner with mutual satisfaction and helpfulness, the capacity to sublimate, the capacity to love.

WILLIAM MENNINGER

Mayflower Compact

...Having undertaken for the glory of God, and advancement of the Christian faith, and the honor of our king and country, a voyage to plant the first colony in the northern parts of

Virginia; [we] do by these presents, solemnly and mutually in the presence of God and one another, covenant and combine ourselves together into a civil body politic, for our better ordering and preservation, and furtherance of the ends aforesaid; and by virtue hereof to enact, constitute, and frame, such just and equal laws, ordinances, acts, constitutions and offices, from time to time, as shall be thought most meet and convenient for the general good of the colony; unto which we promise all due submission and obedience....

Mayonnaise

I always wanted to write a book that ended with the word mayonnaise.
RICHARD BRAUTIGAN

Meddling

Like one who seizes a dog by the ears is a passer-by who meddles in a quarrel not his own.
THE BIBLE: PROVERBS 26:17

Medicine

Formerly, when religion was strong and science weak, men mistook magic for medicine, now, when science is strong and religion weak, men mistake medicine for magic.
THOMAS SZASZ

Mediocrity

Some men are born mediocre, some men achieve mediocrity, and some men have mediocrity thrust upon them.
JOSEPH HELLER

Meekness

Meekness is imperfect if it be not both active and passive, leading us to subdue our own passions and resentments, as well as to bear patiently the passions and resentments of others.

JOHN WATSON FOSTER

Memorableness

If you would not be forgotten as soon as you are dead, either write things worth reading or do things worth writing.

BENJAMIN FRANKLIN

Memories

Money can't buy happiness but it will get you a better class of memories.

RONALD REAGAN

There is nothing like an odor to stir memories.

WILLIAM McFEE

Memory

Memory is the diary we all carry about with us.

OSCAR WILDE

Memory is the cabinet of imagination, the treasury of reason, the registry of conscience, and the council chamber of thought.

BASIL THE GREAT

The secret of a good memory is attention, and attention to a subject depends upon our interest in it. We rarely forget that which has made a deep impression on our minds.

TRYON EDWARDS

They teach us to remember; why do not they teach us to forget? There is not a man living who has not, some time in his life, admitted that memory was as much of a curse as a blessing.

FRANCIS ALEXANDER DURIVAGE

When I was younger, I could remember anything whether it had happened or not; but my faculties are decaying now and soon I shall be so that I cannot remember anything but the things that never happened. It is sad to go to pieces like this but we all have to do it.

MARK TWAIN

Recollection is the only paradise from which we cannot be turned out.

JEAN PAUL RICHTER

Of all the faculties of the human mind, that of memory is the first which suffers from age.

THOMAS JEFFERSON

"I did that," says my memory. "I could not have done that," says my pride, and remains inexorable. Eventually—the memory yields.

FRIEDRICH NIETZSCHE

The beauty of memory is that it still sees beauty when beauty has faded.

PAUL BOESE

The advantage of a bad memory is that one enjoys several times the same good things for the first time.

FRIEDRICH NIETZSCHE

Men

The men that women marry, and why they marry them, will always be a marvel and a mystery to the world.

HENRY W. LONGFELLOW

God give us men! A time like this demands
Strong minds, great hearts, true faith, and ready hands.
Men whom the lust of office does not kill,
Men whom the spoils of office cannot buy,

Men who possess opinions and a will,
Men who have honor, men who will not lie.

JOSIAH GILBERT HOLLAND

Men are nervous of remarkable women.

JAMES M. BARRIE

Merry Heart

He that is of a merry heart hath a continual feast.

THE BIBLE: PROVERBS 15:15 KJV

Middle Age

Middle age is when you are impressed not with the fact that the grass is greener on the other side of the fence but rather how difficult the fence looks to get over.

THE NORTH VERNON SUN

Middle age is when your narrow waist and broad mind begin to change places.

It's called "middle age" because that's where it shows.

Middle of the Road

The middle of the road is where the white line is—and that's the worst place to drive.

ROBERT FROST

We know what happens to people who stay in the middle of the road. They get run over.

ANEURIN BEVAN

Million Dollars

Those who pray for a million dollars would get better results if they prayed for a strong back and a good pair of hands.

Minds

A mind once cultivated will not lie fallow for half an hour.
EDWARD BULWER-LYTTON

The mind is like the stomach. It is not how much you put into it that counts, but how much it digests.
ALBERT JAY NOCK

If thou desirest ease, in the first place take care of the ease of thy mind; for that will make all other sufferings easy. But nothing can support a man whose mind is wounded.
THOMAS FULLER

The mind grows by what it feeds on.
JOSIAH GILBERT HOLLAND

If we work upon marble it will perish; if we work upon brass, time will efface it; if we rear temples, they will crumble into dust; but if we work upon immortal minds, if we imbue them with principles, with just the fear of God and love of our fellow men, we engrave on those tablets something which will brighten all eternity.
DANIEL WEBSTER

I have no idea what the mind of a low-life scoundrel is like, but I know what the mind of an honest man is like: It is terrifying.
ABEL HERMANT

Anguish of mind has driven thousands to suicide, anguish of body, none. This proves that the health of the mind is of far more consequence to our happiness than the health of the body, although both are deserving of much more attention than either of them receives.

Ministry

The Christian ministry is the worst of all trades, but the best of all professions.
JOHN NEWTON

Mirth

Mirth is God's medicine.

HENRY WARD BEECHER

Misery

The surest way to be miserable is to have the leisure to wonder whether or not you are happy. GEORGE BERNARD SHAW

Human misery must somewhere have a stop; there is no wind that always blows a storm. EURIPIDES

A misery is not to be measured from the nature of the evil, but from the temper of the sufferer. JOSEPH ADDISON

Misfortune

Doing what's right is no guarantee against misfortune.

WILLIAM MCFEE

Little minds are tamed and subdued by misfortune; but great minds rise above it.

WASHINGTON IRVING

Misfortunes find their way even on the darkest night.

Most of our misfortunes are more supportable than the comments of our friends upon them.

CHARLES CALEB COLTON

There is a piece of fortune in misfortune.

By speaking of our misfortunes we often seem to get relief.

PIERRE CORNEILLE

Depend upon it that if a man talks of his misfortunes, there is something in them that is not disagreeable to him.

SAMUEL JOHNSON

There is in the worst of fortune the best of chances for a happy change.

EURIPIDES

If all our misfortunes were laid in one common heap, whence everyone must take an equal portion, most people would be content to take their own and depart.

SOCRATES

Let us be of good cheer, however, remembering that the misfortunes hardest to bear are those which never come.

JAMES RUSSELL LOWELL

Mishaps

Mishaps are like knives, that either serve us or cut us, as we grasp them by the blade or the handle.

JAMES RUSSELL LOWELL

Misleading

No matter how much care is taken, someone will always be misled.

Misrepresentation

I have found that it is not entirely safe, when one is misrepresented under his very nose, to allow the misrepresentation to go uncontradicted.

ABRAHAM LINCOLN

Mistakes

A just cause is not ruined by a few mistakes.

FYODOR DOSTOYEVSKY

Learn from the mistakes of others—you can't live long enough to make them all yourself.

MARTIN VANBEE

Everything I say, you know, goes into print. If I make a mistake it doesn't merely affect me or you, but the country. I therefore ought at least try not to make mistakes.

ABRAHAM LINCOLN

Wise men learn by other men's mistakes, fools by their own.

H.G. BOHN

Mistrust

What loneliness is more lonely than mistrust?

GEORGE ELIOT

Misunderstandings

Nine-tenths of the serious controversies which arise in life result from misunderstanding.

LOUIS BRANDEIS

Mobs

A mob is the scum that rises upmost when the nation boils.

JOHN DRYDEN

All assemblages of men are different from the men themselves. Neither intelligence nor culture can prevent a man from acting as a mob. The wise man and the knave lose their identity and merge themselves into a new being.

THOMAS BRACKETT REED

Mockers

Drive out the mocker, and out goes strife; quarrels and insults are ended.

THE BIBLE: PROVERBS 22:10

Models

I think women see me on the cover of magazines and think I never have a pimple or bags under my eyes. You have to realize that's after two hours of hair and makeup, plus retouching. Even I don't wake up looking like Cindy Crawford.

CINDY CRAWFORD

Modesty

Modesty is the citadel of beauty and virtue.   DEMADES

Modesty is the color of virtue.   DIOGENES

Modesty is the only sure bait when you angle for praise.

LORD CHESTERFIELD

Money

If you marry for money only, you will suffer...in comfort.

MURRAY BANKS

No one would remember the Good Samaritan if he'd only had good intentions. He had money as well.

MARGARET THATCHER

Make all you can, save all you can, give all you can.

JOHN WESLEY

Our incomes are like our shoes; if too small, they gall and pinch us; but if too large, they cause us to stumble and to trip.

CHARLES CALEB COLTON

Men who are ashamed of the way their fathers made their money are never ashamed to spend it.

By doing good with his money, a man, as it were, stamps the image of God upon it, and makes it pass current for the merchandise of heaven.

JOHN RUTLEDGE

Money lays waste cities; it sets men to roaming from home; it seduces and corrupts honest men and turns virtue to baseness; it teaches villainy and impiety.

SOPHOCLES

Beware of little expenses; a small leak will sink a great ship.

BENJAMIN FRANKLIN

The love of money is a root of all kinds of evil.

THE BIBLE: 1 TIMOTHY 6:10

Money is a good servant but a bad master.

A fool may make money, but it needs a wise man to spend it.

CHARLES H. SPURGEON

If you would know the value of money, go and try to borrow some.

BENJAMIN FRANKLIN

Monsters

When you fight a monster, beware lest you become a monster.

FRIEDRICH NIETZSCHE

Moral Law

No matter what theory of the origin of government you adopt, if you follow it out to its legitimate conclusions it will bring you face to face with the moral law.

HENRY VAN DYKE

Morality

I have never found a thorough, pervading, enduring morality but in those who feared God.   FRIEDRICH HEINRICH JACOBI

Every young man would do well to remember that all successful business stands on the foundation of morality.
HENRY WARD BEECHER

Morals

To educate a man in mind and not in morals is to educate a menace to society.   THEODORE ROOSEVELT

Morning

The morning hour has gold in its mouth.

Take your thoughts to bed with you, for the morning is wiser than the evening.

Mothers

Stories first heard at a mother's knee are never wholly forgotten—a little spring that never quite dries up in our journey through scorching years.   GIOVANNI RUFFINI

An ounce of mother is worth a pound of clergy.

The mother's heart is the child's schoolroom.
HENRY WARD BEECHER

My mother taught me not only the three R's, but she implanted in my mind the love and purpose of learning. My mother was the making of me. She understood me; she let me follow my bents.

THOMAS EDISON

Moths

What really happened to the buffaloes is just what you might expect if you've ever seen one in a zoo—the moths got into them.

WILL CUPPY

Motives

Men are not only bad from good motives, but also often good from bad motives.

G.K. CHESTERTON

Man sees your actions, but God your motives.

THOMAS À KEMPIS

Never ascribe to an opponent motives meaner than your own.

JAMES M. BARRIE

Mouth

The mouth is easy to open but difficult to close.

Movies

If the man and woman walk away together at the end of the picture, it adds $10 million to the box office.

GEORGE LUCAS

Music

Music is the art of the prophets, the only art that can calm the agitations of the soul; it is one of the most magnificent and delightful presents God has given us.

MARTIN LUTHER

Music is a discipline, and a mistress of order and good manners; she makes the people milder and gentler, more moral and more reasonable.

MARTIN LUTHER

You make as good music as a wheelbarrow.

THOMAS FULLER

Must

Must is a king's word.

Name-dropping

I mustn't go singling out names. One must not be a namedropper, as Her Majesty remarked to me yesterday.

NORMAN ST. JOHN-STEVAS

Narcissists

A narcissist is someone better looking than you are.

GORE VIDAL

National Debt

I, however, place economy among the first and most important of republican virtues, and public debt as the greatest of the dangers to be feared.

THOMAS JEFFERSON

As an individual who undertakes to live by borrowing, soon finds his original means devoured by interest, and next no one left to borrow from—so must it be with a government.

ABRAHAM LINCOLN

I sincerely believe…that banking establishments are more dangerous than standing armies, and that the principle of spending money to be paid by posterity, under the name of funding, is but swindling futurity on a large scale.

THOMAS JEFFERSON

I am for a government rigorously frugal and simple, applying all the possible savings of the public revenue to the discharge of the national debt; and not for a multiplication of officers and salaries merely to make partisans, and for increasing, by every device, the public debt, on the principle of its being a public blessing.

THOMAS JEFFERSON

I wish it were possible to obtain a single amendment to our Constitution. I would be willing to depend on that alone for the reduction of the administration of our government to the genuine principles of its Constitution; I mean an additional article, taking from the federal government the power of borrowing.

THOMAS JEFFERSON

National Defense

It may be laid down as a primary position, and the basis of our system, that every citizen who enjoys the protection of a free government, owes not only a proportion of his property, but even his personal services to the defense of it, and consequently that the citizens of America (with a few legal and official exceptions) from eighteen to fifty years of age should be borne on the militia rolls, provided with uniform arms, and so far accustomed to the use of them, that the total strength of the country might be called forth at a short notice on any very interesting emergency.

GEORGE WASHINGTON

National Honor

If we lose the virile, manly qualities, and sink into a nation of mere hucksters, putting gain over national honor, and subordinate everything to mere ease of life, then we shall indeed reach a condition worse than that of the ancient civilizations in the years of their decay.   THEODORE ROOSEVELT

Nations

Nations, like individuals, are subjected to punishments and chastisements in this world.   ABRAHAM LINCOLN

Necessity

Necessity never made a good bargain.
                                        BENJAMIN FRANKLIN

Necessity, my friend, is the mother of courage, as of invention.

Neighbors

Love your neighbor, yet don't pull down your hedge.
                                        BENJAMIN FRANKLIN

Seldom set foot in your neighbor's house—too much of you, and he will hate you.   THE BIBLE: PROVERBS 25:17

Neurosis

Work and love—these are the basics. Without them there is neurosis.
                                        THEODOR REIK

Neutrality

It is a wicked thing to be neutral between right and wrong.

THEODORE ROOSEVELT

As the poet Dante once said, "The hottest places in hell are reserved for those who, in a time of great moral crisis, maintain their neutrality."

JOHN F. KENNEDY

Newspapers

I fear three newspapers more than a hundred thousand bayonets.

NAPOLEON BONAPARTE

If newspapers are useful in overthrowing tyrants, it is only to establish a tyranny of their own.

JAMES FENIMORE COOPER

But let me beseech you, sir, not to let this letter get into a newspaper. Tranquility, at my age, is the supreme good of life. I think it a duty, and it is my earnest wish, to take no further part in public affairs…The abuse of confidence by publishing my letters has cost me more than all other pains.

THOMAS JEFFERSON

"The papers are not always reliable," Lincoln interjected, "that is to say, Mr. Welles, they lie and then they re-lie."

CARL SANDBURG

It is a melancholy truth, that a suppression of the press could not more completely deprive the nation of its benefits, than is done by its abandoned prostitution of falsehood. Nothing can now be believed which is seen in a newspaper.

THOMAS JEFFERSON

The man who never looks into a newspaper is better informed than he who reads them; inasmuch as he who knows nothing is nearer to truth than he whose mind is filled with falsehoods and errors. He who reads nothing will still learn the great facts, and the details are all false.

THOMAS JEFFERSON

Advertisements contain the only truths to be relied on in a newspaper.

THOMAS JEFFERSON

The art of newspaper paragraphing is to stroke a platitude until it purrs like an epigram.

DON MARQUIS

I do not take a single newspaper, nor read one a month, and I feel myself infinitely the happier for it.

THOMAS JEFFERSON

All successful newspapers are ceaselessly querulous and bellicose. They never defend anyone or anything if they can help it; if the job is forced upon them, they tackle it by denouncing someone or something else.

H.L. MENCKEN

Nicknames

Nicknames stick to people, and the most ridiculous are the most adhesive.

T.C. HALIBURTON

No

One must have the courage to say "no," even at the risk of displeasing others.

FRITZ KUNKEL

Nonessentials

Besides the noble art of getting things done, there is the noble art of leaving things undone. The wisdom of life consists in the elimination of non-essentials.

LIN YUTANG

Normal Times

Most of us have never lived in normal times.

Nothing

He that has done nothing has known nothing.

THOMAS CARLYLE

I started out with nothing. I still have most of it.

MICHAEL DAVIS

In any moment of decision the best thing you can do is the right thing, the next best thing is the wrong thing, and the worst thing you can do is nothing.

He did nothing in particular and did it very well.

W.S. GILBERT

Obedience

I have thoughts about it a great deal, and the more I think, the more certain I am that obedience is the gateway through which knowledge, yes, and love, too, enter the mind of a child.

ANNIE SULLIVAN

Obscenity

But implicit in the history of the First Amendment is the rejection of obscenity as utterly without redeeming social importance.

WILLIAM J. BRENNAN JR.

Obstacles

Discouragements and obstacles can be used to strengthen character as dams make it possible for rivers to generate electricity: They impede the flow but they increase the power. Defeats are inescapable; failures are as certain as the sparks fly upward. By the side of every mountain is a valley, and by the side of every oasis is a desert.

Old Age

Don't resent growing old. A great many are denied the privilege.

He's so old his blood type was discontinued.

BILL DANA

I'm not saying he's old, but his birthday cake has just been declared a fire hazard.

How do you know when you're old? When you double your current age and realize you're not going to live that long.

MICHAEL J. LEYDEN II

The way to live to be one hundred is to reach ninety-nine and then to live very carefully.

At sixty, you realize that grandfather wasn't so old when he died at eighty.

It's not miserable to be old; it's miserable not to be capable of living your age.

EUGENE P. BERTIN

Anyone can get old. All you have to do is live long enough.

GROUCHO MARX

Old age does not announce itself.

Old age and sickness bring out the essential characteristics of a man.
FELIX FRANKFURTER

In youth we run into difficulties, in old age difficulties run into us.
JOSH BILLINGS

Now that I finally know my way around, I don't feel like going.

Old Couples

To see a young couple loving each other is no wonder; but to see an old couple loving each other is the best sight of all.
WILLIAM MAKEPEACE THACKERAY

Once

Once is the beginning of all things.

Openness

Search me, O God, and know my heart: try me, and know my thoughts: and see if there be any wicked way in me.
THE BIBLE: PSALM 139:23,24 KJV

Opera

Going to the opera, like getting drunk, is a sin that carries its own punishment with it, and that a very severe one.
HANNAH MOORE

Opera is when a guy gets stabbed in the back and instead of bleeding, he sings.
ED GARDNER

An unalterable and unquestioned law of the musical world required that the German text of French operas sung by Swedish artists should be translated into Italian for the clearer understanding of English-speaking audiences.

EDITH WHARTON

Opinion

We are so vain that we even care for the opinion of those we don't care for.   MARIE VON EBNER-ESCHENBACH

People do not seem to realize that their opinion of the world is also a confession of character.   RALPH WALDO EMERSON

Do not think of knocking out another person's brains because he differs in opinion from you. It would be as rational to knock yourself on the head because you differ from yourself ten years ago.

HORACE MANN

Literature is strewn with the wreckage of men who have minded beyond reason the opinion of others.

VIRGINIA WOOLF

Opportunities

Small opportunities are often the beginning of great enterprises.

DEMOSTHENES

We are all faced with a series of great opportunities brilliantly disguised as impossible situations.   CHUCK SWINDOLL

Sometimes we stare so long at a door that is closing that we see too late the one that is open.

ALEXANDER GRAHAM BELL

Watch out for emergencies. They are your big chance!

FRITZ REINER

Men do with opportunities as children do at the seashore; they fill their little hands with sand, and then let the grains fall through, one by one, till all are gone.

T. JONES

Too often, the opportunity knocks, but by the time you push back the chain, push back the bolt, unhook the two locks and shut off the burglar alarm, it's too late.

RITA COOLIDGE

Americans want a good standard of living—not simply to accumulate possessions, but to fulfill a legitimate aspiration for an environment in which their families may live meaningful and happy lives. Our people are committed, therefore, to the creation and preservation of opportunity for every citizen, opportunity to lead a more rewarding life. They are equally committed to our alleviation of unavoidable misfortune and distress among their fellow citizens.

DWIGHT D. EISENHOWER

Each problem has hidden in it an opportunity so powerful that it literally dwarfs the problem. The greatest success stories were created by people who recognized a problem and turned it into an opportunity.

JOSEPH SUGARMAN

Optimists

An optimist is one who gets treed by a lion but enjoys the scenery.

The optimist pleasantly ponders how high his kite will fly; the pessimist woefully wonders how soon his kite will fall.

WILLIAM ARTHUR WARD

Original Sin

Original sin is in us, like the beard. We are shaved today and look clean, and have a smooth chin; tomorrow our beard has grown again, nor does it cease growing while we remain on earth. In like manner original sin cannot be extirpated from us; it springs up in us as long as we live. Nevertheless we are bound to resist it to our utmost strength, and to cut it down unceasingly.

MARTIN LUTHER

Originality

Originality is the science of concealing your scores.

He has left off reading altogether, to the great improvement of his originality.

CHARLES LAMB

Others

People love others not for who they are but for how they make us feel!

IRWIN FEDERMAN

Only a life lived for others is the life worthwhile.

ALBERT EINSTEIN

The man who goes alone can start today; but he who travels with another must wait till that other is ready.

HENRY DAVID THOREAU

Oxen

Where there are no oxen, the manger is empty, but from the strength of an ox comes an abundant harvest.

THE BIBLE: PROVERBS 14:4

Pain

Pain nourishes courage. You can't be brave if you've only had wonderful things happen to you.

MARY TYLER MOORE

Remember that pain has this most excellent quality: if prolonged, it cannot be severe, and if severe it cannot be prolonged.

SENECA

Pain is part of being alive, and we need to learn that. Pain does not last forever, nor is it necessarily unbearable, and we need to be taught that.

HAROLD KUSHNER

Paradox

In many ways, mastering paradox is nothing more than having good common sense.

DONALD T. PHILLIPS

Pardoning

Know all and you will pardon all.

THOMAS À KEMPIS

Any man can seek revenge; it takes a king or prince to grant a pardon.

ARTHUR J. REHRAT

One pardons in the degree that one loves.

FRANÇOIS DE LA ROCHEFOUCAULD

Parents

If parents would worry more about when their children turn in, they'd have to worry less about how they'll turn out.

Parties

At a dinner party, one should eat wisely but not too well and talk well but not too wisely.   W. SOMERSET MAUGHAM

Passing Away

It is said an Eastern monarch once charged his wise men to invent him a sentence, to be ever in view, and which should be true and appropriate in all times and situations. They presented him the words: "And this, too, shall pass away." How much it expresses! How chastening in the hour of pride—how consoling in the depth of affliction!   ABRAHAM LINCOLN

Passion

What is man but his passion?   ROBERT PENN WARREN

A strong passion for any object will ensure success, for the desire of the end will point out the means.
   WILLIAM HAZLITT

Be still when you have nothing to say; when genuine passion moves you, say what you've got to say, and say it hot.
   D.H. LAWRENCE

The passions are the only orators which always persuade.
   FRANÇOIS DE LA ROCHEFOUCAULD

What a mistake to suppose that the passions are strongest in youth! The passions are not stronger, but the control over them is weaker! They are more easily excited, they are more violent and apparent; but they have less energy, less durability, less intense and concentrated power than in maturer life.

EDWARD BULWER-LYTTON

Our passions are like convulsion fits, which, though they make us stronger for the time, leave us the weaker ever after.

JONATHAN SWIFT

Passiveness

People seldom want to walk over you until you lie down.

ELMER WHEELER

Past

Your past is always going to be the way it was. Stop trying to change it.

Patches

Better to have an ugly patch than a beautiful hole.

Patience

Never think that God's delays are God's denials. Hold on; hold fast; hold out. Patience is genius.

GEORGES-LOUIS LECLERC DE BUFFON

Patience is the ability to wait until you're too old to care anymore.

To know how to wait is the great secret of success.

JOSEPH MARIE DE MAISTRE

Strength is born in the deep silence of longsuffering hearts; not amidst joy.

FELICIA DOROTHEA BROWNE HEMANS

Patience is a bitter plant, but it has sweet fruit.

The secret of patience…to do something else in the meantime.

Have patience with all things, but chiefly have patience with yourself. Do not lose courage in considering your own imperfections, but instantly set about remedying them—every day begin the task anew.

SAINT FRANCIS DE SALES

The very best and utmost of attainment in this life is to remain still and let God act and speak in thee.

MEISTER ECKHART

A man's wisdom gives him patience; it is to his glory to overlook an offense.

THE BIBLE: PROVERBS 19:11

The string of one's sack of patience is generally tied with a slip-knot.

Plant patience in the garden of thy soul!
The roots are bitter, but the fruit is sweet!
And when at last it stands a tree complete,
Beneath its tender shade the burning heat
And burden of the day shall lose control—
Plant patience in the garden of thy soul!

HENRY AUSTIN DOBSON

There is no royal road to anything. One thing at a time, all things in succession. That which grows fast withers as rapidly; that which grows slowly endures.

JOSIAH GILBERT HOLLAND

One moment of patience may ward off great disaster; one moment of impatience may ruin a whole life.

CHINESE PROVERB

He that can have patience, can have what he will.

BENJAMIN FRANKLIN

Beware the fury of a patient man.

JOHN DRYDEN

A patient person is one who is willing to let somebody teach him something he already knows.

Patriotism

Patriotism is easy to understand in America; it means looking out for yourself by looking out for your country.

CALVIN COOLIDGE

Those who have not risen to the level of patriotism are not likely to rise to higher levels.

RALPH BARTON PERRY

I venture to suggest that patriotism is not a short and frenzied outburst of emotion but the tranquil and steady dedication of a lifetime.

ADLAI STEVENSON

I only regret that I have but one life to lose for my country.

NATHAN HALE

Patriotism depends as much on mutual suffering as on mutual success, and it is by that experience of all fortunes and all feelings that a great national character is created.

BENJAMIN DISRAELI

Patriotism consists not in waving the flag, but in striving that our country shall be righteous as well as strong.

JAMES BRYCE

Patriotism is a mighty precious thing when it costs nothing, but the mass of mankind consider it a very foolish thing when it curtails their self-indulgence.

JOHN BROKENBROUGH

After what I owe to God, nothing should be more dear or more sacred to me than the love and respect I owe my country.

JACQUES-AUGUSTE DE THOU

The patriots are those who love America enough to wish to see her as a model to mankind.

ADLAI STEVENSON

Peace

Peace is not the absence of conflict, but the presence of God no matter what the conflict.

Five great enemies to peace inhabit with us: ...avarice, ambition, envy, anger, and pride. If those enemies were to be banished, we should infallibly enjoy perpetual peace.

PETRARCH

To be prepared for war is one of the most effectual means of preserving peace.

GEORGE WASHINGTON

The currency with which you pay for peace is made up of manly courage, fearless virility, readiness to serve justice and honor at any cost, and a mind and a heart attuned to sacrifice.

WILLIAM FRANKLIN KNOX

Peace, above all things, is to be desired, but blood must sometimes be spilled to obtain it on equable and lasting terms.

ANDREW JACKSON

Peace is a blessing, and like most blessings, it must be earned.

DWIGHT D. EISENHOWER

Better to eat bread in peace than cake amidst turmoil.

With malice toward none, with charity for all, with firmness in the right, as God gives us to see the right, let us strive on to finish the work we are in, to bind up the nation's wounds, to care for him who shall have borne the battle and for his widow and his orphan, to do all which may achieve and cherish a just and lasting peace among ourselves and with all nations.

ABRAHAM LINCOLN

Peace of Mind

Peace of mind is better than giving them a piece of your mind.

J.P. MCEVOY

Peace of mind is that mental condition in which you have accepted the worst.

LIN YUTANG

For peace of mind, resign as general manager of the universe.

Peacemakers

Blessed are the peacemakers: for they shall be called the children of God.

THE BIBLE: MATTHEW 5:9 KJV

People

There are two kinds of people in the world—those who walk into a room and say, "There you are"—and those who say, "Here I am!"

ABIGAIL VAN BUREN

Perfection

He that will have a perfect brother must resign himself to remaining brotherless.

Performance

Gentle in manner, strong in performance.

CLAUDIO AQUAVIVA

When a subordinate is not performing adequately, rather than firing the person outright, some responsibility and authority are removed in the hope that the individual will be able to perform better with fewer responsibilities. Fairness and human dignity are preserved when this first step is employed; it gives the unsatisfactory performer a chance to "turn it around." If behavior and performance are not reversed, the next step is to get the individual out of the decision-making process as much as possible. Having the person report to another superior is a good way to do it.

DONALD T. PHILLIPS

Perseverance

The difference between perseverance and obstinacy is, that one often comes from a strong will, and the other from a strong won't.

HENRY WARD BEECHER

Perseverance is not a long race; it is many short races one after another.

WALTER ELLIOTT

Never give in, never give in, never, never, never, never—in nothing, great or small, large or petty—never give in except to convictions of honor and good sense.

SIR WINSTON CHURCHILL

The will to persevere is often the difference between failure and success.

DAVID SARNOFF

Persistence

Consider the postage stamp: Its usefulness consists in the ability to stick to one thing till it gets there.

JOSH BILLINGS

Nothing in the world can take the place of persistence. Talent will not; nothing is more common than unsuccessful men with talent. Genius will not; unrewarded genius is almost a proverb. Education will not; the world is full of educated derelicts. Persistence and determination are omnipotent. The slogan "press on" has solved and always will solve the problems of the human race.

CALVIN COOLIDGE

Keep on going, and the chances are that you will stumble on something, perhaps when you are least expecting it. I never heard of anyone ever stumbling on something sitting down.

CHARLES KETTERING

Even the woodpecker owes his success to the fact that he uses his head and keeps pecking away until he finishes the job he starts.

COLEMAN COX

This man Wellington is so stupid he does not know when he is beaten, and goes on fighting.

NAPOLEON BONAPARTE

Persistence in one opinion has never been considered a merit in political leaders.

CICERO

An ant hole may collapse an embankment.

The heights by great men reached and kept
Were not attained by sudden flight,

But they, while their companions slept
Were toiling upward in the night.

HENRY W. LONGFELLOW

Hold on with a bulldog grip, and chew and choke as much as possible.

ABRAHAM LINCOLN

Some men give up their designs when they have almost reached the goal; while others, on the contrary, obtain a victory by exerting, at the last moment, more vigorous efforts than before.

POLYBIUS

Drop by drop wears away the stone.

Personal Preferences

Let minor differences and personal preferences, if there be such, go to the winds.

ABRAHAM LINCOLN

Persuasion

When the conduct of men is designed to be influenced, persuasion—kind, unassuming persuasion—should ever be adopted. It is an old and a true maxim, that a "drop of honey catches more flies than a gallon of gall." So with men. If you would win a man to your cause, first convince him that you are his sincere friend. Therein is a drop of honey that catches his heart, which, say what he will, is the great high road to his reason, and which, when once gained, you will find but little trouble in convincing his judgment of the justice of your cause, if indeed that cause really be a just one. On the contrary, assume to dictate to his judgment or to command his action or to mark him as one to be shunned and despised, and he will retreat within himself, close all the avenues to his head and his heart; and, though your cause be naked truth itself,…you shall no more be able to [reach] him, than to penetrate the hard shell of a tortoise with a rye straw. Such is man, and so must he be understood by those who would lead him, even to his own best interest.

ABRAHAM LINCOLN

Pessimists

The pessimist is the man who believes things couldn't possibly be worse, to which the optimist replies, "Oh yes they could."

VLADIMIR BUKOVSKY

No pessimist ever discovered the secrets of the stars, or sailed to an uncharted land, or opened a new heaven to the human spirit.

HELEN KELLER

Peter Principle

In a hierarchy every employee tends to rise to his level of incompetence.

LAURENCE J. PETER

Philanthropy

Where there is the most love to God, there will be there the truest and most enlarged philanthropy.

ROBERT SOUTHEY

Philosophers

There is no record in human history of a happy philosopher.

H.L. MENCKEN

All are lunatics, but he who can analyze his delusion is called a philosopher.

AMBROSE BIERCE

Philosophy

I've developed a new philosophy. I only dread life one day at a time.
CHARLIE BROWN

It is easier to write ten volumes of philosophy than to put one principle into practice.
LEO TOLSTOY

Pictures

A picture is a poem without words.
HORACE

A room hung with pictures, is a room hung with thoughts.
SIR JOSHUA REYNOLDS

Pioneers

The pioneers in any movement are not generally the best people to carry that movement to a successful issue. They often have to meet such hard opposition, and get so battered and bespattered, that afterward, when people find they have to accept reform, they will accept it more easily from others.
ABRAHAM LINCOLN

Pity

Better to be envied than pitied.
HERODOTUS

Pity and forbearance should characterize all acts of justice.
BENJAMIN FRANKLIN

Planning

Before you start looking for a peg, decide what hole you want to fill.

Nothing is particularly hard if you divide it into small jobs.
HENRY FORD

The first and most important step in improving the utilization of your time is planning.

Losers always concentrate on activities, but high achievers concentrate on planning and making every moment count in their efforts to reach progressively higher intermediate goals.

JOHN R. NOE

Plans

A life that hasn't a definite plan is likely to become driftwood.

DAVID SARNOFF

In the space of two days I had evolved two plans, wholly distinct, both of which were equally feasible. The point I am trying to bring out is that one does not plan and then try to make circumstances fit those plans. One tries to make plans fit the circumstances.

GEORGE S. PATTON

Make no little plans; they have no magic to stir men's blood and probably themselves will not be realized. Make big plans; aim high in hope and work, remembering that a noble, logical diagram once recorded will never die, but long after we are gone will be a living thing, asserting itself with ever-growing insistency. Remember that your sons and grandsons are going to do things that would stagger us. Let your watchword be order and your beacon beauty.

DANIEL H. BURNHAM

Play

It is paradoxical that many educators and parents still differentiate between a time for learning and a time for play without seeing the vital connection between them.

LEO BUSCAGLIA

Plays

...the sort of play that gives failures a bad name.

WALTER KERR

Pleasantness

One of the most difficult things to do is to be as pleasant in your own home as you are in the homes of others.

Pleasing

You can please some of the people some of the time; you can please all of the people some of the time; but you can never please all the people all the time. ABRAHAM LINCOLN

If you want to please everybody, you'll die before your time.

Pleasure

The great source of pleasure is variety. SAMUEL JOHNSON

One of the simple but genuine pleasures in life is getting up in the morning and hurrying to a mousetrap you set the night before.

KIN HUBBARD

The greatest pleasure I know is to do a good action by stealth and to have it found out by accident. CHARLES LAMB

Tranquil pleasures last the longest; we are not fitted to bear the burden of great joy. CHRISTIAN NESTELL BOVEE

On an occasion of this kind, it becomes more than a moral duty to speak one's mind. It becomes a pleasure.

OSCAR WILDE

The great pleasure in life is doing what people say you cannot do.

WALTER BAGEHOT

Follow pleasure, and then will pleasure flee. Flee pleasure, and pleasure will follow thee.

JOHN HEYWOOD

That man is the richest whose pleasures are the cheapest.

HENRY DAVID THOREAU

Pledges

Do not be a man who strikes hands in pledge or puts up security for debts; if you lack the means to pay, your very bed will be snatched from under you.

THE BIBLE: PROVERBS 22:26,27

He who puts up security for another will surely suffer, but whoever refuses to strike hands in pledge is safe.

THE BIBLE: PROVERBS 11:15

Poetry

You will not find poetry anywhere unless you bring some of it with you.

JOSEPH JOUBERT

[These] poems have two main characteristics: (1) They are short; (2) they are not short enough.

JOHN SIMON

Then he asked the question that you are all itching to ask me: "How can you tell good poetry from bad?" I answered, "How does one tell good fish from bad? Surely by the smell? Use your nose."

ROBERT GRAVES

Poets

A poet who reads his verse in public may have other nasty habits.

ROBERT HEINLEIN

The man is either crazy or he is a poet.

HORACE

Policy

There is no such thing as a fixed policy because policy, like all organic entities, is always in the making.

LORD SALISBURY

Politeness

Politeness is the art of choosing among one's real thoughts.

ABEL STEVENS

Politeness is an inexpensive way of making friends.

WILLIAM FEATHER

Politeness is not always the sign of wisdom, but the want of it always leaves room for the suspicion of folly.

WALTER SAVAGE LANDOR

Political Parties

Political parties serve to keep each other in check, one keenly watching the other.

HENRY CLAY

The political parties that I would call great, are those which cling more to principles than to consequences; to general, and not to special cases; to ideas, and not to men. Such parties are usually distinguished by a nobler character, more generous passions, more genuine convictions, and a more bold and open conduct than others.

ALEXIS DE TOCQUEVILLE

Political Success

Political success is the ability, when the inevitable occurs, to get credit for it.

LAURENCE J. PETER

Politicians

Bad officials are the ones elected by good citizens who do not vote.

GEORGE JEAN NATHAN

Since a politician never believes what he says, he is surprised when others believe him.

CHARLES DE GAULLE

Ninety percent of the politicians give the other ten percent a bad reputation.

HENRY KISSINGER

Politicians and roosters crow about what they intend to do. The roosters deliver what is promised.

If a political candidate can't get up and make a speech of his own, if he has to hire a press agent to write it for him, then why not let the press agent be the candidate?

RAYMOND CLAPPER

A politician is a man who shakes your hand before election and your confidence afterwards.

If experience teaches us anything at all, it teaches us this: that a good politician, under democracy, is quite as unthinkable as an honest burglar.

H.L. MENCKEN

The politician is an acrobat; he keeps his balance by saying the opposite of what he does.

MAURICE BARRES

He has been called a mediocre man, but this is unwarranted flattery. He was a politician of monumental littleness.

THEODORE ROOSEVELT

Ninety-eight percent of the adults in this country are decent, hard-working, honest Americans. It's the other lousy two percent that get all the publicity. But then—we elected them.

LILY TOMLIN

I don't think it does any harm just once in a while to acknowledge that the whole country isn't in flames, that there are people in the country besides politicians, entertainers, and criminals.

CHARLES KURALT

[Politicians] are the same all over. They promise to build a bridge even where there is no river.

NIKITA KHRUSHCHEV

One thing our founding fathers could not foresee—they were farmers, professional men, businessmen giving of their time and effort to an idea that became a country—was a nation governed by professional politicians who had a vested interest in getting reelected. They probably envisioned a fellow serving a couple of hitches and then looking forward to getting back to the farm.

RONALD REAGAN

We do not elect our wisest and best men to represent us. In general, we elect men of the type that subscribes to only one principle—to get reelected.

TERRY M. TOWNSEND

Politics

Politics are almost as exciting as war, and quite dangerous. In war, you can only be killed once, but in politics many times.

SIR WINSTON CHURCHILL

The penalty good men pay for indifference to public affairs is to be ruled by evil men.

PLATO

The fellow who stays home on election day because he doesn't want to have anything to do with crooked politics has a lot more to do with crooked politics than he thinks.

I believe that biennial elections and quadrennial governorships are inventions which deprive the people of power, and at the same time offer prizes to be captured by the corruption of political life.

THOMAS BRACKETT REED

I looked up the word "politics" in the dictionary and it's actually a combination of two words; "poli," which means many, and "tics," which means bloodsuckers.

JAY LENO

Politics is perhaps the only profession for which no preparation is thought necessary.

ROBERT LOUIS STEVENSON

Man is by nature a political animal.

ARISTOTLE

Politics ought to be the part-time profession of every citizen who would protect the rights and privileges of free people and who would preserve what is good and fruitful in our national heritage.

DWIGHT D. EISENHOWER

The great orators who rule the assemblies by the brilliancy of their eloquence are in general men of the most mediocre political talents; they should not be opposed in their own way, for they have always more noisy words at command than you. Their eloquence should be opposed by a serious and logical argument; their strength lies in vagueness; they should be brought back to the reality of facts; practical arguments destroy them. In the council, there were men possessed of much more eloquence than I was; I always defeated them by this simple argument—two and two make four.

NAPOLEON BONAPARTE

Practical politics consists in ignoring facts.

HENRY ADAMS

Politics is such a torment that I would advise every one I love not to mix with it.

THOMAS JEFFERSON

Poor

There are two things needed in these days; first, for rich men to find out how poor men live; and second, for poor men to know how rich men work.

EDWARD ATKINSON

The best way to help the poor is not to become one of them.

LAING HANCOCK

Pornography

Pornography tells lies about women. But pornography tells the truth about men.

JOHN STOLTENBERG

Possibilities

Our nation was founded as an experiment in human liberty. Its institutions reflect the belief of our founders that men had their origin and destiny in God; that they were endowed by Him with inalienable rights and had duties prescribed by moral law, and that human institutions ought primarily to help men develop their God-given possibilities.

JOHN FOSTER DULLES

Poverty

Neither great poverty, nor great riches will hear reason.

HENRY FIELDING

We are not going to perpetuate poverty by substituting a permanent dole for a paycheck. There is no humanity or charity in destroying self-reliance, dignity and self respect...the very substance of moral fiber. We seek reforms that will, wherever possible, change relief check to paycheck.

RONALD REAGAN

I used to think I was poor. Then they told me I wasn't poor, I was needy. Then they told me it was self-defeating to think of myself as needy, that I was culturally deprived. Then they told me deprived was a bad image, that I was underprivileged. Then they told me underprivileged was overused, that I was disadvantaged. I still don't have a dime, but I do have a great vocabulary.

JULES FEIFFER

Power

Nearly all men can stand adversity, but if you want to test a man's character, give him power.
ABRAHAM LINCOLN

Power for good flows through you from God. It does not originate with you.
W.F. SMITH

I am more and more convinced that man is a dangerous creature and that power, whether vested in many or a few, is ever grasping and like the grave, cries, "Give, give."
ABIGAIL ADAMS

Power may justly be compared to a great river; while kept within its bounds it is both beautiful and useful, but when it overflows its banks, it brings destruction and desolation to ail in its way.
ANDREW HAMILTON

Being powerful is like being a lady. If you have to tell people you are, you aren't.
MARGARET THATCHER

Practicalness

You cannot sell the cow and sup the milk.

Practice

If I miss practicing on the piano one day, I can tell the difference in my playing. If I miss practicing on the piano for two days, my friends can tell the difference. But if I miss the practice for three days, my audience can tell the difference.
JAN PADEREWSKI

Cab drivers are living proof that practice does not make perfect.
HOWARD OGDEN

Praise

Make a joyful noise unto the LORD.

THE BIBLE: PSALM 100:1 KJV

Praise teachers while they are present, subordinates when their work is done, and friends when absent.

Finally, brethren, whatever is true, whatever is honorable, whatever is just, whatever is pure, whatever is lovely, whatever is gracious, if there is any excellence, if there is anything worthy of praise, think about these things.

THE BIBLE: PHILIPPIANS 4:8 RSV

The crucible for silver and the furnace for gold, but man is tested by the praise he receives.

THE BIBLE: PROVERBS 27:21

Let another praise you, and not your own mouth; someone else, and not your own lips.

THE BIBLE: PROVERBS 27:2

I know of no manner of speaking so offensive as that of giving praise, and closing it with an exception.

SIR RICHARD STEELE

If somebody throws a brick at me, I can catch it and throw it back. But when somebody awards a decoration to me, I am out of words.

HARRY S. TRUMAN

We run ourselves down so as to be praised by others.

FRANÇOIS DE LA ROCHEFOUCAULD

Every man needs a blind eye and a deaf ear, so when people applaud, you'll only hear half of it, and when people salute, you'll only see part of it. Believe only half the praise and half the criticism.

CHARLES H. SPURGEON

Prayer

Prayer at its best is the expression of the total life, for all things else being equal, our prayers are only as powerful as our lives.

A.W. TOZER

There are four ways God answers prayer: No, not yet; No, I love you too much; Yes, I thought you'd never ask; Yes, and here's more.

ANNE LEWIS

The potency of prayer hath subdued the strength of fire; it hath bridled the rage of lions, hushed anarchy to rest, extinguished wars, appeased the elements, expelled demons, burst the chains of death, expanded the gates of heaven, assuaged diseases, repelled frauds, rescued cities from destruction, stayed the sun in its course, and arrested the progress of the thunderbolt.

SAINT JOHN CHRYSOSTOM

Confess your trespasses to one another, and pray for one another, that you may be healed. The effective, fervent prayer of a righteous man avails much.

THE BIBLE: JAMES 5:16 NKJV

Dealing in generalities is the death of prayer.

J.H. EVANS

In seasons of distress and grief,
My soul has often found relief,
And oft escaped the tempter's snare,
By thy return, sweet hour of prayer.

W.W. WALFORD

All who call on God in true faith, earnestly from the heart, will certainly be heard, and will receive what they have asked and desired.

MARTIN LUTHER

By prayer we couple the powers of heaven to our helplessness, the powers which can capture strongholds and make the impossible possible.
OLE HALLESBY

Faith, and hope, and patience, and all the strong, beautiful, vital forces of piety are withered and dead in a prayerless life. The life of the individual believer, his personal salvation, and personal Christian graces have their being, bloom, and fruitage in prayer.
E.M. BOUNDS

Seven days without prayer makes one weak.
ALLEN E. BARTLETT

Trouble and perplexity drive me to prayer and prayer drives away perplexity and trouble.
PHILIPP MELANCHTHON

There come times when I have nothing more to tell God. If I were to continue to pray in words, I would have to repeat what I have already said. At such times it is wonderful to say to God, "May I be in Thy presence, Lord? I have nothing more to say to Thee, but I do love to be in Thy presence."
OLE HALLESBY

See to it, night and day, that you pray for your children. Then you will leave them a great legacy of answers to prayer, which will follow them all the days of their life. Then you may calmly and with a good conscience depart from them, even though you may not leave them a great deal of material wealth.
OLE HALLESBY

We can do nothing without prayer. All things can be done by importunate prayer. It surmounts or removes all obstacles, overcomes every resisting force and gains its ends in the face of invincible hindrances.
E.M. BOUNDS

Prayer does not change God, but it changes him who prays.

SØREN KIERKEGAARD

Restraining prayer, we cease to fight;
Prayer keeps the Christian's armor bright;
And Satan trembles when he sees
The weakest saint upon his knees.   WILLIAM COWPER

Prayer is the great engine to overthrow and rout my spiritual
enemies, the great means to procure the graces of which I stand
in hourly need.   JOHN NEWTON

Unless I had the spirit of prayer, I could do nothing.

CHARLES G. FINNEY

We look upon prayer as a means of getting things for ourselves;
The Bible's idea of prayer is that we may get to know God Himself.   OSWALD CHAMBERS

The value of consistent prayer is not that He will hear us, but
that we will hear Him.   WILLIAM McGILL

The purpose of prayer is to reveal the presence of God equally
present, all the time, in every condition.

OSWALD CHAMBERS

No one is a firmer believer in the power of prayer than the
devil; not that he practices it, but he suffers from it.

GUY H. KING

God shapes the world by prayer. Prayers are deathless. They
outlive the lives of those who uttered them.

E.M. BOUNDS

I have been driven many times to my knees by the over-whelming conviction that I had nowhere else to go. My own wisdom and that of all about me seemed insufficient for the day.

ABRAHAM LINCOLN

Though we cannot by our prayers give God any information, yet we must by our prayers give him honor.

MATTHEW HENRY

Some people will say anything except their prayers.

HORACE WYNDHAM

Praying

Praying which does not result in pure conduct is a delusion. We have missed the whole office and virtue of praying if it does not rectify conduct. It is in the very nature of things that we must quit praying, or quit bad conduct.

E.M. BOUNDS

If you can't pray as you want to, pray as you can. God knows what you mean.

VANCE HAVNER

Every time we pray our horizon is altered, our attitude to things is altered, not sometimes but every time, and the amazing thing is that we don't pray more.

OSWALD CHAMBERS

When you pray for anyone you tend to modify your personal attitude toward him.

NORMAN VINCENT PEALE

When you pray, go into your room, and when you have shut your door, pray to your Father who is in the secret place; and your Father who sees in secret will reward you openly.

THE BIBLE: MATTHEW 6:6 NKJV

Do not pray for easy lives, pray to be stronger men. Do not pray for tasks equal to your powers, pray for powers equal to your tasks.

PHILLIPS BROOKS

The less I pray, the harder it gets; the more I pray, the better it goes.

MARTIN LUTHER

Teach us to pray that we may cause
The enemy to flee,
That we his evil power may bind,
His prisoners to free.

WATCHMAN NEE

Don't force your child to pray. Instead, every night set aside fifteen minutes before his bedtime for reading and conversation. Show him pictures of Jesus, and tell him stories of the Savior. Talk to him of the Heavenly Father. Explain to him that God sends the sun and rain. Tell him it is God who makes the flowers grow, and gives us food to eat. Then lead him in prayers of thanksgiving and prayers asking the Heavenly Father for guidance and protection.

BILLY GRAHAM

Preaching

When I hear a man preach, I like to see him act as if he were fighting bees.

ABRAHAM LINCOLN

I preached as never sure to preach again,
And as a dying man to dying men.

RICHARD BAXTER

Prejudice

Prejudice is never easy unless it can pass itself off for reason.

WILLIAM HAZLITT

Racial prejudice is a pigment of the imagination.

GRAFFITO

A prejudiced person is one who doesn't believe in the same things we do.

ART LINKLETTER

One may no more live in the world without picking up the moral prejudices of the world than one will be able to go to hell without perspiring.

H.L. MENCKEN

Everyone is a prisoner of his own experiences. No one can eliminate prejudices—just recognize them.

EDWARD R. MURROW

Presence of Mind

It is by presence of mind in untried emergencies that the native mettle of a man is tested.

JAMES RUSSELL LOWELL

Present

If there is hope in the future, there is power in the present.

JOHN MAXWELL

I don't think we understand the importance of the present; there's nothing more important than what you are doing now.

HAROLD CLURMAN

It is difficult to live in the present, ridiculous to live in the future and impossible to live in the past.

JIM BISHOP

Presentations

A person will accept or reject your proposal in the first nine minutes of your presentation.

President

I know that when things don't go well, they like to blame the president, and that is one of the things presidents are paid for.
JOHN F. KENNEDY

If you are as happy, my dear sir, on entering this house as I am in leaving it and returning home, you are the happiest man in this country.
JAMES BUCHANAN
[TO ABRAHAM LINCOLN UPON LINCOLN'S
ARRIVAL AT THE WHITE HOUSE]

I would take not one step to advance or promote pretensions to the presidency. If that office was to be the prize of cabal and intrigue, of purchasing newspapers, bribing by appointments, or bargaining for foreign missions, I had no ticket in that lottery. Whether I had the qualifications necessary for a President of the United States, was, to say the least, very doubtful to myself. But that I had no talents for obtaining the office by such means was perfectly clear.
JOHN QUINCY ADAMS

If forced to choose between the penitentiary and the White House for four years...I would say the penitentiary, thank you.
WILLIAM T. SHERMAN

I have no ambition to govern men. It is a painful and thankless office.
THOMAS JEFFERSON

I have the consolation...of having added nothing to my private fortune during my public service, and of retiring with hands as clean as they are empty.
THOMAS JEFFERSON

With experience enough in subordinate offices to have seen the difficulties of this the greatest of all, I have learned to expect that it will rarely fall to the lot of imperfect man to retire from this station with the reputation and the favor which bring him into it.

THOMAS JEFFERSON

The president is merely the most important among a large number of public servants. He should be supported or opposed exactly to the degree which is warranted by his good conduct or bad conduct, his efficiency or inefficiency in rendering loyal, able, and disinterested service to the nation as a whole. Therefore it is absolutely necessary that there should be full liberty to tell the truth about his acts, and this means that it is exactly as necessary to blame him when he does wrong as to praise him when he does right. Any other attitude in an American citizen is both base and servile. To announce that there is no criticism of the president, or that we are to stand by the president, right or wrong, is not only unpatriotic and servile, but is morally treasonable to the American public. Nothing but the truth should be spoken about him or anyone else. But it is even more important to tell the truth, pleasant or unpleasant, about him than about anyone else.

THEODORE ROOSEVELT

There has been a lot of talk lately about the burdens of the presidency. Decisions that the president has to make often affect the lives of tens of millions of people around the world, but that does not mean that they should take longer to make. Some men can make decisions and some cannot. Some men fret and delay under criticism. I used to have a saying that applies here, and I note that some people have picked it up: "If you can't stand the heat, get out of the kitchen."

HARRY S. TRUMAN

I am tired of an office where I can do no more good than many others who would be glad to be employed in it. To myself, personally, it brings nothing but unceasing drudgery and daily loss of friends.

THOMAS JEFFERSON

I know well that no man will ever bring out of that office the reputation which carries him into it. The honeymoon would be as short in that case as in any other, and its moments of ecstasy would be ransomed by years of torment and hatred.

THOMAS JEFFERSON

No president who performs his duties faithfully and conscientiously can have any leisure.

JAMES K. POLK

Presumption

Don't sell the skin till you have caught the bear.

Pretense

The best way in which to silence any friend of yours whom you know to be a fool is to induce him to hire a hall. Nothing chills pretense like exposure.

WOODROW WILSON

Price

The highest price we can pay for anything, is to ask it.

WALTER SAVAGE LANDOR

Pride

As Plato entertained some friends in a room where there was a couch richly ornamented, Diogenes came in very dirty, as usual, and getting upon the couch, and trampling on it, said, "I trample upon the pride of Plato." Plato mildly answered, "But with greater pride, Diogenes!"

ERASMUS

It was pride that changed angels into devils; it is humility that makes men as angels.

AUGUSTINE

God resisteth the proud, and giveth grace to the humble.
THE BIBLE: 1 PETER 5:5 KJV

Most of us retain enough of the theological attitude to think that we are little gods.
OLIVER WENDELL HOLMES JR.

Pride is at the bottom of all great mistakes.
JOHN RUSKIN

When a proud man hears another praised, he feels himself injured.

None are more taken in by flattery than the proud, who wish to be the first and are not.
BARUCH SPINOZA

Wounded vanity knows when it is mortally hurt and limps off the field, piteous, all disguises thrown away. But pride carries its banner to the last, and, fast as it is driven from one field, unfurls it in another.
HELEN HUNT JACKSON

There is but a step between a proud man's glory and his disgrace.
PUBLILIUS SYRUS

The prouder a man is, the more he thinks he deserves; and the more he thinks he deserves, the less he really does deserve.
HENRY WARD BEECHER

Principles

The value of a principle is the number of things it will explain.
RALPH WALDO EMERSON

It doesn't pay well to fight for what we believe in.
LILLIAN HELLMAN

We must be willing, individually and as a nation, to accept whatever sacrifices may be required of us. A people that values its privileges above its principles soon loses both.

DWIGHT D. EISENHOWER

It is easier to fight for one's principles than to live up to them.

ALFRED ADLER

I love the man that can smile in trouble, that can gather strength from distress, and grow brave by reflection. 'Tis the business of little minds to shrink; but he whose heart is firm, and whose conscience approves his conduct, will pursue his principles unto death.

THOMAS PAINE

Prison

Prison is a socialist's paradise, where equality prevails, everything is supplied, and competition is eliminated.

ELBERT HUBBARD

Prisoners of War

A prisoner of war is a man who tries to kill you and fails, and then asks you not to kill him.

SIR WINSTON CHURCHILL

Private Enterprise

I believe, I have always believed, and I will always believe in private enterprise as the backbone of economic well-being in America.

FRANKLIN D. ROOSEVELT

The merchants will manage the better, the more they are left free to manage for themselves.

Private Property

What is necessary for the use of land, is not its private ownership, but the security of improvements. It is not necessary to say to a man, "this land is yours," in order to induce him to cultivate or improve it. It is only necessary to say to him, "Whatever your labor or capital produces on this land shall be yours."

HENRY GEORGE

Privileges

What men value in this world is not rights but privileges.

H.L. MENCKEN

Problems

Everybody has a problem, is a problem, or has to live with a problem.

SAM SHOEMAKER

A man with fifty problems is twice as alive as a man with twenty-five. If you haven't got problems, you should get down on your knees and ask, "Lord, don't you trust me anymore?"

JOHN BAINBRIDGE

Every problem contains the seeds of its own solution.

STANLEY ARNOLD

Beware of the danger signals that flag problems: silence, secretiveness, or sudden outburst.

SYLVIA PORTER

If you can talk brilliantly about a problem, it can create the consoling illusion that it has been mastered.

STANLEY KUBRICK

The greatest and most important problems in life are all in a certain sense insoluble. They can never be solved, but only outgrown.

CARL JUNG

The significant problems we face cannot be solved at the same level of thinking we were at when we created them.

ALBERT EINSTEIN

Procrastination

It is an undoubted truth that the less one has to do the less time one finds to do it in. One yawns, one procrastinates, one can do it when one will, and therefore, one seldom does it at all; whereas, those who have a great deal of business must buckle to it; and then they always find time enough to do it.

PHILIP DORMER STANHOPE

Putting off an easy thing makes it hard, and putting off a hard one makes it impossible.

GEORGE HORACE LORIMER

Professionals

A professional is a man who can do his job when he doesn't feel like it. An amateur is a man who can't do his job when he does feel like it.

JAMES AGATE

Professors

There was an old cannibal whose stomach suffered from so many disorders that he could only digest animals that had no spines. Thus, for years, he subsisted only upon university professors.

LOUIS PHILLIPS

Progress

The art of progress is to preserve order amid change, and to preserve change amid order. Life refuses to be embalmed alive.

ALFRED NORTH WHITEHEAD

Progress is the real cure for an over-estimate of ourselves.

GEORGE MACDONALD

He who rejects change is the architect of decay. The only human institution which rejects progress is the cemetery.

HAROLD WILSON

Is it progress if a cannibal uses knife and fork?

STANISLAW J. LEC

Promises

A man apt to promise is apt to forget.   THOMAS FULLER

Magnificent promises are always to be suspected.

THEODORE PARKER

Property

No man acquires property without acquiring with it a little arithmetic also.   RALPH WALDO EMERSON

Prosperity

For every one hundred men who can withstand adversity, there is only one who can withstand prosperity.

THOMAS CARLYLE

The reason American cities are prosperous is that there is no place to sit down.   ALFRED JOSEPH TALLEY

Protestantism

The true force of Protestantism was its signal return to the individual conscience—to the method of Jesus.

MATTHEW ARNOLD

Prudence

[George Washington] was incapable of fear, meeting personal dangers with the calmest unconcern. Perhaps the strongest feature in his character was prudence, never acting until every circumstance, every consideration, was maturely weighed. His integrity was most pure, his justice the most inflexible I have ever known, no motives of interest or consanguinity, of friendship, or hatred, being able to bias his decision. He was, indeed, in every sense of the words, a wise, a good, and a great man.

THOMAS JEFFERSON

Psychobabble

To err is dysfunctional, to forgive co-dependent.

BERTON AVERRE

Psychology

One of the greatest pieces of charlatanic, and satanic, nonsense imposed on a gullible public is the Freudian interpretation of dreams.

VLADIMIR NABOKOV

Psychosis

Neurotic means he is not as sensible as I am, and psychotic means he's even worse than my brother-in-law.

KARL MENNINGER

Public Office

He that puts on a public gown, must put off a private person.

The ordinary affairs of a nation offer little difficulty to a person of any experience; but the gift of office is the dreadful burden which oppresses him.

THOMAS JEFFERSON

When a man assumes a public trust, he should consider himself as public property.

THOMAS JEFFERSON

The duties of all public affairs are, or at least admit of being made, so plain and simple that men of intelligence may readily qualify themselves for their performance; and I cannot but believe that more is lost by the long continuance of men in office than is generally to be gained by their experience.

ANDREW JACKSON

Public officers are the servants and agents of the people, to execute laws which the people have made and within the limits of a Constitution which they have established.

GROVER CLEVELAND

Let no guilty man escape if it can be avoided. Be specially vigilant—or instruct those engaged in the prosecution of fraud to be against all who insinuate that they have high influence to protect them. No personal consideration should stand in the way of performing a public duty.

ULYSSES S. GRANT

My rule, in which I have always found satisfaction, is, never turn aside in public affairs through views of private interest; but to go straight forward in doing what appears to me right at the time, leaving the consequences with Providence.

BENJAMIN FRANKLIN

Public Opinion

When public opinion changes, it is with the rapidity of thought.

THOMAS JEFFERSON

Public Sector

This absorption of revenue by all levels of government, the alarming rate of inflation, and the rising toll of unemployment all stem from a single source: The belief that government, particularly the federal government, has the answer to our ills, and that the proper method of dealing with social problems is to transfer power from the private to the public sector, and within the public sector from state and local governments to the ultimate power center in Washington. This collectivist, centralizing approach, whatever name or party label it wears, has created our economic problems.

         Ronald Reagan

Publicity

What kills a skunk is the publicity it gives itself.

         Abraham Lincoln

Punishment

Distrust all in whom the impulse to punish is powerful.

         Friedrich Nietzsche

Purpose

My research offers impressive evidence that we feel better when we attempt to make our world better...to have a purpose beyond one's self lends to existence a meaning and direction—the most important characteristic of high well-being.

         Gail Sheehy

True happiness...is not attained through self-gratification, but through fidelity to a worthy purpose.   Helen Keller

If a man hasn't discovered something that he will die for, he isn't fit to live.   Martin Luther King Jr.

Great minds have purposes, others have wishes. Little minds are tamed and subdued by misfortune, but great minds rise above them.

         Washington Irving

I cannot believe that the purpose of life is to be "happy." I think the purpose of life is to be useful, to be responsible, to be honorable, to be compassionate. It is, after all, to matter: to count, to stand for something, to have made some difference that you lived at all.

LEO C. ROSTEN

Qualities

Cultivate in yourself the qualities you admire most in others.

ARNOLD GLASON

Quarrels

The quarrel that doesn't concern you is pleasant to hear about.

Quarrelsomeness

As charcoal to embers and as wood to fire, so is a quarrelsome man for kindling strife.

THE BIBLE: PROVERBS 26:21

Better to live on a corner of the roof than share a house with a quarrelsome wife.

THE BIBLE: PROVERBS 25:24

Questioners

He's been that way for years—a born questioner, but he hates answers.

RING LARDNER

Avoid a questioner, for such a man is also a tattler.

HORACE

Questions

No question is so difficult to answer as that which the answer is obvious.

GEORGE BERNARD SHAW

Quitting

Quit now, you'll never make it. If you disregard this advice, you'll be halfway there.

DAVID ZUCKER

Most people give up just when they're about to achieve success. They quit on the one-yard line. They give up at the last minute of the game one foot from a winning touchdown.

ROSS PEROT

Quotations

He wrapped himself in quotations—as a beggar would enfold himself in the purple of emperors.

RUDYARD KIPLING

Next to the originator of a good sentence is the first quoter of it.

RALPH WALDO EMERSON

The wisdom of the wise and the experience of the ages are perpetuated by quotations.

BENJAMIN DISRAELI

I quote others only in order the better to express myself.

MICHEL DE MONTAIGNE

Rabbit's Foot

Depend on the rabbit's foot if you will, but it didn't work for the rabbit!

Radicals

A radical is a man with both feet firmly planted in the air.

FRANKLIN D. ROOSEVELT

Rank

It is an interesting question how far men would retain their relative rank if they were divested of their clothes.

HENRY DAVID THOREAU

Rats

He bears an unmistakable resemblance to a cornered rat.

NORMAN MAILER

Readiness

One sword keeps another in the sheath.

GEORGE HERBERT

Reading

When we read too fast or too slowly, we understand nothing.

BLAISE PASCAL

Reading Christians are growing Christians. When Christians cease to read, they cease to grow.

JOHN WESLEY

To know how to read is to light a lamp in the wind, to release
the soul from prison, to open a gate to the universe.

PEARL S. BUCK

There is a great deal of difference between the eager man who
wants to read a book and the tired man who wants a book to
read.

G.K. CHESTERTON

Realistic Decisions

If someone tells you he is going to make a "realistic decision,"
you immediately understand that he has resolved to do something bad.

MARY MCCARTHY

Realists

You may be sure that when a man begins to call himself a
realist he is preparing to do something that he is secretly
ashamed of doing.

SYDNEY J. HARRIS

Reasons

A man's acts are usually right, but his reasons seldom are.

ELBERT HUBBARD

Rebellion

The spirit of resistance to government is so valuable on certain occasions that I wish it to be always kept alive. It will often
be exercised when wrong, but better so than not to be exercised at all. I like a little rebellion now and then.

THOMAS JEFFERSON

Rebukes

Like an earring of gold or an ornament of fine gold is a wise man's rebuke to a listening ear.

THE BIBLE: PROVERBS 25:12

Reform

Reform must come from within, not from without. You cannot legislate for virtue.

JAMES GIBBONS

The best reformers the world has ever seen are those who commence on themselves.

GEORGE BERNARD SHAW

Regrets

We should have no regrets. The past is finished. There is nothing to be gained by going over it. Whatever it gave us in the experiences it brought us was something we had to know.

REBECCA BEARD

For of all sad words of tongue or pen, the saddest are these: "It might have been."

JOHN GREENLEAF WHITTIER

Relationships

A relationship is a living thing. It needs and benefits from the same attention to detail that an artist lavishes on his art.

DAVID VISCOTT

Relativity

When a man sits with a pretty girl for an hour, it seems like a minute. But let him sit on a hot stove for a minute, and it's longer than any hour. That's relativity.

ALBERT EINSTEIN

Relief

For fast-acting relief try slowing down.   LILY TOMLIN

Religion

I have ever judged of the religion of others by their lives. It is in our lives, and not from our words, that our religion must be read. By the same test the world must judge me. But this does not satisfy the priesthood. They must have a positive, a declared assent to all their interested absurdities. My opinion is that there would never have been an infidel if there had never been a priest. The artificial structures they have built on the purest of all moral systems, for the purpose of deriving from it pence and power, revolt those who think for themselves, and who read in that system only what is really there.

THOMAS JEFFERSON

Most people have some sort of religion. At least they know which church they're staying away from.   JOHN ERSKINE

While just government protects all in their religious rites, true religion affords government its surest support.

GEORGE WASHINGTON

Nothing is so fatal to religion as indifference, which is, at least, half infidelity.   EDMUND BURKE

It is always safe to follow the religious belief that our mother taught us; there never was a mother yet who taught her child to be an infidel.   JOSH BILLINGS

Some would divorce morality from religion; but religion is the root without which morality would die.

CYRUS AUGUSTUS BARTOL

Men will wrangle for religion, write for it, fight for it, die for it, anything but—live for it.   CHARLES CALEB COLTON

Religious Liberty

The love of religious liberty is a stronger sentiment, when fully excited, than an attachment to civil freedom. Conscience, in the cause of religion, prepares the mind to act and to suffer, beyond almost all other causes. It sometimes gives an impulse so irresistible, that no fetters of power or of opinion can withstand it. History instructs us, that this love of religious liberty, made up of the clearest sense of right and the highest conviction of duty, is able to look the sternest despotism in the face, and, with means apparently inadequate, to shake principalities and powers.   DANIEL WEBSTER

Remedies

He that will not apply new remedies must expect new evils.   FRANCIS BACON

Our remedies oft in ourselves do lie.   WILLIAM SHAKESPEARE

Remorse

Remorse begets reform.   WILLIAM COWPER

Renewal

Inside myself is a place where I live all alone, and that's where you renew your springs that never dry up.   PEARL S. BUCK

Repartee

Repartee is a duel fought with the points of jokes.
MAX FORRESTER EASTMAN

Repentance

True repentance is to cease from sinning.
AMBROSE OF MILAN

Repentance is a hearty sorrow for our past misdeeds, and is a sincere resolution and endeavor, to the utmost of our power, to conform all our actions to the law of God. It does not consist in one single act of sorrow, but in doing works meet for repentance; in a sincere obedience to the law of Christ for the remainder of our lives.
JOHN LOCKE

True repentance always involves reform.
HOSEA BALLOU

It is the duty of nations as well as of men to own their dependence upon the overruling power of God, to confess their sins and transgressions in humble sorrow, yet with assured hope that genuine repentance will lead to mercy and pardon.
ABRAHAM LINCOLN

Too late repents the rat when caught by the cat.
JOHN FLORIO

Repose

All mankind's unhappiness derives from one thing: his inability to know how to remain in repose in one room.
BLAISE PASCAL

Repression

Repression is the seed of revolution.
DANIEL WEBSTER

Reproaches

The sting of a reproach is the truth of it.

BENJAMIN FRANKLIN

Reputation

Those who are once found to be bad are presumed so forever.

A reputation once broken may possibly be repaired, but the world will always keep their eyes on the spot where the crack was.

JOSEPH HALL

Much of reputation depends on the period in which it rises. In dark periods, when talents appear, they shine like the sun through a small hole in the window-shutter, and the strong beam dazzles amid the surrounding gloom. Open the shutter, and the general diffusion of light attracts no notice.

SIR ROBERT WALPOLE

A good name is more desirable than great riches; to be esteemed is better than silver or gold.

THE BIBLE: PROVERBS 22:1

Associate with men of good quality, if you esteem your own reputation, for it is better to be alone than in bad company.

GEORGE WASHINGTON

Glass, china, and reputation are easily crack'd and never well mended.

BENJAMIN FRANKLIN

An ill wound, but not an ill name, may be healed.

BENJAMIN FRANKLIN

He who has the reputation of rising early may sleep till noon.

FRENCH PROVERB

I had laid it down as a law to myself, to take no notice of the thousand calumnies issued against me, but to trust my character to my own conduct, and the good sense and candor of my fellow citizens.

THOMAS JEFFERSON

Research

Enough research will tend to support your theory.

A. BLOCK

Resourcefulness

Men are made stronger on realization that the helping hand they need is at the end of their own right arm.

SIDNEY PHILLIPS

Respect

All objects lose by too familiar a view.

JOHN DRYDEN

Any man will command respect if he takes a stand and backs it up with his life.

BOBBY RICHARDSON

Where we do not respect, we cease to love.

BENJAMIN DISRAELI

Responsibility

Responsibility is the thing people dread most of all. Yet it is the one thing in the world that develops us, gives our manhood or womanhood fibre.

FRANK CRANE

Action springs not from thought, but from a readiness for responsibility.

DIETRICH BONHOEFFER

Unto whomsoever much is given, of him shall be much required.
THE BIBLE: LUKE 12:48 KJV

A new position of responsibility will usually show a man to be a far stronger creature than was supposed.
WILLIAM JAMES

In forty hours I shall be in battle, with little information, and on the spur of the moment will have to make the most momentous decisions, but I believe that one's spirit enlarges with responsibility and that, with God's help, I shall make them and make them right.
GEORGE S. PATTON

I believe that every right implies a responsibility; every opportunity, an obligation; every possession, a duty.
JOHN D. ROCKEFELLER JR.

One of the great sources of moral and political breakdown in our day is the reluctance of ordinary people to accept responsibility.
W.T. PURKISER

You must take responsibility for your own development.

Hold yourself responsible for a higher standard than anybody else expects of you.
HENRY WARD BEECHER

Rest

Unless we come apart and rest a while, we may just plain come apart.
VANCE HAVNER

Everywhere I have sought rest and found it not except sitting apart in a nook with a little book.
THOMAS À KEMPIS

Restlessness

Restlessness is discontent—and discontent is the first necessity of progress. Show me a thoroughly satisfied man—and I will show you a failure.

THOMAS EDISON

Restroom

Mark my words, when a society has to resort to the restroom for its humor, the writing is on the wall.

ALAN BENNETT

Retirement

A man is known by the company that keeps him on after retirement age.

Revenge

To refrain from imitation is the best revenge.

MARCUS AURELIUS

Revival

I have long believed there was a divine plan that placed this land here to be found by people of a special kind, that we have a rendezvous with destiny. Yes, there is a spirit moving in this land and a hunger in the people for a spiritual revival. If the task I seek should be given to me, I would pray only that I could perform it in a way that would serve God.

RONALD REAGAN

Revolution

Every revolution was first a thought in one man's mind.

RALPH WALDO EMERSON

I say the right of a state to annul a law of Congress cannot be maintained but on the ground of the inalienable right of man to resist oppression; that is to say, upon the ground of revolution.

DANIEL WEBSTER

This country, with its institutions, belongs to the people who inhabit it. Whenever they shall grow weary of the existing government, they can exercise their constitutional right of amending it or their revolutionary right to dismember or overthrow it.

ABRAHAM LINCOLN

Rewards

What gets rewarded, gets done.

Rhetoric

The best rules of rhetoric are, to speak intelligently; speak from the heart; have something to say, say it; and stop when you've done.

TRYON EDWARDS

Rich

Few things have been more productive of controversy over the ages than the suggestion that the rich should, by one device or another, share their wealth with those who are not.

JOHN KENNETH GALBRAITH

Don't knock the rich. When did a poor person give you a job?

LAURENCE J. PETER

The only way for a rich man to be healthy is by exercise and abstinence, to live as if he were poor.

SIR WILLIAM TEMPLE

Riches

You can't spend yourself rich any more than you can drink yourself sober.
HERMAN E. TALMADGE

Do not wear yourself out to get rich; have the wisdom to show restraint. Cast but a glance at riches, and they are gone, for they will surely sprout wings and fly off to the sky like an eagle.
THE BIBLE: PROVERBS 23:4,5

Riches are gotten with pain, kept with care, and lost with grief.

One day a farmer came to pay his rent to a man whose love of money was very great. After settling the account, the farmer said, "I will give a shilling if you will let me go down to the vault and have a look at your money." The farmer was permitted to see the piles of gold and silver in the miser's big chest. After gazing for a while, the farmer said, "Now I am as well-off as you are." "How can that be?" asked the man. "Why, sir," said the farmer, "you never use any of this money. All you do with it is look at it. I have looked at it, too, so I am just as rich as you are."
NEW CENTURY LEADER

A man is rich in proportion to the number of things he can afford to let alone.
HENRY DAVID THOREAU

Ridicule

Ridicule is the weapon most feared by enthusiasts of every description; from its predominance over such minds it often checks what is absurd, but fully as often smothers that which is noble.
SIR WALTER SCOTT

Ridicule is the deadliest of weapons against a lofty cause.
SAMUEL ADAMS

Ridiculousness

The sublime and the ridiculous are often so nearly related, that it is difficult to class them separately. One step below the sublime, makes the ridiculous; and one step more above the ridiculous, makes the sublime again.   THOMAS PAINE

From the sublime to the ridiculous is but a step.
NAPOLEON BONAPARTE

Right

It's an odd thing about this universe that, though we all disagree with each other, we are all of us always in the right.
LOGAN PEARSALL SMITH

Right wrongs no man.

Aggressive fighting for the right is the noblest sport the world affords.   THEODORE ROOSEVELT

Rightness

Nothing is politically right which is morally wrong.
DANIEL O'CONNELL

We are not satisfied to be right unless we can prove others to be quite wrong.   JOHN W. HAZARD

Rights

Wherever there is a human being, I see God-given rights inherent in the being, whatever may be the sex or the complexion.
WILLIAM LLOYD GARRISON

I believe each individual is naturally entitled to do as he pleases
with himself and the fruit of his labor, so far as it in no wise
interferes with any other man's rights—that each community,
as a state, has a right to do exactly as it pleases with all concerns within that state that interfere with the right of no other
state, and that the general government, upon principle, has no
right to interfere with anything other than that general class
of things that does concern the whole.

ABRAHAM LINCOLN

Risk

Everything is sweetened by risk.   ALEXANDER SMITH

Happiness comes of the capacity to feel deeply, to enjoy simply,
to think freely, to risk life, to be needed.

STORM JAMESON

Only those who will risk going too far can possibly find out
how far one can go.   T.S. ELIOT

In order to find the edge, you must risk going over the edge.

DENNIS DUGAN

Behold the turtle. He makes progress only when he sticks his
neck out.   JAMES BRYANT CONANT

Great deeds are usually wrought at great risks.

HERODOTUS

Living at risk is jumping off the cliff and building your wings
on the way down.   RAY BRADBURY

Robbery

I thank Thee first because I was never robbed before; second because although they took my purse they did not take my life; third, because although they took my all, it was not much; and fourth because it was I who was robbed, and not I who robbed.

MATTHEW HENRY

Rogues

Put a rogue in the limelight, and he will act like an honest man.

NAPOLEON BONAPARTE

Romances

As soon as histories are properly told there is no more need of romances.

WALT WHITMAN

Ruin

All men that are ruined are ruined on the side of their natural propensities.

EDMUND BURKE

Rust

A thought, a sword, and a spade should never be allowed to rust.

IRISH PROVERB

Sadness

No one is more profoundly sad than he who laughs too much.

JEAN PAUL RICHTER

All are not merry that dance lightly.

Safety

If you play it safe in life, you've decided that you don't want to grow anymore.
SHIRLEY HUFSTEDLER

A ship in harbor is safe, but that is not what ships are built for.
JOHN A. SHEDD

Sages

There is a foolish corner even in the brain of the sage.
ARISTOTLE

Saints

Saints are not formed in great crisis but in the ordinary grind of daily life.
EVERYDAY SAINT

Satisfaction

The amount of satisfaction you get from life depends largely on your own ingenuity, self-sufficiency, and resourcefulness. People who wait around for life to supply their satisfaction usually find boredom instead.
WILLIAM MENNINGER

That everyone may eat and drink, and find satisfaction in all his toil—this is the gift of God.
THE BIBLE: ECCLESIASTES 3:13

Saving

Saving is a very fine thing. Especially when your parents have done it for you.
SIR WINSTON CHURCHILL

Scandal

Scandal dies sooner of itself, than we could kill it.

BENJAMIN RUSH

Scandal is like an egg: When it is hatched, it has wings.

Scars

God will not look you over for medals, degrees or diplomas, but for scars.

ELBERT HUBBARD

Scripture

Nobody ever outgrows Scripture; the book widens and deepens with our years.

CHARLES H. SPURGEON

All scripture is given by inspiration of God, and is profitable for doctrine, for reproof, for correction, for instruction in righteousness: that the man of God may be perfect, thoroughly furnished unto all good works.

THE BIBLE: 2 TIMOTHY 3:16,17 KJV

Search the scriptures; for in them ye think ye have eternal life: and they are they which testify of me.

THE BIBLE: JOHN 5:39 KJV

Sculptors

You show me a sculptor who works in the basement and I'll show you a low-down chiseler!

SOUPY SALES

Secrets

To know that one has a secret is to know half the secret itself.

HENRY WARD BEECHER

To keep your secret is wisdom; but to expect others to keep it is folly.
OLIVER WENDELL HOLMES JR.

Secrets are things we give to others to keep for us.
ELBERT HUBBARD

If you wish to preserve your secret, wrap it up in frankness.
ALEXANDER SMITH

A woman can keep one secret—the secret of her age.
VOLTAIRE

Nothing is so burdensome as a secret.

To whom thy secret thou dost tell,
To him thy freedom thou dost sell.
BENJAMIN FRANKLIN

A secret stays long in darkness, but it will see the light.

Secrets, after all, do serve a purpose. Those you tell them to get so much pleasure out of telling them to somebody else.

Security

If you want total security, go to prison. There you're fed, clothed, given medical care and so on. The only thing lacking... is freedom.
DWIGHT D. EISENHOWER

Security is not the absence of danger, but the presence of God, no matter what the danger.

We spend our time searching for security and hate it when we get it.
JOHN STEINBECK

Security is mostly a superstition. It does not exist in nature, nor do the children of men as a whole experience it. Avoiding danger is no safer in the long run than outright exposure. Life is either a daring adventure, or nothing. Serious harm, I am afraid, has been wrought to our generation by fostering the idea that they would live secure in a permanent order of things. They have expected stability and find none within themselves or in their universe. Before it is too late they must learn and teach others that only by brave acceptance of change and all-time crisis-ethics can they rise to the height of superlative responsibility.

HELEN KELLER

No matter what may be the test,
God will take care of you;
Lean, weary one, upon His breast,
God will take care of you.

C.D. MARTIN

Seeking

He that seeks, finds, and sometimes what he would rather not.

Self-centeredness

Edith was a little country bounded on the north, south, east, and west by Edith.

MARTHA OSTENSO

Men are not against you; they are merely for themselves.

GENE FOWLER

Self-control

The best time for you to hold your tongue is the time you feel you must say something or bust.

JOSH BILLINGS

He that hath no rule over his own spirit is like a city that is broken down, and without walls.

THE BIBLE: PROVERBS 25:28 KJV

Self-deception

Nothing is so easy as to deceive one's self; for what we wish, that we readily believe.

DEMOSTHENES

Do you see a man wise in his own eyes? There is more hope for a fool than for him.

THE BIBLE: PROVERBS 26:12

Lying to ourselves is more deeply ingrained than lying to others.

FYODOR DOSTOYEVSKY

Self-denial

What a curious phenomenon it is that you can get men to die for the liberty of the world who will not make the little sacrifice that is needed to free themselves from their own individual bondage.

BRUCE BARTON

Self-discipline

No steam or gas ever drives anything until it is confined. No Niagara is ever turned into light and power until it is tunneled. No life ever grows until it is focused, dedicated, disciplined.

HARRY EMERSON FOSDICK

What we do upon some great occasion will probably depend on what we already are; and what we are will be the result of previous years of self-discipline.

HENRY PARRY LIDDON

Self-entrapment

He who digs a pit for others falls into it himself.

Self-evaluation

If you don't like something about yourself, change it. If you can't change it, accept it.   TED SHACKELFORD

We judge ourselves by what we feel capable of doing, while others judge us by what we have already done.
HENRY W. LONGFELLOW

Still as of old, men by themselves are priced—for thirty pieces Judas sold himself, not Christ.   HESTER H. CHOLMODELEY

We are all inclined to judge ourselves by our ideals; others by their acts.
HAROLD NICHOLSON

Self-examination

Sometimes it is more important to discover what one cannot do, than what one can do.   LIN YUTANG

It is doubtless a vice to turn one's eyes inward too much, but I am my own comedy and tragedy.
RALPH WALDO EMERSON

The life which is unexamined is not worth living.
PLATO

Self-hatred

He who despises himself esteems himself as a self-despiser.
SUSAN SONTAG

Self-improvement

When an archer misses the mark, he turns and looks for the fault within himself. Failure to hit the bull's-eye is never the fault of the target. To improve your aim, improve yourself.

GILBERT ARLAND

Selfishness

Selfishness is the root and source of all natural and moral evils.

NATHANIEL EMMONS

He who lives only to benefit himself confers on the world a benefit when he dies.

TERTULLIAN

If you wish to be miserable, think about yourself; about what you want, what you like, what respect people ought to pay you, what people think of you; and then to you nothing will be pure. You will spoil everything you touch; you will make sin and misery for yourself out of everything God sends you; you will be as wretched as you choose.

CHARLES KINGSLEY

Self-knowledge

People travel to wonder at the height of mountains, at the huge waves of the sea, at the long courses of rivers, at the vast compass of the ocean, at the circular motion of the stars, and they pass by themselves without wondering.

AUGUSTINE

Know thyself? If I knew myself, I'd run away.

JOHANN WOLFGANG VON GOETHE

Know yourself. Don't accept your dog's admiration as conclusive evidence that you are wonderful.

ANN LANDERS

As we advance in life, we learn the limits of our abilities.
J.A. FROUD

Though you may see another's back, you cannot see your own.

Self-respect

Self-respect cannot be hunted. It cannot be purchased. It is never for sale. It cannot be fabricated out of public relations. It comes to us when we are alone, in quiet moments, in quiet places, when we suddenly realize that, knowing the good, we have done it; knowing the beautiful, we have served it; knowing the truth, we have spoken it.
ALFRED WHITNEY GRISWOLD

Self-sufficiency

The proverb warns that, "You should not bite the hand that feeds you." But maybe you should, if it prevents you from feeding yourself.
THOMAS SZASZ

Selling

If everyone thought alike, no goods would be sold.

Senate

I believe if we introduced the Lord's Prayer here, senators would propose a large number of amendments to it.
ABRAHAM LINCOLN

Sermon on the Mount

We have grasped the mystery of the atom and rejected the Sermon on the Mount.
OMAR BRADLEY

Serving

The high destiny of the individual is to serve rather than to rule.

ALBERT EINSTEIN

I am a little pencil in the hand of a writing God who is sending a love letter to the world.

MOTHER TERESA

For anything worth having one must pay the price; and the price is always work, patience, love, self-sacrifice—no paper currency, no promises to pay, but the gold of real service.

JOHN BURROUGHS

Shame

Better a pain in your heart than shame before men.

Shoes

I did not have three thousand pairs of shoes, I had one thousand and sixty.

IMELDA MARCOS

Shopping

A place where a woman goes when she's got nothing to wear.

Silence

Silence is not always golden—sometimes it's guilt.

Silence is one great art of conversation.

WILLIAM HAZLITT

Silence: the unbearable repartee.

G.K. CHESTERTON

To sit by in silence, when they should protest, makes cowards of men.
                                    ABRAHAM LINCOLN

Silence is the most perfect expression of scorn.
                                    GEORGE BERNARD SHAW

Silence is one of the hardest arguments to refute.
                                    JOSH BILLINGS

Drawing on my fine command of language, I said nothing.
                                    ROBERT BENCHLEY

Sometimes you have to be silent to be heard.
                                    STANISLAW J. LEC

Sin

Sin is first pleasing, then it grows easy, then delightful, then frequent, then habitual, then confirmed; then the man is impenitent, then he is obstinate, then he is resolved never to repent, and then he is ruined.
                                    ROBERT LEIGHTON

St. Augustine teaches that there is in each man a Serpent, an Eve, and an Adam. Our senses and natural propensities are the Serpent; the excitable desire is Eve; and the reason is the Adam. Our nature tempts us perpetually; criminal desire is often excited; but sin is not completed till reason consents.
                                    BLAISE PASCAL

It is base to filch a purse, daring to embezzle a million, but it is great beyond measure to steal a crown. The sin lessens as the guilt increases.
                                    FRIEDRICH VON SCHILLER

Sin has always been an ugly word, but it has been made so in a new sense over the last half-century. It has been made not only ugly but passé. People are no longer sinful, they are only immature or underprivileged or frightened or, more particularly, sick.

PHYLLIS MCGINLEY

Singing
Give me a man who sings at his work.

THOMAS CARLYLE

Sins
Every sin is the result of a collaboration.

STEPHEN CRANE

Old sins cast long shadows.

One leak will sink a ship, and one sin will destroy a sinner.

JOHN BUNYAN

Commit the oldest sins the newest kind of ways.

WILLIAM SHAKESPEARE

The seven sins are wealth without works, pleasure without conscience, knowledge without character, commerce without morality, science without humanity, worship without sacrifice, and politics without principle.

MAHATMA GANDHI

Men are punished by their sins, not for them.

ELBERT HUBBARD

Situation
An actor entering through the door, you've got nothing. But if he enters through the window, you've got a situation.

BILLY WILDER

Sixty-five

My, my—65! I guess this marks the first day of the rest of our life savings.

H. MARTIN

Slackness

One who is slack in his work is brother to one who destroys.

THE BIBLE: PROVERBS 18:9

Slander

No one is safe from slander. The best way is to pay no attention to it, but live in innocence and let the world talk.

MOLIÈRE

The slanderer and the assassin differ only in the weapon they use; with the one it is the dagger, with the other the tongue. The former is worse than the latter, for the last only kills the body, while the other murders the reputation and peace.

TRYON EDWARDS

Next to the slanderer, we detest the bearer of the slander to our ears.

MARY CATHERWOOD

To speak ill of others is a dishonest way of praising ourselves; let us be above such transparent egotism....If you can't say good and encouraging things, say nothing. Nothing is often a good thing to say, and always a clever thing to say.

WILL DURANT

Character assassination is at once easier and surer than physical assault; and it involves far less risk for the assassin. It leaves him free to commit the same deed over and over again, and may, indeed, win him the honors of a hero even in the country of his victims.

ALAN BARTH

Slander is like a hornet; if you cannot kill it dead at the first blow, better not strike at it.

JOSH BILLINGS

Slang

Slang is a language that rolls up its sleeves, spits on its hands and goes to work.

CARL SANDBURG

Slavery

From my earliest youth I have regarded slavery as a great moral and political evil. I think it unjust, repugnant to the natural equality of mankind, founded only in superior power; a standing and permanent conquest by the stronger over the weaker. The religion of Christ is a religion of kindness, justice, and brotherly love: but slavery is not kindly affectionate; it does not seek another's and not its own; it does not let the oppressed go free; it is but a continual act of oppression.

DANIEL WEBSTER

I am not going to be terrified by an excited populace, and hindered from speaking my honest sentiments upon this infernal subject of human slavery.

ABRAHAM LINCOLN

In this enlightened age, there are few, I believe, but what will acknowledge that slavery as an institution is a moral and political evil in any country.

ROBERT E. LEE

Although volume upon volume is written to prove slavery a very good thing, we never hear of the man who wishes to take the good of it by being a slave himself.

ABRAHAM LINCOLN

Whenever [I] hear anyone arguing for slavery, I feel a strong impulse to see it tried on him personally.

ABRAHAM LINCOLN

Sluggards

The sluggard craves and gets nothing, but the desires of the diligent are fully satisfied.   THE BIBLE: PROVERBS 13:4

As a door turns on its hinges, so a sluggard turns on his bed.
THE BIBLE: PROVERBS 26:14

Smiles

A smile is the whisper of a laugh.

Wear a smile and have friends; wear a scowl and have wrinkles.
GEORGE ELIOT

No matter how grouchy you're feeling,
You'll find the smile more or less healing.
It grows in a wreath
All around the front teeth—
Thus preserving the face from congealing.

ANTHONY EUWER

Smoke

We better know there is fire whence we see much smoke rising than we could know it by one or two witnesses swearing to it. The witnesses may commit perjury, but the smoke cannot.

ABRAHAM LINCOLN

Sneers

Who can refute a sneer? It is independent of proof, reason, argument, or sense, and may as well be used against facts and truth, as against falsehood.   CHARLES SIMMONS

Sniffles

Life is made up of sobs, sniffles, and smiles, with sniffles pre-dominating.

O. HENRY

Society

What can you say about a society that says God is dead and Elvis is alive?

IRV KUPCINET

To get into the best society nowadays, one has either to feed people, amuse people, or shock people.

OSCAR WILDE

A society of sheep must in time beget a government of wolves.

JUVENAL

Songs

A song will outlive all sermons in the memory.

HENRY GILES

Sorrow

We have no right to ask when a sorrow comes, "Why did this happen to me?" unless we ask the same question for every joy that comes our way.

PHILIP E. BERNSTEIN

Sorrow is like a precious treasure, shown only to friends.

Have courage for the great sorrows of life and patience for the small ones. And when you have finished your daily task, go to sleep in peace. God is awake.

VICTOR HUGO

Sorrow will pay no debt.

Experiencing a great sorrow is like entering a cave. We are overwhelmed by the darkness and the loneliness. We feel that there is no escape from the prison-house of pain. But God in His loving kindness has placed on the invisible wall the lamp of faith, whose beams shall lead us back to the sunlit world, where work and friends and service await us.

HELEN KELLER

I walked a mile with Pleasure—
She chattered all the way
But left me none the wiser
For all she had to say.
I walked a mile with Sorrow
And ne'er a word said she,
But, oh, the things I learned from her
When Sorrow walked with me.

ROBERT BROWNING HAMILTON

Soul

Money is not required to buy one necessity of the soul.

HENRY DAVID THOREAU

What good will it be for a man if he gains the whole world, yet forfeits his soul? Or what can a man give in exchange for his soul?

THE BIBLE: MATTHEW 16:26

Sowing and Reaping

Sow a thought, you reap an act; sow an act, you reap a habit; sow a habit, you reap a character; sow a character, you reap a destiny.

Speaking Ill

Never speak ill of yourself; your friends will always say enough on that subject.

CHARLES-MAURICE DE TALLEYRAND

He who speaks ill of himself is praised by no one.

Speech

If you your lips would keep from slips,
Five things observe with care;
To whom you speak, of whom you speak,
And how, and when, and where.

WILLIAM EDWARD NORRIS

Not only to say the right thing in the right place, but far more difficult, to leave unsaid the wrong thing at the tempting moment.

GEORGE AUGUSTUS HENRY SALA

Think twice before you speak, and then say it to yourself.

ELBERT HUBBARD

The human brain starts working the moment you are born and never stops until you stand up to speak in public.

SIR GEORGE JESSEL

If you don't say anything, you won't be called on to repeat it.

CALVIN COOLIDGE

Speak little, do much.

BENJAMIN FRANKLIN

He who guards his lips guards his life, but he who speaks rashly will come to ruin.

THE BIBLE: PROVERBS 13:3

The man who says what he thinks is finished, and the man who thinks what he says is an idiot.

ROLF HOCHHUTH

It is good speaking that improves good silence.

Men are born with two eyes, but with one tongue, in order that they should see twice as much as they say.

It often shows a fine command of language to say nothing.

If you haven't struck oil in your first three minutes, stop boring!

GEORGE JESSEL

Speeches

In my present position, it is hardly proper for me to make speeches. Every word is so closely noted that it will not do to make trivial ones.

ABRAHAM LINCOLN

The best impromptu speeches are those written well in advance.

RUTH GORDON

It usually takes me more than three weeks to prepare a good impromptu speech.

MARK TWAIN

Spending

I don't think you can spend yourself rich.

GEORGE HUMPHREY

If you know how to spend less than you get, you have the philosopher's stone.

BENJAMIN FRANKLIN

Spirit

There are only two forces in the world, the sword and the spirit. In the long run the sword will always be conquered by the spirit.

NAPOLEON BONAPARTE

Spiritual Darkness

Man is stumbling blindly through a spiritual darkness while toying with the precarious secrets of life and death. The world has achieved brilliance without wisdom, power without conscience. We know more about war than we know about peace, more about killing than we know about living.

OMAR BRADLEY

Squeaking

The wheel that squeaks the loudest is the one that gets grease.

JOSH BILLINGS

Stages of Life

The seven ages of man: spills, drills, thrills, bills, ills, pills, wills.

RICHARD J. NEEDHAM

Every stage of life has its troubles, and no man is content with his own age.

AUSONIUS

Standing Still

People may get tireder by standing still than by going on.

When you're trying to get something done, don't worry too much about stepping on someone else's toes. Nobody gets his toes stepped on unless he is standing still or sitting down on the job.

ARLEIGH A. BURKE

Stars

I always thought I should be treated like a star.

MADONNA

States

What an augmentation of the field for jobbing, speculating, plundering, office-building, and office-hunting would be produced by an assumption of all the state powers into the hand of the general government! The true theory of our Constitution is surely the wisest and best, that the states are independent as to everything within themselves and united as to everything respecting foreign nations. Let the general government be reduced to foreign concerns only.

THOMAS JEFFERSON

Asking one of the states to surrender part of her sovereignty is like asking a lady to surrender part of her chastity.

JOHN RANDOLPH

The maintenance inviolate of the rights of the states, and especially the right of each state to order and control its own domestic institutions according to its own judgment exclusively, is essential to that balance of powers on which the perfection and endurance of our political fabric depends.

ABRAHAM LINCOLN

The states should be left to do whatever acts they can do as well as the general government.

THOMAS JEFFERSON

Statesmen

You can always get the truth from an American statesman after he has turned seventy, or given up all hope of the presidency.

WENDELL PHILLIPS

Statistics

He uses statistics as a drunken man uses lampposts—for support rather than for illumination.

ANDREW LANG

Staying

"Stay" is a charming word in a friend's vocabulary.

AMOS BRONSON ALCOTT

Stories

There are only two or three human stories, and they go on repeating themselves as fiercely as if they had never happened before.

WILLA CATHER

Storms

Where there was a storm, there is calm.

The world is a great ocean upon which we encounter more tempestuous storms than calms.

Strangers

If a man be gracious to strangers, it shows that he is a citizen of the world, and his heart is no island, cut off from other islands, but a continent that joins them.

FRANCIS BACON

I do desire we may be better strangers.

WILLIAM SHAKESPEARE

A stranger's eye sees clearest.

Strength

Don't expect to build up the weak by pulling down the strong.

CALVIN COOLIDGE

Strenuous Life

I wish to preach, not the doctrine of ignoble ease, but the doctrine of the strenuous life.   THEODORE ROOSEVELT

Stress

Don't be afraid to enjoy the stress of a full life nor too naive to think you can do so without some intelligent thinking and planning. Man should not try to avoid stress any more than he would shun food, love or exercise.   HANS SELYE

Most stress is caused by people who overestimate the importance of their problems.   MICHAEL LeBOEUF

Times of stress and difficulty are seasons of opportunity when the seeds of progress are sown.   THOMAS F. WOODLOCK

Strong Defense

A strong defense is the surest way to peace. Strength makes detente attainable. Weakness invites war, as my generation— my generation—knows from four very bitter experiences.   GERALD R. FORD

On the presidential coat of arms, the American eagle holds in his right talon an olive branch, while in his left he holds a bundle of arrows. We intend to give equal attention to both.   JOHN F. KENNEDY

If we desire to avoid insult, we must be able to repel it; if we desire to secure peace, one of the most powerful instruments of our rising prosperity, it must be known that we are at all times ready for war.   GEORGE WASHINGTON

Struggle

The struggle alone pleases us, not the victory.

BLAISE PASCAL

Success

Flaming enthusiasm, backed up by horse sense and persistence, is the quality that most frequently makes for success.

DALE CARNEGIE

The secret of my success is that at an early age I discovered I was not God.

OLIVER WENDELL HOLMES JR.

One of the biggest factors in success is the courage to undertake something.

JAMES A. WORSHAM

God may allow His servant to succeed when He has disciplined him to a point where he does not need to succeed to be happy. The man who is elated by success and is cast down by failure is still a carnal man. At best his fruit will have a worm in it.

A.W. TOZER

All you need in this life is ignorance and confidence; then success is sure.

MARK TWAIN

If you wish success in life, make perseverance your bosom friend, experience your wise counselor, caution your elder brother, and hope your guardian genius.

JOSEPH ADDISON

I have learned that success is to be measured not so much by the position that one has reached in life as by the obstacles which he has overcome while trying to succeed.

BOOKER T. WASHINGTON

Success is counted sweetest by those who ne'er succeed.

EMILY DICKINSON

It takes twenty years to be an overnight success.

EDDIE CANTOR

It is only as we develop others that we permanently succeed.

HARVEY S. FIRESTONE

Success: A subtle contrivance of Nature for bringing about a man's defeat.

ELBERT HUBBARD

The secret of success is constancy of purpose.

BENJAMIN DISRAELI

The difference between failure and success is doing a thing nearly right and doing a thing exactly right.

EDWARD SIMMONS

Someday I hope to enjoy enough of what the world calls success so that somebody will ask me, "What's the secret of it?" I shall say simply this: "I get up when I fall down."

PAUL HARVEY

Anybody can become a success in America if he's willing to work while everybody else is killing time.

One of the first things a person must do to climb the ladder of success is to take his hands out of his pockets.

Men who have attained things worth having in this world have worked while others idled, have persevered when others gave up in despair, have practiced early in life the valuable habits of self-denial, industry, and singleness of purpose. As a result, they enjoy in later life the success so often erroneously attributed to good luck.

GRENVILLE KLEISER

The key to executive success is the ability to inspire teamwork.
                                            HENRY L. DOHERTY

Success is just a matter of luck. Ask any failure.
                                            EARL WILSON

The people who succeed are the few who have the ambition
and the willpower to develop themselves.
                                            HERBERT N. CASSON

All it takes to be successful today is a willingness to start an
eight-hour day immediately after you finish the first one.

Success is a journey, not a destination.   BEN SWEETLAND

When a man succeeds, he does it in spite of everybody, and
not with the assistance of everybody.
                                            EDGAR WATSON HOWE

I was successful because you believed in me.
                                            ULYSSES S. GRANT

Suffering

He who fears he shall suffer, already suffers what he fears.
                                            MICHEL DE MONTAIGNE

What really raises one's indignation against suffering is not
suffering intrinsically, but the senselessness of suffering.
                                            FRIEDRICH NIETZSCHE

The chief pang of most trials is not so much the actual suffering itself as our own spirit of resistance to it.
                                            JEAN-NICHOLAS GROU

We are healed of a suffering only by experiencing it to the full.
                                            MARCEL PROUST

I have often noticed that the suffering which is most difficult, if not impossible, to forgive is unreal, imagined suffering...The worst, most obstinate grievances are imagined ones.

LAURENS VAN DER POST

To live is to suffer; to survive is to find meaning in suffering.

VIKTOR FRANKL

Supporting

People support what they help to create.

Surprise

When I was born I was so surprised I didn't talk for a year-and-a-half.

GRACIE ALLEN

Suspense

Even cowards can endure hardships; only the brave can endure suspense.

MIGNON MCLAUGHLIN

Suspicion

Suspicion is the poison of true friendship.   AUGUSTINE

Suspicion is far more apt to be wrong than right; oftener unjust than just. It is no friend to virtue and always an enemy to happiness.

HOSEA BALLOU

Swearing

He that will swear, will lie.

You do not swear at your serious troubles. One only swears at trifling annoyances.

G.F. TURNER

The foolish and wicked practice of profane cursing and swearing is a vice so mean and low that every person of sense and character detests and despises it.

GEORGE WASHINGTON

It chills my blood to hear the blest Supreme
Rudely appealed to on each trifling theme.
Maintain your rank, vulgarity despise.
To swear is neither brave, polite, nor wise.

WILLIAM COWPER

Swearing was invented as a compromise between running away and fighting.

FINLEY PETER DUNNE

Tact

Tact consists in knowing how far we may go too far.

JEAN COCTEAU

Silence is not always tact, and it is tact that is golden, not silence.

SAMUEL BUTLER

In the battle of existence, talent is the punch; tact is the clever footwork.

WILSON MIZNER

Talent

You cannot define talent. All you can do is build the greenhouse and see if it grows.

WILLIAM P. STEVEN

Talk Shows

In the Soviet Union a writer who is critical, as we know, is taken to a lunatic asylum. In the United States, he's taken to a talk show.

CARLOS FUENTES

Talking

You may talk too much on the best of subjects.

BENJAMIN FRANKLIN

There are very few people who don't become more interesting when they stop talking.

MARY LOWRY

Tasks

I long to accomplish a great and noble task, but it is my chief duty to accomplish humble tasks as though they are great and noble. The world is moved along, not only by the mighty shoves of its heroes, but also by the aggregate of the tiny pushes of each honest worker.

HELEN KELLER

Attempt easy tasks as if they were difficult, and difficult as if they were easy; in the one case that confidence may not fall asleep, in the other that it may not be dismayed.

BALTASAR GRACIAN

Nothing is so fatiguing as the eternal hanging on of an uncompleted task.

WILLIAM JAMES

Taxes

The power to tax is the power to destroy.

DANIEL WEBSTER

Teachers

A teacher affects eternity; he can never tell where his influence stops.

HENRY ADAMS

Teaching

Teach the small and the lowly gently; the needle with a small eye should be threaded slowly.

Good teaching is one-fourth preparation and three-fourths theater.

GAIL GODWIN

Teamwork

No matter how outstanding teamwork may be in accomplishing something great, history will identify it with a single name years or centuries later.

Tears

The bitterest tears shed over graves are for words left unsaid and deeds left undone.

HARRIET BEECHER STOWE

Teenagers

In the 1940s a survey listed the top seven discipline problems in public schools: talking, chewing gum, making noise, running in the halls, getting out of line, wearing improper clothes, and not putting paper in wastebaskets.

A more recent survey lists these top seven: drug abuse, alcohol abuse, pregnancy, suicide, rape, robbery, and assault. (Arson, gang warfare, and venereal disease are also-rans.)

GEORGE F. WILL

Television

Television is now so desperately hungry for material that they're scraping the top of the barrel. GORE VIDAL

Temper

We must interpret a bad temper as a sign of inferiority. ALFRED ADLER

Men lose their tempers in defending their taste. RALPH WALDO EMERSON

There's no quicker way of cooking your goose than by letting your temper boil over.

Temptation

Temptation is a part of life. No one is immune—at any age. For temptation is present wherever there is a choice to be made, not only between good and evil, but also between a higher and lower good. For some, it may be a temptation to misuse their gifts, to seek a worthy aim by unworthy means, to lower their ideal to win favor with the electorate, or with their companions and associates. ERNEST TRICE THOMPSON

Some temptations come to the industrious, but all temptations attack the idle. CHARLES H. SPURGEON

If thou wouldst conquer thy weakness thou must never gratify it. No man is compelled to evil; only his consent makes it his. It is no sin to be tempted; it is to yield and be overcome. WILLIAM PENN

Keep yourself from opportunity, and God will keep you from sins. JACOB CATS

Ten Commandments

1. You shall have no other gods before me.

2. You shall not make for yourself an idol in the form of anything in heaven above or on the earth beneath or in the waters below. You shall not bow down to them or worship them; for I, the LORD your God, am a jealous God, punishing the children for the sin of the fathers to the third and fourth generation of those who hate me, but showing love to a thousand [generations] of those who love me and keep my commandments.

3. You shall not misuse the name of the LORD your God, for the LORD will not hold anyone guiltless who misuses his name.

4. Remember the Sabbath day by keeping it holy. Six days you shall labor and do all your work, but the seventh day is a Sabbath to the LORD your God. On it you shall not do any work, neither you, nor your son or daughter, nor your manservant or maidservant, nor your animals, nor the alien within your gates. For in six days the LORD made the heavens and the earth, the sea, and all that is in them, but he rested on the seventh day. Therefore the LORD blessed the Sabbath day and made it holy.

5. Honor your father and your mother, so that you may live long in the land the LORD your God is giving you.

6. You shall not murder.

7. You shall not commit adultery.

8. You shall not steal.

9. You shall not give false testimony against your neighbor.

10. You shall not covet your neighbor's house. You shall not covet your neighbor's wife, or his manservant or maidservant, his ox or donkey, or anything that belongs to your neighbor.

THE BIBLE: EXODUS 20:3-17

The first anticrime bill was called the Ten Commandments.

IRV KUPCINET

Tenacity

Let me tell you the secret that has led me to my goal: my strength lies solely in my tenacity.

LOUIS PASTEUR

Theories

A little experience often upsets a lot of theory.

CADMAN

Thieves

Set a thief to catch a thief.

The eye of the thief glances about.

Things

The best things in life aren't things.

ART BUCHWALD

Thinking

Crises and deadlocks when they occur have at least this advantage, that they force us to think.

JAWAHARLAL NEHRU

As he thinketh in his heart, so is he.

THE BIBLE: PROVERBS 23:7 KJV

Thoughts

Our best friends and our worst enemies are our thoughts. A thought can do us more good than a doctor or a banker or a faithful friend. It can also do us more harm than a brick.

FRANK CRANE

If we were all to be judged by our thoughts, the hills would be swarming with outlaws.

JOHANN SIGURJONSSON

If we are not responsible for the thoughts that pass our doors, we are at least responsible for those we admit and entertain.

CHARLES B. NEWCOMB

Every event that a man would master must be mounted on the run, and no man ever caught the reins of a thought except as it galloped past him.

OLIVER WENDELL HOLMES JR.

Tigers

Some days you tame the tiger. And some days the tiger has you for lunch.

TUG MCGRAW

Time

Time is an equal opportunity employer. Each human being has exactly the same number of hours and minutes every day. Rich people can't buy more hours. Scientists can't invent new minutes. And you can't save time to spend it on another day. Even so, time is amazingly fair and forgiving. No matter how much time you've wasted in the past, you still have an entire tomorrow. Success depends upon using it wisely—by planning and setting priorities.

DENIS WAITLEY

Much may be done in those little shreds and patches of time which every day produces, and which most men throw away.

CHARLES CALEB COLTON

Time is like a river of fleeting events, and its current is strong; as soon as something comes into sight, it is swept past us, and something else takes its place, and that too will be swept away.

MARCUS AURELIUS

If we are willing to spend hours on end to learn to play the piano, operate a computer, or fly an airplane, it is sheer nonsense for us to imagine that we can learn the high art of getting guidance through communion with the Lord without being willing to set aside time for it.

PAUL REES

Lost, yesterday, somewhere between sunrise and sunset, two golden hours, each set with sixty diamond minutes. No reward is offered, for they are gone forever.

HORACE MANN

Time is:
Too slow for those who wait,
Too swift for those who fear,
Too long for those who grieve,
Too short for those who rejoice.
But for those who love, time is not.

HENRY VAN DYKE

Pick my left pocket of its silver dime,
But spare the right—it holds my golden time!

OLIVER WENDELL HOLMES JR.

I resolve to live with all my might while I do live. I resolve never to lose one moment of time and to improve my use of time in the most profitable way I possibly can. I resolve never to do anything I wouldn't do, if it were the last hour of my life.

JONATHAN EDWARDS

Time is the herb that cures all diseases.

BENJAMIN FRANKLIN

If we lose our money, it gives us some concern. If we are cheated or robbed of it, we are angry. But money lost may be found; what we are robbed of may be restored. The treasure of time, once lost, can never be recovered; yet we squander it as though it were nothing of worth or we had no use of it.

BENJAMIN FRANKLIN

Dost thou love life? Then do not squander time, for that is the stuff life is made of.
BENJAMIN FRANKLIN

Time flies; but remember, you are the navigator.

Don't be fooled by the calendar. There are only as many days in the year as you make use of. One man gets only a week's value out of a year while another man gets a full year's value out of a week.
CHARLES RICHARDS

Today

Live each day as you would climb a mountain. An occasional glance toward the summit keeps the goal in mind, but many beautiful scenes are to be observed from each new vantage point. So climb slowly, enjoying each passing moment; and then the view from the summit will serve as a more rewarding climax for your journey.
FULTON J. SHEEN

The days come and go like muffled and veiled figures sent from a distant friendly party, but they say nothing, and if we do not use the gifts they bring, they carry them as silently away.
RALPH WALDO EMERSON

We can easily manage if we will only take, each day, the burden appointed to it. But the load will be too heavy for us if we carry yesterday's burden over again today, and then add the burden of the morrow before we are required to bear it.
JOHN NEWTON

Do not look back on happiness, or dream of it in the future. You are only sure of today; do not let yourself be cheated out of it.
HENRY WARD BEECHER

It is a mistake to look too far ahead. Only one link in the chain of destiny can be handled at a time.

SIR WINSTON CHURCHILL

Yesterday is but a dream, tomorrow is only a vision. But today, well lived, makes every yesterday a dream of happiness, and every tomorrow a vision of hope. Look well, therefore, to this day, for it is life, the very life of life.   SANSKRIT PROVERB

The past, the present, and the future are really one: they are today.

HARRIET BEECHER STOWE

Today is the first day of the rest of your life.

One today is worth two tomorrows.   BENJAMIN FRANKLIN

Tolerance
Nothing makes you more tolerant of a neighbor's noisy party than being there.

FRANKLIN P. JONES

Tombs
Tombs are the clothes of the dead; a grave is but a plain suit; a rich monument is an embroidered one.

THOMAS FULLER

Tongue
The tongue has the power of life and death, and those who love it will eat its fruit.   THE BIBLE: PROVERBS 18:21

He who guards his mouth and his tongue keeps himself from calamity.
                                        THE BIBLE: PROVERBS 21:23

Teach thy tongue to say "I do not know." MAIMONIDES

Toupee

His toupee makes him look twenty years sillier.
                                        BILL DANA

Trade

He that hath a trade, hath an estate. BENJAMIN FRANKLIN

He who has a trade may travel through the world.

Tradition

Time consecrates; and what is gray with age becomes religion.
                                        FRIEDRICH VON SCHILLER

Tranquility

Great tranquility of heart is his who cares for neither praise nor blame.
                                        THOMAS À KEMPIS

Travel

In America, there are two classes of travel: first class and with children.
                                        ROBERT BENCHLEY

Treachery

No one can guard against treachery.

Treason

Is there not some chosen curse, some hidden thunder in the stores of heaven, red with uncommon wrath, to blast the man who owes his greatness to his country's ruin!

JOSEPH ADDISON

Trees

He that plants a tree plants for posterity.

Trials

We are always in the forge, or on the anvil; by trials God is shaping us for higher things.

HENRY WARD BEECHER

It is not until we have passed through the furnace that we are made to know how much dross there is in our composition.

CHARLES CALEB COLTON

What seem to us bitter trials are often blessings in disguise.

OSCAR WILDE

Triumph

Triumph—umph added to try.

Trivial Matters

From trivial things great contests oft arise.

Trouble

If winter comes, can spring be far behind?

PERCY BYSSHE SHELLEY

It is a painful thing to look at your own trouble and know that you yourself, and no one else, had made it.

SOPHOCLES

There is no man in this world without some manner of tribulation or anguish, though he be king or pope.

THOMAS À KEMPIS

Man is born unto trouble, as the sparks fly upward.

THE BIBLE: JOB 5:7 KJV

No one would have crossed the ocean if he could have gotten off the ship in the storm.

CHARLES KETTERING

Trouble creates a capacity to handle it.

OLIVER WENDELL HOLMES JR.

It never rains but it pours.

He who fumes at his quandaries becomes their victim.

DAVID SEABURY

Trouble is the thing that strong men grow by. Met in the right way, it is a sure-fire means of putting iron into the victim's will and making him a tougher man to down forever after.

H. BERTRAM LEWIS

When things go wrong, don't go with them.

I have learned much from my teachers, more from my books, but most from my troubles.

THE MIDRASH

Trust

I know God will not give me anything I can't handle. I just wish that He didn't trust me so much.   MOTHER TERESA

You may be deceived if you trust too much, but you will live in torment if you don't trust enough.   FRANK CRANE

Blessed is the man that trusteth in the LORD, and whose hope the LORD is.   THE BIBLE: JEREMIAH 17:7 KJV

Trust men, and they will be true to you; treat them greatly, and they will show themselves great.   RALPH WALDO EMERSON

Trust is the emotional glue that binds followers and leaders together.   WARREN BENNIS AND BERT NANUS

Be courteous to all but intimate with few, and let those few be well-tried before you give them your confidence.

GEORGE WASHINGTON

Truth

Everyone wishes to have truth on his side, but not everyone wishes to be on the side of truth.   RICHARD WHATELY

The truth is incontrovertible: malice may attack it, ignorance may deride it, but in the end, there it is.

SIR WINSTON CHURCHILL

And in the end, through the long ages of our quest for light, it will be found that truth is still mightier than the sword.

DOUGLAS MACARTHUR

Truth has no special time of its own. Its hour is now—always.
ALBERT SCHWEITZER

I never give them hell. I just tell the truth, and they think it's hell.
HARRY S. TRUMAN

Let the people know the truth and the country is safe.
ABRAHAM LINCOLN

Let my name stand among those who are willing to bear ridicule and reproach for the truth's sake, and so earn some right to rejoice when the victory is won.
LOUISA MAY ALCOTT

Truth is tough. It will not break, like a bubble, at a touch. Nay, you may kick it about all day, and it will be round and full at evening.
OLIVER WENDELL HOLMES JR.

It is easier to perceive error than to find truth, for the former lies on the surface and is easily seen, while the latter lies in the depth, where few are willing to search for it.
JOHANN WOLFGANG VON GOETHE

Seize upon truth, wherever it is found,
Amongst your friends, amongst your foes,
On Christian or on heathen ground;
The flower's divine where'er it grows.
ISAAC WATTS

I like better for one to say some foolish thing upon important matters than to be silent. That becomes the subject of discussion and dispute, and the truth is discovered.
DENIS DIDEROT

Have patience awhile; slanders are not longlived. Truth is the child of time; ere long she shall appear to vindicate thee.
IMMANUEL KANT

Truth is always consistent with itself, and needs nothing to help it out; it is always near at hand, sits upon our lips, and is ready to drop out before we are aware; a lie is troublesome, and sets a man's invention upon the rack, and one trick needs a great many more to make it good. It is like building upon a false foundation, which continually stands in need of props to shore it up, and proves at last more chargeable than to have raised a substantial building at first upon a true and solid foundation.

JOSEPH ADDISON

Men occasionally stumble over the truth, but most of them pick themselves up and hurry off as if nothing happened.

SIR WINSTON CHURCHILL

Craft must have clothes, but truth loves to go naked.

JONATHAN SWIFT

It is error alone which needs the support of government. Truth can stand by itself.

THOMAS JEFFERSON

You'll never get mixed up if you simply tell the truth. Then you don't have to remember what you have said, and you never forget what you have said.

SAM RAYBURN

Who speaks the truth stabs falsehood to the heart.

JAMES RUSSELL LOWELL

From the cowardice that shrinks from new truth,
From the laziness that is content with half-truths,
From the arrogance that thinks it knows all truth,
O, God of Truth, deliver us.

PRAYER OF THE SCHOLAR

Truthful lips endure forever, but a lying tongue lasts only a moment.

THE BIBLE: PROVERBS 12:19

A truth that's told with bad intent beats all the lies you can invent.

WILLIAM BLAKE

Half the misery in the world comes of want of courage to speak and to hear the truth plainly and in a spirit of love.

HARRIET BEECHER STOWE

Are we disposed to be of the number of those who, having eyes, see not, and having ears, hear not the things which so nearly concern their temporal salvation? For my part, whatever anguish of spirit it might cost, I am willing to know the whole truth, to know the worst and to provide for it.

PATRICK HENRY

A man that should call everything by its right name, would hardly pass the streets without being knocked down as a common enemy.

LORD HALIFAX

Truth always lags behind, limping along on the arm of time.

BALTASAR GRACIAN

I have discovered the art of fooling diplomats; I speak the truth, and they never believe me.

BENSO DI VACOUR

There is nothing so powerful as truth—and often nothing so strange.

DANIEL WEBSTER

As scarce as truth is, the supply has always been in excess of the demand.

JOSH BILLINGS

A man had rather have a hundred lies told to him than one truth which he does not wish should be told.

SAMUEL JOHNSON

Sometimes the kindest thing you can do for a person is to tell him a truth that will prove very painful. But in so doing, you may have saved him from serious harm or even greater pain. In a world such as ours, people must learn to "take it." A painless world is not necessarily a good world.

SYLVANUS AND EVELYN DUVALL

If you're going to tell people the truth, make them laugh, or they'll kill you.

BILLY WILDER

Speaking the truth in love may mean, at times, keeping silence.

WILLARD L. SPERRY

The most casual student of history knows that, as a matter of fact, truth does not necessarily vanquish. What is more, truth can never win unless it is promulgated. Truth does not carry within itself an antitoxin to falsehood. The cause of truth must be championed, and it must be championed dynamically.

WILLIAM F. BUCKLEY JR.

He who has the right needs not to fear...truth is generally the best vindication against slander.

ABRAHAM LINCOLN

The truth is often a terrible weapon of aggression. It is possible to lie, and even to murder, with the truth.

Truthfulness

He who is truthful may be the enemy of many.

Truthfulness is a cornerstone in character, and if it be not firmly laid in youth, there will ever after be a weak spot in the foundation.

JEFFERSON DAVIS

Pretty much all the honest truth-telling there is in the world is done by children.
OLIVER WENDELL HOLMES SR.

Tyranny

There is a secret pride in every human heart that revolts at tyranny. You may order and drive an individual, but you cannot make him respect you.
WILLIAM HAZLITT

The time to guard against corruption and tyranny is before they have gotten hold of us. It is better to keep the wolf out of the fold than to trust to drawing his teeth and talons after he shall have entered.
THOMAS JEFFERSON

I have sworn upon the altar of God, eternal hostility against every form of tyranny over the mind of man.
THOMAS JEFFERSON

Tyrants

Any excuse will serve a tyrant.
AESOP

With reasonable men, I will reason; with humane men, I will plead; but to tyrants I will give no quarter, nor waste arguments where they will certainly be lost.
WILLIAM LLOYD GARRISON

It is time to fear when tyrants seem to kiss.

Men must be governed by God or they will be ruled by tyrants.
WILLIAM PENN

Uncertainty

Without measureless and perpetual uncertainty the drama of human life would be destroyed.

SIR WINSTON CHURCHILL

Uncomfortableness

Those people who are uncomfortable in themselves are disagreeable to others.

WILLIAM HAZLITT

Understanding

Nothing in life is to be feared. It is only to be understood.

MARIE CURIE

With different persons, we may be quite different individuals. We cling, however, to the illusion that we remain identical for all persons and every situation.

LUIGI PIRANDELLO

Unemployment

The thing that really worries business today is the great number of people still on their payroll who are unemployed.

Unfaithfulness

Like a bad tooth or a lame foot is reliance on the unfaithful in times of trouble.

THE BIBLE: PROVERBS 25:19

Unfaithfulness in the keeping of an appointment is an act of clear dishonesty. You may as well borrow a person's money as his time.

HORACE MANN

Unionism

Unionism, seldom, if ever, uses such power as it has to insure better work; almost always it devotes a large part of that power to safeguarding bad work.

H.L. MENCKEN

University Politics

University politics are vicious precisely because the stakes are so small.

HENRY KISSINGER

Unknown

Many live in dread of what is coming. Why should we? The unknown puts adventure into life....The unexpected around the corner gives a sense of anticipation and surprise. Thank God for the unknown future.

E. STANLEY JONES

Unskilled Labor

Don't condescend to unskilled labor. Try it for a half a day first.

BROOKS ATKINSON

Vacation

A period of travel and relaxation when you take twice the clothes and half the money you need.

Value

The harder the conflict, the more glorious the triumph. What we obtain too cheaply, we esteem too lightly; 'tis dearness only that gives everything its value.

THOMAS PAINE

Try not to become a man of success but rather try to become a man of value.

ALBERT EINSTEIN

Vanity

Of all our infirmities, vanity is the dearest to us; a man will starve his other vices to keep that alive.

BENJAMIN FRANKLIN

The only cure for vanity is laughter, and the only fault that's laughable is vanity.

HENRI BERGSON

Vengeance

Nothing is more costly, nothing is more sterile, than vengeance.

SIR WINSTON CHURCHILL

Vice President

My country has in its wisdom contrived for me the most insignificant office that ever the invention of man contrived or his imagination conceived.

JOHN ADAMS

The vice president is like a man in a cataleptic state: he cannot speak, he cannot move, he suffers no pain, and yet he is perfectly conscious of everything that is going on around him.

THOMAS MARSHALL

Once there were two brothers. One ran away to sea, the other was elected vice president, and nothing was ever heard of them again.

Thomas Marshall

The vice presidency is sort of like the last cookie on the plate. Everybody insists he won't take it, but somebody always does.

Bill Vaughan

Will you please tell me what you do with all the vice presidents a bank has? I guess that's to get you more discouraged before you can see the president. Why, the United States is the biggest business institution in the world, and they only have one vice president, and nobody has ever found anything for him to do.

Will Rogers

Vices

Search others for their virtues, thy self for thy vices.

Benjamin Franklin

Viewpoint

The hues of the opal, the light of the diamond, are not to be seen if the eye is too near.

Ralph Waldo Emerson

Vigilance

When good people in any country cease their vigilance and struggle, then evil men prevail.

Pearl S. Buck

Villains

One may smile, and smile, and be a villain.

William Shakespeare

The more successful the villain, the more successful the picture.

ALFRED HITCHCOCK

Virtue

Order your soul; reduce your wants; live in charity; associate in Christian community; obey the laws; trust in Providence.

AUGUSTINE

Virtue, though in rags, will keep me warm.

JOHN DRYDEN

We are apt to mistake our vocation by looking out of the way for occasions to exercise great and rare virtues, and by stepping over the ordinary ones that lie directly in the road before us.

HANNAH MORE

What does the LORD require of you? To act justly and to love mercy and to walk humbly with your God.

THE BIBLE: MICAH 6:8

A Bible and a newspaper in every house, a good school in every district—all studied and appreciated as they merit—are the principle support of virtue, morality, and civil liberty.

BENJAMIN FRANKLIN

These are times in which a genius would wish to live. It is not in the still calm of life, or the repose of a pacific station, that great characters are formed....Great necessities call out great virtues.

ABIGAIL ADAMS

Visa Cards

I just recently had my Visa card stolen....Right now it's everywhere I want to be.

SCOTT WOOD

Vision

Vision is the art of seeing things invisible.

JONATHAN SWIFT

Give us clear vision that we may know where to stand and what to stand for—because unless we stand for something, we shall fall for anything.

MEGIDDO MESSAGE

Vote

Giving every man a vote has no more made men wise and free than Christianity has made them good.

H.L. MENCKEN

Always vote for principle, though you may vote alone, and you may cherish the sweetest reflection that your vote is never lost.

JOHN QUINCY ADAMS

Perhaps the best way to get people out to vote would be to propose a law which wouldn't let them.

The right of voting for representatives is the primary right by which other rights are protected. To take away this right is to reduce a man to slavery, for slavery consists in being subject to the will of another, and he that has not a vote in the election of representatives is in this case.

THOMAS PAINE

Vulnerability

Men are taught that women respect them for their strength and that may well be true, but they love them for their vulnerability.

MERLE SHAIN

Waiting

Wait! Wait! To children it seems this is all they hear. Yet the very act of waiting is valuable training, for waiting is something they will have to do all their lives. The youth must wait for his right to drive a car, the student for his diploma, the lawyer for his degree, the worker for the salary increase, the married couple for the home they want. Teaching a child to wait is just as important as the training in manners and morals that he receives at his mother's knee.

DOROTHY BRANT WARRICK

There are two kinds of people in one's life: people whom one keeps waiting and the people for whom one waits.

S.N. BEHRMAN

The man who has done nothing but wait for his ship to come in has already missed the boat.

Walking

Thoughts come clearly while one walks.

THOMAS MANN

War

It is fatal to enter any war without the will to win it.

DOUGLAS MACARTHUR

There is many a boy here today who looks on war as all glory, but boys, it is all hell. You can bear this warning voice to generations yet to come. I look upon war with horror.

WILLIAM T. SHERMAN

My first wish is to see this plague to mankind banished from off the earth, and the sons and daughters of this world employed in more pleasing and innocent amusements than in preparing implements and exercising them for the destruction of mankind.

GEORGE WASHINGTON

Older men declare war. But it is the youth that must fight and die.

HERBERT HOOVER

The four great motives which move men to social activity are hunger, love, vanity, and fear of superior powers. If we search out the causes which have moved men to war, we find them under each of these motives or interests.

WILLIAM GRAHAM SUMNER

Washington, D.C.

Things get very lonely in Washington sometimes. The real voice of the great people of America sometimes sounds faint and distant in that strange city. You hear politics until you wish that both parties were smothered in their own gas.

WOODROW WILSON

Watching

You observe a lot by watching.

YOGI BERRA

Water

Water never rises above its level.

Weak Character

He is a sheep in sheep's clothing.

SIR WINSTON CHURCHILL

Wealth

Wealth unused might as well not exist.   AESOP

Wedding Cake

The most dangerous food is a wedding cake.

Welfare

Doing for people what they can and ought to do for themselves is a dangerous experiment. In the last analysis, the welfare of the workers depends upon their own initiative. Whatever is done under the guise of philanthropy or social morality which in any way lessens initiative is the greatest crime that can be committed against the toilers. Let social busybodies and professional "public morals experts" in their fads reflect upon the perils they rashly invite under this pretense of social welfare.   SAMUEL GOMPERS

Whining

Boys, this is only a game. But it's like life in that you will be dealt some bad hands. Take each hand, good or bad, and don't whine and complain, but play it out. If you're men enough to do that, God will help and you will come out well.

DWIGHT D. EISENHOWER'S MOTHER

Wickedness

I never wonder to see men wicked, but I often wonder to see them not ashamed.   JONATHAN SWIFT

The wicked flee when no man pursueth, but they make better time when someone is after them.

CHARLES HENRY PARKHURST

If men are so wicked (as we see them now) with religion, what would they be without it?

Winners

The winners in life think constantly in terms of "I can," "I will," and "I am." Losers, on the other hand, concentrate their waking thoughts on what they should have done or what they don't do.

DENIS WAITLEY

Wisdom

All human wisdom is summed up in two words—wait and hope.

ALEXANDRE DUMAS

Be wiser than other people if you can, but do not tell them so.

LORD CHESTERFIELD

Wisdom grows when knowledge is lived.

SIDNEY B. SIMON

Wisdom is knowledge that has been cured in the brine of tears.

RICHARD ARMOUR

Nine-tenths of wisdom consists in being wise in time.

THEODORE ROOSEVELT

The art of being wise is the art of knowing what to overlook.

WILLIAM JAMES

Though a man may become learned by another's learning, he can never be wise but by his own wisdom.

MICHEL DE MONTAIGNE

Pain makes man think. Thought makes man wise. Wisdom makes life endurable.

JOHN PATRICK

True wisdom lies in gathering the precious things out of each day as it goes by.

E.S. BOUTON

If you find a wise sentence or apt phrase, commit it to your memory.

HENRY SIDNEY

Wit

Wit makes its own welcome, and levels all distinctions. No dignity, no learning, no force of character, can make any stand against good wit.

RALPH WALDO EMERSON

Wit is a sword; it is meant to make people feel the point as well as see it.

G.K. CHESTERTON

Witnessing

Every week our preacher tells us to go out and "witness" to others. But nothing strikes more fear in my heart than having to share my faith with a complete stranger. It's gotten so bad I've enrolled in a Witness Relocation Program.

ROBERT G. LEE

Wives

A good wife makes a good husband.

Every man can rule an ill wife but him that has her.

JOHN RAY

A quarrelsome wife is like a constant dripping on a rainy day; restraining her is like restraining the wind or grasping oil with the hand.

THE BIBLE: PROVERBS 27:15,16

The wife of Willis Anderson came again to petition for his pardon. She hinted that her husband did not wish to be discharged from prison himself, and that it would be no relaxation of his punishment to turn him over to her.

JOHN QUINCY ADAMS

An ideal wife is any woman who has an ideal husband.

BOOTH TARKINGTON

She would have made a splendid wife, for crying only made her eyes more bright and tender.

O. HENRY

Women

Next to God, we are indebted to women, first for life itself, and then for making it worth having.

Woman begins by resisting a man's advances and ends by blocking his retreat.

OSCAR WILDE

You see, dear, it is not true that woman was made from man's rib; she was really made from his funny bone.

JAMES M. BARRIE

When a woman says, "They say," she means herself.

KIN HUBBARD

Not ten yoke of oxen
Have the power to draw us
Like a woman's hair!

HENRY W. LONGFELLOW

Women forgive injuries but never forget slights.

T.C. HALIBURTON

To a woman there is something indescribably inviting in a man whom other women favor.

HONORÉ DE BALZAC

Wondering

The world will never starve for want of wonders, but for want of wonder.

G.K. CHESTERTON

As knowledge increases, wonder deepens.

CHARLES MORGAN

Words

Like apples of gold in settings of silver is a word spoken in right circumstances.

THE BIBLE: PROVERBS 25:11 NASB

Man does not live by words alone, despite the fact that sometimes he has to eat them.

ADLAI STEVENSON

My words fly up, my thoughts remain below;
Words without thoughts never to heaven go.

WILLIAM SHAKESPEARE

All epoch-making revolutionary events have been produced not by the written but the spoken word.

ADOLF HITLER

Words that come from the heart enter the heart.

THE SAGES

During a long life I have had to eat my own words many times, and I have found it a very nourishing diet.

SIR WINSTON CHURCHILL

No one means all he says, and yet very few say all they mean, for words are slippery and thought is viscous.

HENRY ADAMS

Reckless words pierce like a sword, but the tongue of the wise brings healing.

THE BIBLE: PROVERBS 12:18

The more the words, the less the meaning, and how does that profit anyone?

THE BIBLE: ECCLESIASTES 6:11

Pleasant words are a honeycomb, sweet to the soul and healing to the bones.

THE BIBLE: PROVERBS 16:24

He can compress the most words into the smallest ideas of any man I ever met.

ABRAHAM LINCOLN

There's small revenge in words, but words may be greatly revenged.

BENJAMIN FRANKLIN

The more articulate one is, the more dangerous words become.

MARY SARTON

Work

Work is the meat of life, pleasure the dessert.

BERTIE CHARLES FORBES

Find your place and hold it: find your work and do it. And put everything you've got into it.

EDWARD WILLIAM BOK

A truly American sentiment recognizes the dignity of labor and the fact that honor lies in honest toil.

GROVER CLEVELAND

Go and wake up your luck.

Of all the tonics devised by man, none is as stimulating as a good day's work.

Better to wear out shoes than sheets.

Everything considered, work is less boring than amusing one-self.
　　　　　　　　　　　　　　　　CHARLES BAUDELAIRE

Work is the best method devised for killing time.
　　　　　　　　　　　　　　　　WILLIAM FEATHER

I do not know anyone who has gotten to the top without hard work. That is the recipe.
　　　　　　　　　　　　　　　　MARGARET THATCHER

Perhaps the most damaging form of personal rejection is to tell a man there is nothing in the world for him to do. For worklessness equals meaninglessness; and meaninglessness eats at the foundation of all law, all morality, all joy in human relationships.
　　　　　　　　　　　　　　　　TIMOTHY L. SMITH

Nothing is really work unless you would rather be doing something else.
　　　　　　　　　　　　　　　　JAMES M. BARRIE

Too many people quit looking for work when they find a job.

Fine work is its own flattery.

The best eraser in the world is an eight-hour dose of hard work.

At the workingman's house, hunger looks in but dares not enter.
BENJAMIN FRANKLIN

To work without payment is better than sitting idle.

As a remedy against all ills—poverty, sickness, and melancholy—only one thing is absolutely necessary: a liking for work.
CHARLES BAUDELAIRE

Do not waste a minute...not a second...in trying to demonstrate to others the merits of your performance. If your work does not indicate yourself, you cannot vindicate it.
THOMAS W. HIGGINSON

All hard work brings a profit, but mere talk leads only to poverty.
THE BIBLE: PROVERBS 14:23

Work expands so as to fill the time available for its completion.
C. NORTHCOTE PARKINSON

Nothing ever comes to one, that is worth having, except as a result of hard work.
BOOKER T. WASHINGTON

The most unhappy of all men is the man who cannot tell what he is going to do, who has got no work cut out for him in the world, and does not go into it. For work is the grand cure for all the maladies and miseries that ever beset mankind—honest work, which you intend getting done.
THOMAS CARLYLE

With a good conscience our only sure reward, with history the final judge of our deeds, let us go forth to lead the land we love, asking His blessing and His help, but knowing that here on earth God's work must truly be our own.
JOHN F. KENNEDY

I never did anything worth doing by accident, nor did any of my inventions come by accident; they came by work.

THOMAS EDISON

Property is the fruit of labor; property is desirable, is a positive good in the world. That some should be rich shows that others may become rich, and hence is just encouragement to industry and enterprise. Let not him who is houseless pull down the house of another, but let him work diligently and build one for himself, thus by example assuring that his own shall be safe from violence when built.

ABRAHAM LINCOLN

As a cure for worrying, work is better than whiskey.

THOMAS EDISON

The best inheritance a parent can leave a child is a will to work.

HIPPOCRATES

A man's health seldom suffers from the work he loves and does for its own sake.

HONORÉ DE BALZAC

When your work speaks for itself, don't interrupt.

HENRY J. KAISER

The lady-bearer of this says she has two sons who want to work. Set them at it, if possible. Wanting to work is so rare a merit that it should be encouraged.

ABRAHAM LINCOLN

I like work; it fascinates me. I can sit and look at it for hours. I love to keep it by me; the idea of getting rid of it nearly breaks my heart.

JEROME K. JEROME

There is no substitute for hard work.

THOMAS EDISON

My observation is that whenever one person is found adequate to the discharge of duty by close application thereto, it is worse executed by two persons, and scarcely done at all if three or more are employed therein.

GEORGE WASHINGTON

If the hand would do what the tongue says, there would be no poverty.

Anyone can do any amount of work, provided it isn't the work he is supposed to be doing at that moment.

ROBERT BENCHLEY

Work as if you were to live one hundred years;
Pray as if you were to die tomorrow.

BENJAMIN FRANKLIN

When a man tells you that he got rich through hard work, ask him, "Whose?"

DON MARQUIS

When work is a pleasure, life is a joy! When work is a duty, life is slavery.

MAXIM GORKY

Labor is man's greatest function. He is nothing, he can do nothing, he can achieve nothing, he can fulfill nothing, without working.

ORVILLE DEWEY

Worry

Worry is a futile thing,
It's somewhat like a rocking chair,
Although it keeps you occupied,
It doesn't get you anywhere.

There is nothing so wretched or foolish as to anticipate misfortunes. What madness is it in expecting evil before it arrives?

SENECA

How much pain they have cost us, the evils which have never happened.

THOMAS JEFFERSON

The reason why worry kills more people than work is that more people worry than work.

ROBERT FROST

Worry affects circulation, the heart and the glands, the whole nervous system and profoundly affects the heart. I have never known a man who died from overwork, but many who died from doubt.

CHARLES H. MAYO

Which of you by worrying can add one cubit to his stature?

THE BIBLE: MATTHEW 6:27 NKJV

Worry is a thin stream of fear trickling through the mind. If encouraged, it cuts a channel into which all other thoughts are drained.

ARTHUR SOMERS ROCHE

Every evening I turn worries over to God. He's going to be up all night anyway.

MARY C. CROWLEY

Worry does not empty tomorrow of its sorrow; it empties today of its strength.

CORRIE TEN BOOM

Don't hurry, don't worry. You're only here for a short visit. So be sure to stop and smell the flowers.

WALTER HAGEN

How futile is worry? Just try to recall what you were worrying about one year ago today.

Worth

Now that it's all over, what did you really do yesterday that's worth mentioning?

COLEMAN COX

There is no readier way for a man to bring his own worth into question, than by endeavoring to detract from the worth of other men.

JOHN TILLOTSON

We never know the worth of water till the well is dry.

For anything worth having one must pay the price; and the price is always work, patience, love, self-sacrifice.

JOHN BURROUGHS

Go to bed. What you're staying up for isn't worth it.

ANDY ROONEY

Wrath

When wrath speaks, wisdom veils her face.

Writers

The writer must be willing, above everything else, to take chances, to risk making a fool of himself—or even to risk revealing the fact that he is a fool.

JESSAMYN WEST

About the most originality that any writer can hope to achieve honestly is to steal with good judgment.

JOSH BILLINGS

After being turned down by numerous publishers, he decided to write for posterity.

GEORGE ADE

A painter can hang his pictures, but a writer can only hang himself.

EDWARD DAHLBERG

There are three reasons for becoming a writer: The first is that you need the money; the second that you have something to say that you think the world should know; the third is that you can't think what to do with the long winter evenings.

QUENTIN CRISP

If you want to be a writer—stop talking about it and sit down and write!

JACKIE COLLINS

I love being a writer. What I can't stand is the paperwork.

PETER DE VRIES

Like most writers, I don't like to write; I like to have written.

WILLIAM ZINSSER

I want to pay tribute to my four writers: Matthew, Mark, Luke, and John.

FULTON J. SHEEN

He inquired of an old man whether it were sinful to write for money. And the old man answered, "There be two kinds of writers, my son: to wit, those who write for money and get it, and those who write for money and don't get it."

T.W.H. CROSLAND

Writing

A drop of ink may make a million think.

LORD BYRON

The profession of book writing makes horse racing seem like a solid, stable business.
                                                      JOHN STEINBECK

Two or more people getting together to write something is like three people getting together to make a baby.
                                                      EVELYN WAUGH

The greatest part of a writer's time is spent in reading, in order to write. A man will turn over half a library to make one book.
                                                      SAMUEL JOHNSON

When I face the desolate impossibility of writing five hundred pages, a sick sense of failure falls on me, and I know I can never do it. This happens every time. Then gradually I write one page and then another. One day's work is all I can permit myself to contemplate, and I eliminate the possibility of ever finishing.
                                                      JOHN STEINBECK

The great struggle of a writer is to learn to write as he would talk.

The most important sentence in any article is the first one. If it doesn't induce the reader to proceed to the second sentence, your article is dead. And if the second sentence doesn't induce him to continue to the third sentence, it's equally dead. Of such a progress of sentences, each tugging the reader forward until he is safely hooked, a writer constructs that fateful unit: the "lead."
                                                      WILLIAM ZINSSER

When something can be read without effort, great effort has gone into its writing.
                                                      ENRIQUE JARDIEL PONCELA

Your manuscript is both good and original, but the part that is good is not original, and the part that is original is not good.

SAMUEL JOHNSON

Most people won't realize that writing is a craft. You have to take your apprenticeship in it like anything else.

KATHERINE ANNE PORTER

The secret of all good writing is sound judgment.

HORACE

You don't write because you want to say something; you write because you've got something to say.

F. SCOTT FITZGERALD

There is no subject so old that something new cannot be said about it.

FYODOR DOSTOEVSKY

Find a subject you are about and which you in your heart feel others should care about. It is the genuine caring, and not your games with language, which will be the most compelling and seductive element in your style.

KURT VONNEGUT

As a general rule, run your pen through every other word you have written; you have no idea what vigor it will give your style.

SYDNEY SMITH

Make 'em laugh; make 'em cry; make 'em wait.

CHARLES READE

What is written without effort is in general read without pleasure.

SAMUEL JOHNSON

Originality is nothing but judicious imitation. The most original writers borrowed one from another. The instruction we find in books is like fire. We fetch it from our neighbor's, kindle it at home, communicate it to others, and it becomes the property of all.

VOLTAIRE

Writing is easy. All you do is stare at a blank sheet of paper until drops of blood form on your forehead.

GENE FOWLER

Vigorous writing is concise. A sentence should contain no unnecessary words, a paragraph no unnecessary sentence, for the same reason that a drawing should have no unnecessary lines and a machine no unnecessary parts. This requires not that the writer make all his sentences short, or that he avoid all detail and treat his subjects only in outline, but that every word tell.

WILLIAM STRUNK JR.

Wrong

The man who says "I may be wrong, but—" does not believe there can be any such possibility.

KIN HUBBARD

Wrongs

To be wronged is nothing unless you continue to remember it.

CONFUCIUS

All wrongdoing is done in the sincere belief that it is the best thing to do.

ARNOLD BENNETT

Yawning

Why doth one man's yawning make another yawn?

ROBERT BURTON

Youth

It is better to be a young June-bug than an old bird of paradise.

MARK TWAIN

To be seventy years young is sometimes far more cheerful and hopeful than to be forty years old.

The young always have the same problem: how to rebel and conform at the same time. They have now solved this by defying their parents and copying one another.

QUENTIN CRISP

Youth is a wonderful thing: what a crime to waste it on children.

GEORGE BERNARD SHAW

Oh, this age! How tasteless and ill-bred it is!   CATULLUS

It is not possible for civilization to flow backwards while there is youth in the world.

HELEN KELLER

Youth comes but once in a lifetime.

HENRY W. LONGFELLOW

Youth is not entirely a time of life; it is a state of mind. Nobody grows old by merely living a number of years. People grow old by deserting their ideals. You are as young as your faith, as old as your doubt; as young as your self-confidence, as old as your fear; as young as your hope, as old as your despair.

DOUGLAS MACARTHUR

The Youth of a Nation aren't the trustees of Posterity.

BENJAMIN DISRAELI

Don't laugh at a youth for his affectations; he is only trying on one face after another to find his own.

LOGAN PEARSALL SMITH

I love the acquaintance of young people, because, in the first place, I don't like to think myself growing old. In the next place, young acquaintances must last longest, if they do last; and then young men have more virtue than old men; they have more generous sentiments in every respect.   SAMUEL JOHNSON

The denunciation of the young is a necessary part of the hygiene of older people, and greatly assists the circulation of their blood.   LOGAN PEARSALL SMITH

The young do not know enough to be prudent, and therefore they attempt the impossible—and achieve it, generation after generation.   PEARL S. BUCK

For God's sake, give me the young man who has brains enough to make a fool of himself.   ROBERT LOUIS STEVENSON

Zeal

The world is moved by highly motivated people, by enthusiasts, by men and women who want something very much or believe very much.

JOHN GARDNER

Books by Bob Phillips

For information on how to purchase any of the above books, contact your local bookstore or send a self-addressed stamped envelope to:
Family Services
P.O. Box 9363
Fresno, CA 93702